A SHORT HISTORY

OF

RENAISSANCE

EUROPE

Dances over Fire and Water

Jonathan W. Zophy
University of Houston Clear Lake

PRENTICE HALL, UPPER SADDLE RIVER, NEW JERSEY 07458

Library of Congress Cataloging-in-Publication Data

Zophy, Jonathan W. (date)
   A short history of Renaissance Europe : dances over fire and water
   / by Jonathan W. Zophy.
        p.   cm.
   Includes bibliographical references and index.
   ISBN 0–13–181579–2
   1. Europe—History—476–1492.   2. Europe—History—1492–1648.
   3. Renaissance.   I. Title.
   D200.Z665   1997
   940.2'1—dc20   96-14364
                                                             CIP

This book was set in Palatino and Zapf Chancery by The Composing Room of Michigan, Inc.
It was printed and bound by Hamilton Printing Company.
The cover was printed by Phoenix Color Corp.

Acquisitions editor: Sally Constable
Editorial production/supervision: F. Hubert
Manufacturing buyer: Lynn Pearlman
Cover art: Albrecht Dürer, *Dancing Peasants,* Giraudon/Art Resource

Printed in the United States of America
10 9 8 7 6 5 4 3 2 1

ISBN 0-13-181579-2

Prentice-Hall International (UK) Limited,London
Prentice-Hall of Australia Pty. Limited, Sydney
Prentice-Hall Canada Inc., Toronto
Prentice-Hall Hispanoamericana, S.A., Mexico
Prentice-Hall of India Private Limited, New Delhi
Prentice-Hall of Japan, Inc., Tokyo
Pearson Education Asia Pte. Ltd., Singapore
Editora Prentice-Hall do Brasil, Ltda., Rio de Janeiro

CONTENTS

10 The Renaissance in the North 157

PREFACE

This book originated from the concerns of my students that my course in Renaissance Europe needed a suitable textbook. They argued that the various texts I have been using over the past three decades are too detailed, too boring, and do not pay sufficient attention to the roles of women. Although I do not agree with them about some Renaissance texts being either too lengthy or insufficiently stimulating, student concerns did remind me how much of a gap there is between those of us who have studied a period intensely for a number of years and those who are learning about it in some cases almost for the first time. This text, like its companion volume on Reformation Europe, is an effort to provide a bridge between the often different worlds of the professor and the student.

I seek to make the Renaissance more accessible to students, many of whom have not had much prior exposure to the subject. Deliberately adopting a conversational tone in my prose, I have attempted to write what might be called a student-friendly text by, for example, avoiding technical and foreign language terms as much as possible and attempting to introduce historical figures and concepts as they appear in the narrative. Since this is a brief history, it is more representative than comprehensive. This means, for example, that some important Renaissance painters are not discussed in much detail. This is somewhat compensated for by the greater coverage given to important women artists such as Sofonisba Anguissola or thinkers such as Christine de Pizan, who are usually not found in traditional Renaissance textbooks.

This textbook is organized around topics such as "Italian Renaissance Art" (Chapter 6 and 7) or "Northern Humanism" (Chapter 11). However, topics are presented roughly in a chronological order throughout the book. Hence, the Black Death of 1347 to 1350 appears in Chapter 3 of the book and the development of printing is discussed in the last chapter. Subtopics are presented in chronological order in each chapter. All but the second chapter on "The Peoples of Europe" feature a *Chronology* of important persons and events. My students have found these chronologies to be a helpful review aid in preparing for examinations. Even though I refuse to test them on their recall of specific dates, I do wish them to have a relative sense of sequence—to know, for example, that Giotto lived before Artemisia Gentileschi or that Francesco Petrarca preceded Thomas More. It seems to me that to tell a good story it is usually a sensible notion to begin at the beginning and proceed to the end, even if life itself is a seamless web.

Each chapter also ends with a list of

suggestions for *Further Reading*. These are meant to recommend some of the best and most recent English-language scholarship on various topics covered in each chapter and in some cases throughout the book. Usually, I have selected books and collections of translated sources that I think serious students will enjoy reading, although I do not include novels or nonfiction works written by nonprofessional historians. In the interest of brevity, the lists have been kept relatively short with only limited annotation. They are not at all comprehensive bibliographies. I do refer readers to some of the bibliographical literature such as Merry Wiesner's *Women in the Sixteenth Century: A Bibliography* or my own *Annotated Bibliography of the Holy Roman Empire*. Obviously, the scholarly monographs included have a wealth of citations in their notes and bibliographies.

Although I try to give some attention to the intellectual developments of the era, my emphasis for the most part has been on people of all ages and both genders. My experience is that the ideas of the period can best be learned by small group discussions of documents and texts. This brief text is meant to be used in conjunction with collections of documents such as Kenneth Bartlett's *The Civilization of the Italian Renaissance* or Benjamin Kohl and Alison Andrews Smith's *Major Problems in the History of the Italian Renaissance*. For intellectual currents north of the Alps, I have found Lewis Spitz, Jr.'s *The Northern Renaissance* to be a useful sourcebook for students. This text should also be supplemented by more specialized monographs. It is meant solely as a brief introduction to some of the major personalities, issues, events, and ideas of the Renaissance. It is not a compendium or a grand *summa*. My hope is to capture your attention and interest and stimulate you to make additional explorations of this rich and complex period in human history.

Acknowledgments

Since this book has grown out of more than twenty-five years of teaching college and university courses on Renaissance-Reformation Europe, I want to begin by thanking my students and colleagues at eight different institutions for their advice and their enthusiasm. They are: Carthage College, Lane College, Michigan State University, the Ohio State University, University of Houston Clear Lake, University of Maryland European Division, University of West Florida, and University of Wisconsin-Parkside. I have learned more from them than they have from me and have taken their specific suggestions for this book seriously. I particularly want to thank the students of History 3332 (fall of 1994) at the University of Houston Clear Lake. They graciously consented to serve as guinea pigs in using a draft of this text. Their comments and criticisms have been invaluable.

I also dared to assign the draft text to my graduate seminar in the fall of 1994 for their oral and written criticisms. They had great fun critiquing the work of their genial professor, but in the process helped make this a much more usable text. I was particularly pleased that they succeeded in using their imaginations to criticize the book as a text not for their own interests but for undergraduates. I want to mention the following students in particular for going beyond my assignment and providing detailed suggestions for the improvement of the text. Those stalwarts include: Mary Demeny, Diane De Vusser, Lisa Edwards, Gloria Flores, Deborah Goldman, Sue Grooms,

Haydn Hutson, Piper Madland, Sandra Petrovich, Rita Starostenko, and Sasha Tarrant. One of them, Karen Raines-Pate, deserves special mention for she had helped me with the text for the past two years as my research assistant. Her work on this project has been exemplary and invaluable. She is already a student-sensitive teacher.

As with my previous books, I received a great deal of help and inspiration from a variety of colleagues, friends, and family members. For example, one friend, Kathy Reeves, helped catch several mistakes. Several colleagues at the University of Houston Clear Lake went over all or parts of the early drafts, including Vivian Atwater, Marjolijn Avé Lallemant, Roger Bilstein, and Gretchen Mieszkowski. Lawrence Buck (Widener University), John Patrick Donnelly, S. J. (Marquette University), and William Wright (University of Tennessee-Chattanooga), experienced teachers of courses on Renaissance-Reformation Europe, all went painstakingly over drafts of the manuscript and made incredibly useful corrections and suggestions for further improvement. Colleagues at various meetings of the Renaissance Society of America, the Sixteenth Century Studies Conference and the Society for Reformation Research have also offered various forms of aid and encouragement. My late mentors Harold Grimm and John Harrison taught me a great deal about the importance of textbooks as teaching tools. Such is the cooperative spirit of Renaissance and Reformation scholars and teachers. Readers for Prentice Hall also wrote perceptive comments in evaluating an earlier version of the manuscript: James R. Banker, North Carolina State University, Carl Christensen, University of Colorado at Boulder, Merry Wiesner-Hanks, University of Wisconsin at Milwaukee. Other scholarly debts are hinted at in the narrative, in the suggestions for *Further Reading*, and in the *Notes*.

At Prentice Hall, I owe special thanks to former executive editor Steven Dalphin for his wise counsel and support for this project. Carmine Batsford first persuaded me to approach Steve Dalphin about doing this book. Sally Constable, Frank Hubert, Serena Hoffman, Tamara Mann, Justin Belinsky, and many others at Prentice Hall have done an excellent job in putting this text together. Annette Weir of Art Resource in New York deserves a special mention for her good taste and help in securing illustrations. The various art galleries listed with the illustrations throughout the text are also thanked for their help, as is the library staff of the University of Houston Clear Lake.

Finally, I must again thank the members of the Howard and Zophy families for their continued support and encouragement. My colleague-spouse, Dr. Angela Howard Zophy, who teaches Women and U.S. History in superb fashion at the University of Houston Clear Lake, continues to provide me with great inspiration and character-building lessons. I have dedicated a previous book to her so this book is in honor of two other wonderful teacher-scholars, Marjolijn Avé Lallemant of the University of Houston at Clear Lake and Donald M. Michie of Carthage College. They are two of the best friends and role models that anyone could ever know.

Jonathan W. Zophy

1

INTRODUCTION:
THE BEST AND WORST
OF TIMES

" . . . as if on a given signal, splendid talents are stirring."
Erasmus, 1517

"This is the worst age of history."
Erasmus, 1536

The Problem of the Renaissance

The conflicting attitudes toward his age expressed by the influential humanist scholar Erasmus of Rotterdam quoted above suggest something of the fundamental problem of Europe in the time of Renaissance and Reformation. It truly was one of the best and worst of times. In painting, for example, between 1300 and 1700 many parts of Europe experienced an incredible era of superb achievement with such luminaries as Jan van Eyck, Botticelli, Albrecht Dürer, Raphael, Michelangelo, Titian, Artemisia Gentileschi, and many others all producing masterpieces in abundance. Seldom in history have so many artistic geniuses appeared at one special moment in time on one continent.

Artists such as the Italian master Leonardo da Vinci used newly perfected techniques in oil painting, perspective, and the use of light and shade to produce revolutionary paintings such as his *Virgin of the Rocks*, of which he painted two versions (see Chapter 6). This work reveals the left-handed Leonardo as a man fascinated by na-

ture, who painted scientifically accurate versions of human anatomy, plant life, and rock formations. Da Vinci is a man in love with nature and nature's God. His Virgin Mary, baby Jesus, and John the Baptist are depicted as both heroes of the Bible and yet touchingly human. *The Virgin of the Rocks* represents a culminating manifestation of many important Renaissance trends, including the rise of humanism and scientific naturalism in art.

The accomplishments of Leonardo da Vinci and his colleagues in painting and other fine arts were paralleled by the almost equally spectacular developments in letters, music, science, theology, and other areas. As the fifteenth-century philosopher Marsilio Ficino expressed it, "This age, like a golden age, has restored to light the liberal arts that were almost extinct: grammar, poetry, rhetoric, painting, sculpture, architecture, music."[1] Many intellectuals of the period had the sense that they were living at a special moment in history. We moderns share the sense that something unique was going on during the Renaissance partly because of the rich cultural legacy it has left us.

Leonardo da Vinci, *The Virgin of the Rocks.* National Gallery, London, Great Britain. Photo courtesy of Alinari/Art Resource.

In literature, the Renaissance was also the age of such cultural giants as Boccaccio, Cervantes, Marguerite of Navarre, Petrarca, Rabelais, and Shakespeare, to drop only a few of the greatest names. Important thinkers such as Christine de Pizan challenged many of the medieval world's fundamental notions about the roles of women in society. Others such as Niccolò Machiavelli boldly questioned the traditional understandings of the connection between ethics and politics. The great classical scholars and humanists of the period such as Erasmus and Lorenzo Valla helped to revive the wisdom of classical Greece and Rome and strengthen our understanding of the Judeo-Christian tradition. Classical models and humanist ideas also helped Renaissance artists with their pathbreaking work. The word *renaissance* means literally "rebirth" and refers to the revived interest in classical and Judeo-Christian sources. The humanist slogan *ad fontes* (to the sources) sums up this attitude nicely. Many humanists urged their followers to immerse themselves in ancient languages and literature as a means of individual and societal improvement.

Some of the extraordinary accomplishments of the time also challenged the ideas of revered ancients. In science, for example, the notions of the universe developed by

Aristotle and Ptolemy were discredited to some degree by the Pole Nicholas Copernicus and the Italian Galileo. The Fleming Andreas Vesalius respectfully revised some of the time-honored notions about anatomy put forth by the Greek physician Galen in the second century A.D. Indeed, during the Renaissance we find the beginnings of the Western scientific revolution. Inspirational religious leaders such as John Wycliffe, Jan Hus, Savonarola, and others also confronted many existing traditions while reviving others. Similarly, the writing of history and political theory would never be the same after Guicciardini and Machiavelli.

Yet the Renaissance was also a period of almost incessant warfare, periodic famine, high infant mortality, rapid aging, widespread epidemics, peasant and artisan revolts, intolerance of any form of diversity, grinding poverty, massive illiteracy, forced conversions and migrations, cruelly elaborate public executions of ethnic and religious minorities, and a ferocious witchcraft craze that occurred mostly after the 1590s. For much of the fifteenth century, the European economy suffered a serious depression. The Renaissance began against the background of a series of natural and human disasters and ended in the bloody religious conflicts of the Reformation era. Women, for the most part, did not have much of a "renaissance," as the modern historian Joan Kelly has noted. The age started with females generally subordinated to males and restricted by law and custom. It ended up much the same way, since patriarchy (the rule of the father in the family and society) continued and in some ways was enhanced. Those relatively few people who consumed the dazzling higher culture of the period were supported by the drudgery of the masses. For many Europeans who lived through it, what we call the Renaissance must have often seemed like the worst of times, as the influential humanist Erasmus called it shortly before his death in 1536.

This book will use the label *Renaissance* to refer both to a period of European history and to the international cultural movement which emerged during the fourteenth century in Italy and spread to much of the rest of the world by the seventeenth century. Although we may have ambivalent feelings about the period or even the use of the term *Renaissance,* there is little doubt about the historical and cultural importance of the years between the lives of the painter Giotto (c. 1267–1337) and the naturalist Maria Sibylla Merian (1647–1717). For the nineteenth-century Swiss historian Jacob Burckhardt, the Italian Renaissance brought forth the triumph of "individualism" and helped usher in the modern world. The twentieth-century historian Richard Goldthwaite recently paid homage to Burckhardt's modernity thesis by describing Renaissance Italy as the birthplace of modern consumer society, such was the obsession with things among the wealthy elites of the time. This lust for acquisition also helped to fuel the rise of capitalism and the movement toward a world economy.

During the fourteenth through the seventeenth centuries, merchants learned to make better use of international banking and found new ways to raise capital. Simple innovations such as the use of double entry bookkeeping and bills of exchange greatly improved business practices. Navigational techniques became more sophisticated and ships were made bigger and better. Trade expanded and the standard of living improved greatly, at least for the prosperous. Capitalism also helped lead to an expansion in the horrific practices of the slave trade and to the voyages of discovery, which in turn led to the creation of vast colonial empires and the spread of lethal diseases throughout the so-called "New World." The controversial navigator Christopher Columbus was a child of the Renaissance, as was Francesco Pizzaro, who conquered and looted the Inca Empire in Peru. Although life for most Renaissance people changed little, for others it was an era of transformation.

Even though many things about the Renaissance, including the term itself, are subjects of great debate among modern scholars, the period clearly featured the rise of the modern territorial state as feudal monarchies in Europe gave way to more bureaucratized and centralized power structures. Even a massive state like the Holy Roman Empire, which remained largely decentralized and supranational, attempted to regularize its medieval organizational structure. In 1356 the empire codified its tradition of electing its monarchs in a document known as the Golden Bull. Some even thought divided Italy should be made into a unified kingdom. Feudal levies were frequently replaced by mercenaries, who fought for anyone who would pay them. The lance and sword became more and more obsolete, challenged first by the bow and arrow and then by new gunpowder weapons. A military revolution ensued which was to have profound consequences as general superiority in warfare allowed Europeans to dominate and exploit the rest of the world economically until well into the twentieth century.

Dances over Fire and Water?

Regardless of what one calls this age in history, it was, indeed, the best and worst of times, which is why we can think of it as a series of dances over fire and water. The modern historian and novelist Sydney Alexander first used that stimulating image to refer to the Renaissance. "Dances over Fire and Water" may be a useful way to think about certain aspects of the period. After all, most of its intellectuals still believed that the world was made up of four basic elements: earth, fire, air, and water. Although firmly rooted in the soil that most of its people farmed for an often meager living, this era seemed to soar above most earlier periods in terms of its cultural achievements. Some of its major figures such as Botticelli, Machiavelli, Michelangelo, William Shakespeare, or Elizabeth Tudor appear nearly superhuman at times. One can imagine them capable of doing anything, including dancing over fire and water. Not since classical Athens or Rome of the first century had Europe witnessed such an age of stunning artistic and intellectual accomplishments set against a background of incredible suffering. So many splendid successes set against a background of so many painful societal failures.

Although the Middle Ages was hardly like "a thousand years without a bath," even its great Gothic cathedrals and magnificent theological summas seemed to moderns to be overshadowed by the series of dances over fire and water that was Europe in the age of Renaissance. Sometimes it was a dance of death caused at times by the new gunpowder weapons which had substantially increased the "firepower" available to the period's military. Sometimes it was a dance of death caused by the outbreak of pandemic diseases.

The ancient Greek philosopher Heraclitus thought of fire and water as elements of change. Change is one of the great themes of the Renaissance. While some of these transformations were for the better, this was not always the case. The Renaissance was also a period of almost constant misery, especially for the many whose lives were fundamentally unaffected by most of what went on during the period. The Renaissance has always meant different things to different people. Despite the difficulties of com-

Albrecht Dürer, *Dancing Peasants and the Bagpipe Player* (1514). Musee du Petit Palais, Paris, France. Giraudon/Art Resource.

prehending the swirling dances that were the Renaissance, it is an effort well worth making. With these cautions in mind, let the dances begin!

General Chronology

c. 1267–1337	Life of the painter Giotto.
1304–1374	Life of the humanist Petrarca.
1305–1376	The Babylonian Captivity (the popes at Avignon).
1313–1375	Life of the humanist Boccaccio.
1337–1453	The Hundred Years' War between England and France.
1347–1350	The Black Death (plague epidemics).
1356	Peasant Revolt in France.
1364–1430	Life of Christine de Pizan.
1378–1417	Western papal schism.
1384	Death of John Wycliffe.
1414–1418	Reform Council of Constance.
1415	Death of Jan Hus.
1431	Death of Joan of Arc.
1441	Death of Jan van Eyck.
1449–1492	Life of Lorenzo de' Medici.
1453	Fall of Constantinople to the Ottomans.
1454	Johann Gutenberg prints a Bible at Mainz.
1455–1485	War of the Roses in England.
1469	Marriage of Isabella of Castile to Ferdinand of Aragon.
1471	Birth of Albrecht Dürer in Nuremberg.
1492	Christopher Columbus's first voyage to the Americas; birth of Marguerite of Navarre.
1494	King Charles VIII of France invades Italy; Rabelais born.

1495	Leonardo da Vinci begins *The Last Supper.*
1512	Michelangelo completes the Sistine chapel ceiling.
1513	Machiavelli writes *The Prince.*
1516	Erasmus's edition of the Greek New Testament and Thomas More's *Utopia* published.
1519	Cortés begins the conquest of Mexico.
1543	Publication of Copernicus's *On the Revolution of Celestial Spheres* and Vesalius's *On the Fabric of the Human Body.*

1558–1603	Reign of Elizabeth I of England.
1576	Death of Titian.
1602	Shakespeare's *Hamlet.*
1605	Cervantes publishes *Don Quixote.*
1625	Death of Sofonisba Anguissola.
1616	Artemisia Gentileschi admitted to the Florentine Academy of Art; deaths of Shakespeare and Cervantes; Galileo ordered to cease and desist his new astronomy.
1647–1717	Life of Sibylla Merian.

Further Reading

GENERAL SURVEYS

Sidney Alexander, *Lions and Foxes: Men and Ideas in the Italian Renaissance* (1974). Written by a novelist.

Ernst Breisach, *Renaissance Europe, 1200–1517* (1973).

Peter Burke, *The Italian Renaissance: Culture and Society in Renaissance Italy* (1987).

Wallace Ferguson, *Europe in Transition, 1300–1520* (1962).

Myron Gilmore, *The World of Humanism, 1453–1517* (1952).

John Hale, *The Civilization of Europe in the Renaissance* (1994).

Denys Hay, *The Italian Renaissance in Its Historical Background*, 2nd ed. (1976).

De Lamar Jensen, *Renaissance Europe: Age of Recovery and Reconciliation*, 2nd ed. (1992). A first-rate, comprehensive text which includes some material on women and a very useful set of bibliographical essays.

Theodore Rabb, *Renaissance Lives: Portraits of an Age* (1993). Handsomely illustrated character sketches of such diverse figures as Petrarca, Hus, Dürer, Artemisia Gentileschi, Teresa of Avila, and others.

Eugene Rice with Anthony Grafton, *The Foundations of Early Modern Europe, 1460–1559*, 2nd ed. (1994). A valuable synthesis.

Lewis Spitz, Jr., *The Renaissance Movement*, 2nd ed. (1987). A lively text.

S. Harrison Thomson, *Europe in Renaissance and Reformation* (1963). Still a worthwhile store of information.

REFERENCE WORKS

Catherine Avery, ed., *The New Century Italian Renaissance Encyclopedia* (1972).

Thomas Bergin and Jennifer Speake, eds., *Encyclopedia of the Renaissance* (1987).

Thomas Brady, Jr., Heiko Oberman, and James Tracy, eds., *Handbook of European History, 1400–1600.* 2 vols. (1994 and 1995). Important essays and bibliographies by leading international scholars on diverse topics such as "Population," "Trade," "Family," and various political entities.

John Hale, ed., *A Concise Encyclopedia of the Italian Renaissance*, 2nd ed. (1992).

New Cambridge Modern History, vol. 1, *The Renaissance, 1493–1520* (1957); vol. 2, *The Reformation*, 2nd ed. (1990).

Frederick Schweitzer and Harry Wedick, *Dictionary of the Renaissance* (1967).

COLLECTIONS OF SOURCES

Kenneth Bartlett, ed., *The Civilization of the Italian Renaissance: A Sourcebook* (1992). Includes more well-selected materials by and about women than is usually the case.

Julia Conaway Bondadella and Mark Musa, eds., *The Italian Renaissance Reader* (1992).

Eric Cochrane and Julius Kirshner, eds., *The Renaissance* (1986).

G. R. Elton, ed., *Renaissance and Reformation, 1300–1648*, 3rd ed. (1976).

David Englander, et al., eds., *Culture and Belief in Europe 1450–1600: An Anthology of Sources* (1993).

Werner Gundersheimer, ed., *The Italian Renaissance*, 2nd ed. (1993).

Benjamin Kohl and Alison Andrews Smith, *Major Problems in the History of the Italian Renaissance* (1995). An excellent selection of source materials and essays by leading modern scholars concerned with family, gender, and cultural issues.

James Bruce Ross and Mary Martin McLaughlin, eds., *The Portable Renaissance Reader* (1967). Excerpts from the writings of 100 fifteenth- and sixteenth-century thinkers from all over Europe.

INTERPRETATIONS

William Bousma, *A Usable Past: Essays in European Cultural History* (1990). Provocative essays by a leading interpreter.

Jacob Burckhardt, *The Civilization of the Italian Renaissance* (1860). This highly influential study has been frequently reprinted.

Karl Dannenfeldt, ed., *The Renaissance: Basic Interpretations*, 2nd ed. (1974).

Wallace Ferguson, *The Renaissance in Historical Thought* (1948).

Richard Goldthwaite, *Wealth and the Demand for Art in Italy, 1300–1600* (1993).

Joan Kelly, *Women, History, and Theory* (1984).

William Kerrigan and Gordon Braden, *The Idea of the Renaissance* (1989).

Erwin Panofsky, *Renaissance and Renascences in Western Art* (1971).

Mary Beth Rose, ed., *Women in the Middle Ages and the Renaissance* (1986).

There are also useful English translations of the works of many of the writers discussed in the pages that follow.

Note

1. Cited in John Hale, *The Civilization of Europe in the Renaissance* (New York: Atheneum, 1993), p. 586.

2

THE PEOPLES
OF EUROPE

The Peasantry

The Europe of the Renaissance and Reformation was much like Europe of the present
in languages and weather, but that is about
all. In sharp contrast to today's highly populated, polluted, and urbanized world, the
world of the fourteenth through seventeenth centuries was thinly populated and
mostly rural and agricultural. If only 1 to 2
percent of a modern, industrialized country's workforce is necessary to feed the rest,
nearly the opposite was true in the Renaissance. Crop yields were still minimal by
modern standards despite the wider use of
horse collars and oxen yokes, iron-tipped
plows, and a greater reliance on the three-
field system than had been the case in the
early Middle Ages. The three-field system
allowed a farmer to plant one field with
wheat in the fall and barley or rye in another
in the spring, while letting one field lie fal-
low each year. Even though this system improved the yield over the two-field system,
agricultural production was less than abundant. The result was that every able-bodied
person in a Renaissance farm family, including women and children, had to
work the land intensively. Toddlers under
seven were allowed to play at home and
were looked after by the disabled or older
children.

A CULTURE OF POVERTY: VILLAGE LIFE

Most Europeans in the sixteenth century
lived in small farming villages of 500 to 700
inhabitants. Generally connected to self-suf-
ficient agricultural estates called *manors*,
typical villages would be filled with win-
dowless, thatch-roofed huts with dirt floors.
Usually peasant huts had only two rooms
plus an attic and a barn or a cowshed. Privacy in our sense was unheard of. Furthermore, lice and vermin abounded, ventila-
tion was poor, and the smoke of the central
fire of the hearthstone mingled with the
smells of humans and animals.

In addition to the peasant huts and
sheds, a village might have a miller to grind
grain, a tavern, a blacksmith shop, perhaps
a general store, a parish church, and maybe
the manor house of the principal landowner
of the region. Some agricultural communities were attached to monasteries and some
were located near the walls of a town. Other
manorial estates were remote and isolated.
The level of prosperity varied from year to
year and place to place. A village like Sen-
nely in France outside of Orléans was constantly on the edge of poverty because it had
poor soil, although it never faced an all-out
famine. Other villages were not so lucky.

The peasants of Europe usually wore
simple, homespun clothes of sturdy fibers.

A fourteenth-century manuscript page of *Ovide Moralise* by Chrétien Legouais. The miniature depicts a man obliged to work in order to live. Bibliotheque Municipale, Rouen, France. Photo courtesy of Giraudon/Art Resource.

Their underwear was usually made of wool with wool or linen outerwear. Many wore wooden shoes equivalent to modern clogs. Some well-off farmers had leather boots, whereas others went barefoot at times. Peasants tended to age rapidly and they were often bent over from frequent stooping in the fields. Some had yellowish skin, and others were deeply tanned in the summer from long hours in the sun. Almost every adult had poor teeth and fetid breath. Frequent bouts of ill health were a common occurrence for adults.

Coarse, dark bread was the staple of peasant diets throughout Europe, whether from grains of barley, rye, millet, wheat or some combination of several grains. Corn or maize did not come into Europe until after Christopher Columbus's voyages to the so-called "New World" in the 1490s. Potatoes from Peru followed corn by two generations, first appearing in Spain in 1573 and then arriving in Italy by 1601. Even with the introduction of corn and potatoes, grains—whether baked as bread or mixed with water—remained the core of the European peasant diet.

When grain crops failed, starving peasants substituted acorns, tree bark, grass seeds, and even earth mixed with wheat flour. Fruit was usually too expensive for peasant households and green vegetables were rare. Dried beans, peas, and fish provided much needed protein and vitamins. Meat in any form was rare. King Henri IV, in the late sixteenth century, expressed the hope that every French rural family would be able to have "a chicken in its cooking pot every Sunday." Had this wish been fully realized in the Renaissance, it would have represented a considerable advance in the nutritional life of the French peasantry in many areas.

Such a dramatic change in the living standards of the peasantry did not occur during the Renaissance, and their meager diets were reflected in the high levels of disease and malnutrition present throughout Europe and in the fact that some girls in northern Europe did not menstruate until the age of eighteen. Peasant girls in most of the rest of Europe typically had menarche between ages twelve and fourteen. Women in the northern parts of Europe married at about age twenty-three, usually to older husbands. An estimated one third of all babies died in their first year. Couples averaged three to four children, with only about 45 percent reaching adulthood. Life spans were about half of what they are now and few peasant households had living grandparents.

In some senses, however, things were slowly improving for Europe's peasantry during the Renaissance. Most European peasants were no longer "bound to the soil" as serfs. Serfdom did linger on in parts of eastern Europe and in Russia until well into the nineteenth century, but many western European peasants owned some land. Better off peasants might possess their own horses for plowing and even their own wooden plows. A prosperous peasant family in France often had an estate worth about 2,000 livres. Those farmers just below them on the social scale who did not own horses and plows might be worth about 600 livres. They often rented most of their land and were in constant danger of falling into the status of hired hands. Hired hands often owned nothing other than a hut, a garden, and maybe a pig.

Regardless of their relative wealth or poverty, all peasants, including most children, worked exceedingly hard for most of the year. Men worked the fields, gathered wood, and repaired equipment. Children assisted their parents in all farm activities as soon as they were able. Peasant women usually helped the men with the plowing, manure spreading, weeding, reaping, and threshing. Women were expected to do all the internal household chores, as well as to gather kindling, haul well water, garden, tend animals, suckle infants, cook, sweep, and tend the fires. In addition to doing laundry for themselves and sometimes others, peasant women often sold cheese and butter, cared for children, and made the family's clothes. As a nineteenth-century Sicilian proverb put it, "If the father is dead, the family suffers. If the mother dies, the family cannot exist."[1]

THE CONTINUITIES OF LIFE FOR MEN, WOMEN, AND CHILDREN

Other constants in the peasants' world besides hard work included death and taxes. Peasants who lived on manors had to pay fees to use the lord's grain mill or to breed livestock. They had to perform certain seasonal duties for the lord, such as road and fence repairs. A peasant son had to surrender his best animal to inherit his father's tenancy. Normally a family had to pay about a third of their harvests to landlords, priests, and tax collectors. When the harvest was bad, people starved to death and infants were abandoned in larger numbers than usual. Survival was always the central issue for the peasantry in the culture of poverty that was Renaissance Europe.

In parts of Europe such as the Mediterranean basin, northern England, Scotland, Ireland, and Scandinavia, agricultural production was not as tightly organized as in regions of richer soils, where the communal farming of the manors predominated. Regardless of regional differences, the lives of the rural working men, women, and children of Renaissance Europe can be described as difficult and only slightly improved over that of their medieval ancestors. That superstitions still persisted, such as belief in the magical powers of bull's blood for example, is hardly surprising for people who sought help in a variety of ways.

Given the lives of drudgery that most peasants experienced, it is little wonder that church holidays, weddings, services, games of all sorts, visits to market towns, and occasional fairs meant so much to them. These were among the few occasions when a peasant family did not have to labor from sunrise to sunset. Fairs allowed a peasant family to buy a few items, such as magical potions they could not make for themselves, and to dance, drink, and swap stories with friends. If peasant dancing was often frenetic, that is understandable, considering the hardships of their lives.

Even an occasional holiday, however, could not disguise the essential harshness of peasant life nor the contempt which they sometimes experienced from the more privileged estates. Crude jests about "dumb and illiterate" peasants abounded. To be a peasant was often to be looked down upon and taken for granted by those whom you fed and served. Sometimes the level of anger was so intense that peasants risked everything to rebel against their often absentee landlords. Major peasant revolts had broken out in Flanders between 1323 and 1328; in France in 1358; in 1381 in England; and in various places in Germany throughout the fifteenth century (called *Bundschuh* revolts for the clog-like shoes most peasants wore). Between 1524 to 1526 a major Peasants' War was fought in southern Germany and spread to Austria. Since the peasantry was not generally trained in the use of arms and military leadership, all their revolts were brutally crushed by the authorities. These occasional, violent eruptions reflected the deep-seated desperation that often lay just below the surface calm of "those who work."

Town Dwellers

Although most Europeans lived in rural villages during the Renaissance, the third estate of commoners also included those who lived in walled towns. As an old legal maxim confirmed: "Only a wall separates the burgher from the peasant." Even though the feudal nobility may have lumped the town dwellers with the peasants, the wealthiest members of an early modern urban community considered themselves to be more closely allied with Europe's noble families. Indeed, sometimes the leading citizens of a powerful and wealthy city might declare themselves to be noble, as did the wealthy merchant families of Venice in the fourteenth century. Other urban elites simply styled themselves patricians, thereby forging a link with the aristocrats of ancient Rome.

The so-called patricians of the towns of Europe seldom numbered more than 5 to 6 percent of a community's populace, although they often had more than their share of political power. Ranking below the patriciate were the smaller merchants, skilled artisans, shop owners, lawyers, and teachers. The size of the clerical populations varied, but even a town without a resident bishop, such as sixteenth-century Nuremberg, might have had as many as 10 percent of its population in the ranks of the clergy. Since the clerical estate made up roughly 2 to 4 percent of the European population as a whole, the figure for Nuremberg shows how the clergy would often cluster around the protective walls of towns. Towns that were seats of bishops would have large clerical populations, whereas remote rural parishes often had difficulty in keeping enough priests.

At least a third of a typical town's population were apprentices, journeymen, gardeners, servants, prostitutes, unskilled laborers, paupers, and peddlers. In times of economic difficulties, the ranks of a city's poor would swell. Nuremberg, for example, distributed free bread on a daily basis to 13,000 people in 1540 and 1541. Famine was always a possibility even inside a town with its grain storage warehouses, but usually cities seemed much more prosperous than the countryside. This can also be seen in the hordes of beggars who lined the roads leading to most urban centers. The upper echelon of urban society, in sharp contrast, ate the best the surrounding countryside could provide, including white bread made of the finest available grains, as well as fresh vegetables and meat on a regular basis.

While Europe remained predominantly rural throughout the preindustrial age, towns had generally increased in size and wealth since the eleventh century. Even though urban populations may have fallen by as much as a third during the disasters associated with the widespread and lethal effects of the Black Death between 1347 and 1350, by the late fifteenth century trade and towns began to grow again. By 1500 modest increases had brought the European population up to 60 to 75 percent of what they had been before the mid-fourteenth century. Europe's population would continue to increase gradually over the course of the sixteenth century.

Most towns, however, numbered only a few thousand inhabitants. There were a few large communes such as Cologne in Germany and Marseilles in France, both of which had about 40,000 residents inside their walls in the beginning of the sixteenth century. Ghent in the Low Countries had around 50,000 inhabitants, as did London, Lyon, and Seville. Readers should be aware that all Renaissance era population figures are a matter of considerable debate. However, it appears that Florence, Milan, Rome, Venice, and Palermo in Sicily all had populations nearing 100,000, as did Lisbon in Portugal. Paris may have had almost 200,000 residents. Mighty Naples had perhaps as many as 230,000 people, thus rivaling Constantinople and the Aztec capital of Tenochtitlán in Mexico before its destruction in 1521 by Hernan Cortés and his allies.

All of these comparatively large cities had great ports or were near major land trade routes. Nuremberg, for example, was not a port city or on a navigable river, but it was located near twelve different trade routes in the heart of central Europe. Bruges in the Low Countries was in rapid decline throughout the fifteenth century. Its port entrance had silted over, and large ships would go to other nearby ports such as Amsterdam and Antwerp, which grew apace in the sixteenth and seventeenth centuries, as did London.

Most towns had surrounding clusters of peasant villages and sometimes smaller client towns as well. People liked the feeling of security that came from being near walled, fortified places. Some Renaissance towns bristled with armaments and fortifications, such as wealthy Nuremberg with its several rings of walls, large trenches, eighty-four towers on the inner wall and forty on the outer wall, and protected gates. York in northern England had fortifications going back to the Norman conquest; Chester's walls and gates dated to Roman times, as did Trier's in Germany and Lyon's in France. Spanish towns such as Avila and Segovia bristled with barriers and defenses that had been used in the wars with the Muslims.

Inside even the largest of towns, people lived close together and their behavior was closely regulated by the community's leading male citizens. The majority of town dwellers lived in small, half-timbered cabins with some of the poor huddled in crude sheds clustered alongside town walls. Shopkeepers and their families and servants usually lived in a few rooms above their places of business. Only a few rich merchants and bankers such as the Medici of Florence or the Fuggers of Augsburg had imposing town houses with brick and stone facades and sometimes country homes as well. Goods were displayed for sale on the lower floor and sometimes sold on the streets and in the market square. Every town had its Weavers' Lane, its Butchers' Row, and its Fishmongers' Alley. The narrow streets

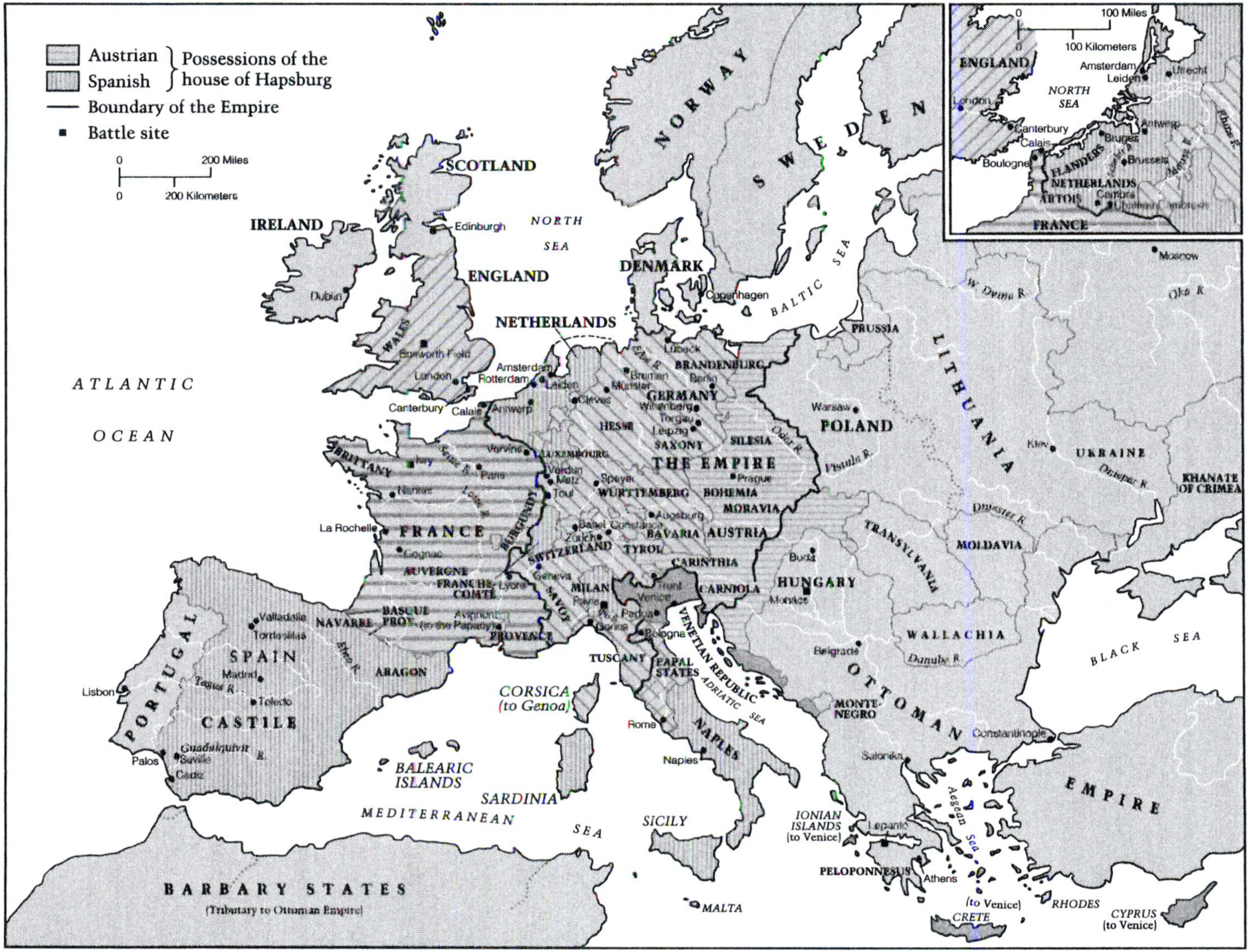
Austrian
Spanish
Possessions of the house of Hapsburg
Boundary of the Empire
Battle site
0 200 Miles
0 200 Kilometers
ATLANTIC OCEAN
NORTH SEA
BALTIC SEA
BLACK SEA
MEDITERRANEAN SEA
ADRIATIC SEA
Aegean Sea
IRELAND
SCOTLAND
ENGLAND
WALES
NORWAY
SWEDEN
DENMARK
NETHERLANDS
FRANCE
BRITTANY
BURGUNDY
AUVERGNE
FRANCHE COMTÉ
PROVENCE
BASQUE PROV.
NAVARRE
ARAGON
SPAIN
CASTILE
PORTUGAL
THE EMPIRE
GERMANY
HESSE
SAXONY
BRANDENBURG
SILESIA
BOHEMIA
MORAVIA
WURTTEMBERG
BAVARIA
AUSTRIA
TYROL
CARINTHIA
CARNIOLA
SWITZERLAND
LUXEMBOURG
SAVOY
MILAN
TUSCANY
PAPAL STATES
VENETIAN REPUBLIC
NAPLES
CORSICA (to Genoa)
SARDINIA
SICILY
MALTA
BALEARIC ISLANDS
PRUSSIA
POLAND
LITHUANIA
UKRAINE
KHANATE OF CRIMEA
HUNGARY
TRANSYLVANIA
MOLDAVIA
WALLACHIA
MONTENEGRO
OTTOMAN EMPIRE
IONIAN ISLANDS (to Venice)
PELOPONNESUS
CRETE (to Venice)
RHODES
CYPRUS (to Venice)
BARBARY STATES
(Tributary to Ottoman Empire)
Dublin
Edinburgh
London
Canterbury
Calais
Amsterdam
Rotterdam
Leiden
Antwerp
Cleves
Münster
Bremen
Lübeck
Berlin
Wittenberg
Torgau
Leipzig
Prague
Speyer
Augsburg
Constance
Basel
Zürich
Geneva
Lyons
Avignon (to the Papacy)
Verdun
Metz
Toul
Vervins
Paris
Nantes
La Rochelle
Cognac
Trent
Venice
Padua
Pavia
Bologna
Rome
Naples
Copenhagen
Warsaw
Kiev
Moscow
Buda
Belgrade
Constantinople
Salonika
Lepanto
Athens
Lisbon
Palos
Seville
Cadiz
Madrid
Toledo
Valladolid
Tordesillas
Tagus R.
Ebro R.
Guadalquivir R.
Loire R.
Seine R.
Elbe R.
Oder R.
Vistula R.
Danube R.
Dniester R.
Dnieper R.
W. Dvina R.
Oka R.
NORTH SEA
ENGLAND
London
Canterbury
Calais
Boulogne
Amsterdam
Leiden
Utrecht
Antwerp
Bruges
Brussels
Cambrai
FLANDERS
NETHERLANDS
ARTOIS
FRANCE
Rhine R.
0 100 Miles
0 100 Kilometers

Europe in the Renaissance

were crowded with people, animals (scavenging pigs being a particular favorite), and various kinds of refuse, including human excrement, often dumped from upper-floor windows. The practice of burying the dead within town walls did nothing to lower the threshold of disease.

DAILY LIFE

Church and town hall bells awoke the burghers and punctuated their days. Bells were also used to warn the inhabitants of the danger of approaching enemies. During the day, towns were filled with activity. Goods were made, bought, and sold, as were the food products of the countryside. Inns and taverns were filled with travelers and locals. Religious processions, holy days, and civic festivals provided welcome distractions from the routine work activities. At sundown, gates were locked, vagrants were expelled, and curfews were enforced as darkness and quiet descended over the towns. City streets at night were places for honest citizens to avoid, even though crime was severely and publicly punished. Entrance gates to towns were often "decorated" with the severed, eyeless heads of executed criminals.

Despite the severity of punishment, Renaissance towns could often be dangerous places. The presence of unmarried journeymen away from the restraints of their hometowns posed a constant threat. Sexual assaults and drunken brawls were common. In sixteenth-century Venice, violence was ritualized to the point where several times each year, workers and artisans would gather on a Sunday or a holiday afternoon to battle with sticks and fists for the possession of a bridge. These prearranged, organized "wars" would be watched regularly by thousands of spectators. Violence, whether organized or not, was as much a part of urban life as barter in the marketplace or high-quality craft production in the workshops.

Maintaining law and order was the great preoccupation of most urban governments. Renaissance towns were usually governed by councils made up of the leading male merchants, who were sometimes joined by prosperous guildsmen. Crafts were still organized in the form of economic associations, called *guilds*, which regulated production and employment standards, set prices, and provided benefits for the widows and orphans of their members. The guilds also served as social and religious brotherhoods and typically sponsored floats in carnival parades and religious processions. Therefore, they were something like labor unions, but with management functions and a firm commitment to religion as well.

URBAN WOMEN

Women were typically not allowed to be members of guilds and go through the full training course of being apprentices, journeymen, and finally masters. Girls might be apprenticed to makers of silk thread, to dressmakers, or to embroiderers. Often wives and daughters of a master craftsman learned the skills of the trade, and sometimes widows were allowed to take over their deceased husband's shop for a limited period of time. This was done chiefly to avoid having to provide financial support for widows and their children out of collective guild funds. As was the case of farm families, everyone was expected to work. Guild widows had to pay guild fees, but had no voice in the running of the guilds. Although most urban women worked as housekeepers, others found additional employment primarily as shopkeepers, tavern maids, and servants. Legal restrictions made it difficult for women to own much property or to conduct business.

Because women were denied economic power, they also had little political power in most towns. They were not eligible for public office and not allowed to make public policy decisions. The laws that bound them were made exclusively by males. Inside families, men ruled supreme and were able to enforce their power by brute force if necessary. Wife beating was common, even though the church made efforts to limit it. While theorists such as the architect Leon Battista Alberti (c. 1404–1472) urged husbands to treat their wives and children with kindness, there was no question where ultimate power resided.

Renaissance governments mirrored family and household structure in being not only patriarchal, but also paternalistic. Tight social control was the supposedly divinely sanctioned order of the day and it was exerted by wealthy men over men of lower status, all women, and children. Households consisted of family members, relatives, and servants. City fathers took responsibility for regulating not only all aspects of market life, but also the personal lives of their fellow citizens. For example, a typical town council spent time deliberating "how the extravagance of children in dressing during Holy Week might be prevented" or whether or not a woman "was too ardent in bed with her husband."[2] Nothing was considered beneath the notice of the paternalistic rulers of towns, whether they were bishops, dukes, or councils of merchants and guildsmen.

SOCIAL TENSIONS

Although animosities between men and women seldom erupted into public violence, many Renaissance towns experienced considerable tension between rich merchants, professionals, and the mostly illiterate masses who worked with their hands. The patriciate considered themselves to be "honorable men who earn their living in respectable business, not lowly manual work," as the lawyer Christoph Scheurl (1481–1542) put it.[3] Increasingly the business of government required more and more lawyers to transact. Towns kept lawyers on their payrolls as consultants and used men with legal training as bureaucrats despite the reputation of the legal profession for avarice, as Marinus van Reymerswaele's 1545 painting of a law office reveals. The artist was responding to a Dutch proverb: "If you go to a lawyer to get back your cow, you will have to bring the lawyer another to pay his fee." Despite the presence of those trained in the law and other public officials preoccupied with maintaining law and order, Renaissance towns were filled with festering jealousies and social grievances that often threatened to erupt into public violence.

Sometimes the struggles over employment, status, and representation on city councils, among other issues, boiled over into class warfare, as when the artisans of Nuremberg revolted in 1348 to 1349 or when the hungry cloth workers of Florence revolted in the summer of 1378. The unskilled Florentine cloth workers (called *Ciompi*) were crushed by their more prosperous brothers in the guilds. The Nuremberg craft workers were defeated by the patriciate allied with the Holy Roman Emperor Charles IV. In times of crisis, the privileged tended to stick together. The patricians of Nuremberg then used the artisans' revolt as an excuse to keep guildsmen off the city's elite governing small council, whereas other German towns such as Augsburg and Strasbourg found means of accommodating the most powerful guildsmen.

At times public violence erupted between members of the same social class, but who lived in different neighborhoods with

Marinus van Reymerswaele, *The Lawyer's Office* (1545). Courtesy of the New Orleans Museum of Art, Ella West Freeman Foundation Matching Fund.

which they identified, as was the case of the famous bridge battlers of Venice. Factional violence could be almost as dangerous as class warfare. Further complicating the situation in many communes were family rivalries, such as that between the Albizzi and the Ricci families in fourteenth-century Florence. Often family and factional disputes were related to political matters—for example, the rivalry in Italy between the supporters of the German Holy Roman emperor and his frequent rival the pope (Ghibellines versus Guelfs) or factions within the larger groupings. Although life in many Renaissance towns was sometimes turbulent, it was seldom dull. Urban centers were busy, colorful places of hard work and sometimes intense interactions.

THE RISE OF THE CAPITALISTS

The growth of towns in the late Middle Ages had accompanied the rise of capitalism. Capitalism involves private or corporate ownership of capital goods and investment decisions. Capitalists usually favor letting free markets determine prices, production, and distribution. During the Middle Ages, capitalists had struggled against the Old Testament injunction against "taking usury or increase" on loans. The highly influential theologian St. Thomas Aquinas (c. 1225–1274) and other leading church intellectuals agreed with Aristotle that "money is sterile" and that a good Christian should not take advantage of a neighbor in need.

Generally the Europeans lagged behind the Asians and Muslims as merchants and in technology and medicine during much of the medieval period. None of the European overland trade routes compared to the Asian "silk road" from Samarkand to Beijing in China. The Asians also had better ships and navigational instruments than the Europeans until the time of the Renaissance.

All of this began to change even before the fourteenth century. For example, the idea of usury became more and more acceptable as Christian bankers helped fund the Crusades and endowed chapels and hospitals at home and abroad. The medieval Crusades to the Holy Land (1096 to 1291) helped stimulate demand in Europe for luxury goods such as cottons, silks, muslin, dye-stuffs, medicines, perfumes, spices, and much else. Once Europeans had sampled ginger and nutmeg, they were never going to be content again with just plain, but still expensive, salt as their main spice.

Italian merchants from port cities such as Genoa and Venice had long been active in trading with Byzantine and Arab merchants. Several members of the thirteenth-century Polo merchant family of Venice had spent decades in the Asia of Kublai Khan, grandson of the Mongol conqueror Genghis Khan (c. 1160–1227). Marco Polo (c. 1254–1324) eventually published his *Travels*, a widely read account of his time spent in the East, whose accuracy has recently been called into question. Be that as it may, by the thirteenth and fourteenth centuries, dozens of Italian cities were heavily involved in the growing trade in the Mediterranean.

That trade also included a lucrative traffic in human flesh as the thirteenth century witnessed a resurgence of the slave trade. Prisoners of war and children of desperate parents were sold in the markets of various towns such as bustling Genoa. Slaves came from Africa as well as the Balkans and the Black Sea regions. Africans, Asians, and Ottomans were especially valued as house servants and for tasks in the expanding cloth industries of Italy. This shameful traffic in human beings also fueled the growth of capitalism.

To facilitate expanding and increasingly long-distance trade, banking operations had to be expanded and modernized. Bills of exchange and other written instruments of credit, together with more stable currencies such as the gold florin of Florence and the ducat of rich Venice, all helped increase long-distance trade. Florence became the banking capital of Europe as eighty banking houses were located there by 1338. Florentine trading houses such as the Bardi and Peruzzi used their banking operations to enhance trade and make easy profits on exchange rates. Pope Boniface VIII used Bardi banks for collecting papal taxes and transmitting money to Rome from all over Europe. Florentine bankers also loaned large sums of money to the crowned heads of Europe, sometimes to their financial peril.

JACOB FUGGER THE RICH (1459–1525)

What the Italians mastered, other Europeans emulated. Great financial centers such as Antwerp, Amsterdam, London, and Paris emerged in the north of Europe. In the Holy Roman Empire, the mighty banking empire of Jacob Fugger the Rich became the major bankroll behind Emperor Maximilian I. A native of a prominent Augsburg banking family, Jacob's mother, Barbara (d. 1497), was one of the leading businesswomen of the period. Jacob had studied bookkeeping and business in Venice as a youth. Families involved in international business typically sent their sons to work abroad. This allowed them to expand their horizons and learn foreign business techniques, customs, currencies, and languages. Business was not studied in schools, but learned on the job. In 1485 Jacob took charge of a Fugger branch bank in Innsbruck, Austria, and made several successful ventures into the growing mining industry in the Tyrolian Alps. By 1502, after extending the family's mining interests into Hungary and Silesia, he became the virtual head of the Fugger family business. The Habsburgs, whose loans Fugger shrewdly secured by a claim against the royal salt mines, were among his most notable customers.

Amazingly successful, Jacob the Rich's motto was "I shall gain while I am able." To do that, Fugger not only loaned money to powerful princes at a high rate of interest, but he also involved his firm in the new East India spice trade opened up by the recent voyages of discovery. He also hired theologians such as Dr. Johann Eck of Ingolstadt to write defenses of usury. It was Jacob Fugger who loaned Albrecht of Brandenburg the 29,000 gulden necessary to secure the archbishopric of Mainz, which triggered Martin Luther's famous protests against the sale of indulgences. Fugger also secured Charles V's election as Holy Roman emperor in 1519 by loaning him 544,000 gulden in bribe money. Jacob the Rich also used some of his wealth to found the Fuggerei in Augsburg, the world's first housing project for poor and retired workers. Towns all over Europe could only dream of having families like the

Portrait engraving of Jacob Fugger. Bibliotheque Nationale, Paris, France. Giraudon/Art Resource.

Fuggers in their midst. Capitalists with or without consciences were here to stay.

MUSLIMS

Added to the social mix of some sixteenth-century communities were a small number of religious and ethnic minorities. It should be remembered that the overwhelming majority of Europe's people at the beginning of the sixteenth century were Roman Catholics. A minority in the eastern parts of Europe were Orthodox Christians, who used either the Greek or the Slovonic rites. People thought of themselves not as Europeans, but as part of the body of Christ (Christendom). Diversity in religion was not tolerated in very many parts of Christian Europe. Muslims predominated only in southern Spain until the fall of their last major stronghold, Granada, in 1492 to the armies of Isabella of Castile (1451–1504), the pious warrior-queen. After a period of initial toleration, Queen Isabella found herself under intense pressure to end religious pluralism. For many prominent Christians, those who kept other religious traditions were in danger of losing their immortal souls and infecting those around them. There was doubtless also a great deal of Christian jealousy about the sophisticated business and medical practices of a number of the Muslims. Therefore, the only allowed option for the thousands of Spanish Muslims was to convert to Christianity or leave the Iberian peninsula. Thousands converted, but even more surrendered their property and fled to various places in Europe, Africa, and the Middle East, often with dire consequences.

Although Islam was severely reduced in what became the Spanish kingdom, it grew apace on Europe's eastern flank after the Ottoman conquest of Constantinople, or Byzantium, in 1453. Sultan Mehmed II (r. 1451–1481) used cannons to breach the huge sea walls which protected the mighty city on the straits. Known to contemporaries for his intellectual curiosity, Mehmed then advanced to besiege Athens, which fell in 1456. His forces then moved on to conquer the rest of Greece and pushed on up the Balkans to take Serbia, Bosnia, Herzegovina, and Albania while spreading Islam in their wake.

After a period of consolidation and expansion to the east against the Persians, the Ottomans renewed their war of conquest against the Christian West under the leadership of the poetry-writing Sultan Süleyman I (r. 1520–1566), the Lawgiver. Süleyman's great armies took Belgrade in 1521, crushed the Hungarians in central Hungary in 1526, and threatened Vienna in 1529. Had well-fortified Vienna fallen, it is hard to imagine any force in Europe strong enough to resist the Ottomans. In fact, the Ottomans would have been an even greater threat had their feudal officers not found it necessary to return periodically to their home estates around Constantinople (now known as Istanbul). Such sudden departures by many members of the officer corps made sustaining lengthy sieges and campaigns difficult. Sultan Süleyman also worried about the effects of European winters on his beloved herds of cavalry horses. Nevertheless, his western campaigns permanently established Islam in the Balkans.

SLAVES FROM AFRICA AND THE LEVANT

In addition to Muslims, Europe's minority populations also included Africans of various religious and tribal backgrounds, who served primarily as domestic slaves in prosperous homes in Italy during the fifteenth century with the beginning of the Portuguese black slave trade in West Africa. Captured Africans as well as Tartars and

Gentile Bellini, *Sultan Mehmed II Fahti, "The Conqueror"* (c. 1479–1481). National Gallery, London, Great Britain. Erich Lessing / Art Resource.

Turks from the Levant were sold at the slave markets in Ancona, Genoa, Pisa, and Venice. It is difficult to determine how much cultural influence they exerted on their masters, but some cross-cultural stimulation was inevitable. Black faces fascinated a number of Renaissance artists, including Albrecht Dürer. Merchants from Africa had appeared in England by the 1550s. William Shakespeare's play *Othello* uses black-white relations and racial prejudice as powerful themes.

During the sixteenth century the supply of domestic slaves in Italy was sharply reduced by rising costs and the growing domination of the Ottomans, who fought to gain control of the slave markets. Slaves and prisoners continued to row galleys that plied the Mediterranean, although most

Albrecht Dürer, *Head of a Black* (1508). Charcoal drawing. Graphisches Sammlung Albertina, Vienna, Austria. Foto Marburg/Art Resource.

rowers were free men. Domestic slavery did not develop in other parts of Europe in part because of the abundance of poorly paid workers, but became a major part of the growing slave trade to the "New World" of the Americas. There slave labor came to be in great demand.

JEWS

Europe also had a small Jewish population in the sixteenth century despite periodic waves of expulsions, forced conversions, and judicial murder. Although often placed under the protection of a ruling prince, Jews were prohibited from owning land in most parts of Europe and barred from many other occupations. They worked for the most part as butchers, bookbinders, domestic workers, notaries, scribes, itinerant peddlers, money lenders, pawnbrokers, and physicians. Given the many restrictions that Jews lived under, they played only a minor part in the economy.

During the fourteenth century, Jewish communities were often blamed for such great disasters as the Black Death (1347–1350). Looking for scapegoats, some Christians accused their Jewish neighbors of poisoning wells and spreading the plague in other ways. Actually the Jews had nothing to do with the spread of the various epidemics that killed almost a third of the population of Europe in less than three years. As we shall see in the next chapter, the various epidemics that made up the Black Death were spread mostly by germs that lived on fleas which were hosted by black Asian rats. This was, of course, not understood by people in the fourteenth century, most of whom thought God was punishing them for their sins. As a vulnerable minority, Jews were sometimes unjustly blamed for spreading the plague, allegedly by poisoning wells. Therefore, Europe's Jews in many places suffered waves of terror in the fourteenth century, which further reduced their population.

At the end of the fifteenth century, Jews in Castile and Aragon were forced to convert to Christianity or to leave. Thousands converted, but continued to be treated with great suspicion and suffered waves of persecution as "New Christians." Others risked everything to migrate to Africa, the Middle East, and other parts of Europe, especially Italy. Many Jews and "New Christians" were the victims of the notorious Spanish Inquisition. Ritual public burnings of Jews in Spain continued until late in the seventeenth century, with a particularly elaborate *auto de fé* held in Madrid's "Theater of Blood" in 1680. Portugal in 1496 under King Joao also forced its Jewish population to convert to Christianity or to flee. By 1517 Jews had been almost completely driven out of Spain and southern Italy.

During the sixteenth century, Jews had made something of a comeback in other parts of Europe, although they still made up less than 1 percent of the Continent's population. Even the largest known Jewish communities outside Italy such as those in Prague and Vienna did not number more than 500 to 700 members. Most others were considerably smaller. Some large towns such as Nuremberg had no Jewish citizens in the sixteenth century. Nuremberg had been given permission to expel its Jews in 1498 by Emperor Maximilian I (r. 1493–1519). Some of those driven from Nuremberg moved only a few miles away to the smaller town of Fürth, but their synagogue on the city's market square was torn down and replaced with a church dedicated to the Virgin Mary. Maximilian's grandson and successor, Charles V (r. 1519–1555), inspired by the Renaissance humanists, took a more benevolent attitude toward the empire's Jews. He was also impressed by the elo-

quence of Rabbi Joseph of Rosheim from Alsace. Emperor Charles did allow a few persecutions in the Holy Roman Empire, but conditions for Jews gradually improved throughout much of the empire and in Europe as a whole during the later part of the sixteenth century despite the scorn and neglect of the predominantly Christian society.

The Nobility

Although some rich city folk claimed to be noble, they were generally looked down upon by the remnants of the old feudal nobility or, as contemporaries viewed it, "those who fight." For the most part, the "nobles of the sword," who made up the second estate, were in relative decline for much of the later part of the Renaissance. Their landed estates did not produce as much wealth as could be secured from international trade by merchants and bankers. Some nobles tried to expand their incomes by changing the forms of peasant obligations, substituting cash for customary services, for example. These so-called commutations helped to free up peasant living conditions to a degree, but they failed to make some of the lesser nobility feel more economically secure.

Innovations in warfare had made the nobility as the major source of military strength largely obsolete even as early as the fourteenth century. Longbows and gunpowder made knights in shining armor a thing of the past, except for the tournaments, which continued to flourish until King Henri II of France died after receiving a fragment of a shattered lance in the eye during a joust in 1559. The premature death of this chivalrous king had a chilling effect on the noble sport of tournament jousting, which began to fall out of fashion in respectable circles.

MERCENARY AND ROBBER NOBLES

To meet rising expenses, some nobles were reduced to the role of mercenaries—hired paladins at the beck and call of the highest bidder. Although some such as Federigo da Montefeltro (1422–1482) of Urbino were honest, pious, and highly cultivated, others lapsed into thuggery or worse. Sigismondo Malatesta (c. 1417–1468), ruler of Rimini, was convicted of murder, rape, wife beating, sacrilege, perjury, incest, and adultery. Yet he was also an important patron of art and scholarship. Trained to kill from their early youth, it is not surprising that some nobles resorted to crime and robbery. Gangs of noble thugs and their armed retainers attacked merchant caravans moving from town to town.

One such robber knight was Götz von Berlichingen (c. 1480–1562). Götz was born to a German noble family and took service at the court of the margrave of Brandenburg-Ansbach. In 1504 he lost his right hand in combat in the War of the Bavarian Succession. Berlichingen hired a craftsperson to make him an iron hand, which he used to strike terror into the hearts of his enemies. Those enemies came to include the prosperous citizens of towns such as Bamberg, Mainz, and Nuremberg, whose merchant caravans he plundered for many years. In 1519 he fought as a mercenary for Duke Ulrich of Württemberg. Six years later, Berlichingen lowered himself socially by fighting for cash on the side of rebellious peasants, but deserted them in time to avoid being destroyed by their defeat in the summer of 1525.

Although placed under imperial ban as an outlaw on four occasions and jailed twice, Berlichingen fought for Emperor Charles V against the Ottomans in 1542 and against the French in 1544. Robber knights like Berlichingen often had family and friends in high places and were difficult to suppress. As much as princes might decry robber barony, they still needed skilled warriors to make up their officer corps.

THE REFINEMENT OF MANNERS

Those nobles of the higher strata who stayed out of trouble and had sufficient revenues saw their lifestyles improve in the course of the Renaissance. Castles became better heated and more luxuriously furnished and much better designed. Country estates came to be surrounded by lovely gardens, stocked fishponds, and ample facilities for leisure. During the sixteenth century, the nobility of Europe withdrew more and more from their contact with the lower orders. They stopped eating with their retainers in great halls and withdrew into separate dining rooms. Nobles in Lombardy stopped wrestling with their peasants and stopped killing bulls in public in Spain.

To further set themselves apart, nobles learned to talk and behave in a more formal and self-conscious style. Manners improved and became more refined as more was expected of the nobility than just skill in combat. Baldassare Castiglione's 1528 *Book of the Courtier* set new standards for noble behavior. To succeed at court, noblemen were expected by the humanist and former diplomat Castiglione (1478–1529) to be able to dance, play games, ride, recite and understand poetry, speak clearly, and give good advice. As for the noblewomen of the court, according to Castiglione:

> I wish this Lady to have knowledge of letters, of music, of painting, and know how to dance and how to be festive, adding a discrete modesty and the giving of a good impression of herself to those other things that are required of the Courtier.[4]

Noblewomen of all ranks were responsible for producing meals, supervising servants, and doing all sorts of needlework.

Although the nobility of Renaissance Europe may have been in a state of relative and gradual decline, overall it was a most privileged elite. Its male members especially had an enviable existence. After all, the nobility was still at the top of the social heap. Those at the top of the top were part of the extended family of the crowned heads of Europe. They held vast amounts of lands and had many privileges. Nobles had virtual monopolies on the best offices in the royal governments and in the military. Some received generous pensions from the crown. Noble sons and daughters received preferential treatment in the church and, like the clergy, the nobility in many places enjoyed widespread exemption from direct taxes. While revenues from lands may have failed to keep pace with inflation in the sixteenth century, it is still important to remember that the nobility, which made up only about 2 percent of the population of Europe, controlled as much as half of the best land in many areas. So even though their incomes in many cases may have been falling during the period, they were still among the wealthiest people in Europe, and many rich commoners were eager to marry their daughters into the ranks of the nobility or to be made "noble" by royal favor.

Even though it was difficult even for a rich commoner to secure a patent of nobility, many prosperous merchants attempted to imitate noble lifestyles. The sons of the merchant elite as well as the nobility enjoyed hunting, dancing, jousting, and feasting. Merchants also emulated the social pretensions of the nobility. Indeed, with their sumptuous meals of meat soup, boiled beef, roasted mutton, capons fattened on oats, pigeon, fresh or salted fish, white bread, jams, juices, gravies, fruits, vegetables, and cheeses, all washed down by beer or watered wine, there was a great deal in a typical noble's gastronomic life to be envied.

Noblewomen, while hardly creatures of total leisure, still had much better lives than those below them, especially if their fathers and husbands were kind, something that could never be taken for granted. As with the women of other social groups, noble females were brought up to expect a far different destiny from noble males. Their lives would revolve around family and domestic life. Some would go into the church as "brides of Christ." All women were taught that they held lower status than the males, for as the poplar saying expressed it, "He is the sun and she is the moon."

Everyone in the nobility and the upper ranks of the merchant elite seemed to dress very sumptuously indeed when compared to the peasantry. Furs and fine fabrics, eventually including silk, made the "men in tights" (actually hose) of the era and their sumptuously clad and bejeweled ladies of lace and brocade appear to be figures worlds apart from the woolen-clad poor people who surrounded them and even the armies of servants who cooked for them and waited upon them. Clearly, the nobility of Europe were a privileged elite who often loved to display their power, status, and wealth in increasingly conspicuous consumption. Their "honor" demanded no less of them.

The Clergy

Also set apart from the roughly clad hordes of poor working people were the members of the first estate—the clergy—"those who pray." They were first, theoretically, in the medieval social hierarchy because they were considered to be closest to God. They were to pray, dispense charity, do good works, and sacrifice worldly pleasures for the sake of everyone's salvation. Therefore, they, like some in the second estate, were exempted from taxation by the state. They had

Limbourg, Month of March, Ploughing the Field. Manuscript illumination from the *Trés Riches Heures du Duc de Berry*. Musee Conde, Chantilly, France. Giraudon/Art Resource.

their own legal code (canon law) and court system, which punished clerics less severely than secular courts punished the laity for similar crimes. Only the celebrant could receive both the cup and the bread during the Eucharist, among other signs of God's favor. The clergy made up from 2 to 4 percent of the population at the beginning of the sixteenth century. This made them a relatively large group of people to have so many privileges in a culture where so many had so little except hard work and deprivation. Like the laity, the clergy were divided along class lines. Although those at the higher levels had large incomes, many priests, especially those in rural parishes, were paid very poorly.

The Renaissance clergy were made up of two main groups: the secular clergy, or those who were in the world, and the regu-lar clergy, who followed a religious rule and were either cloistered monks or worked among the laity as friars. The clergy was technically a male monopoly; women were not candidates for ordination. Even cloistered nuns had to receive the sacraments from males. The higher ranks of the secular clergy administered the church's elaborate sacramental system: baptism, confirmation, penance, the Eucharist, ordination (for the clergy only), marriage (for the laity only), and final rites. The seven sacraments were considered outward signs of God's favor and were essential in order to achieve salvation. They helped instill a feeling of God's presence in the world and bound people of all stations into a sacred community of believers throughout the European world. They provided important rites of passage for all stages of a Christian's life on earth.

The Latin of the Roman church and the Greek and Slovonic of the Orthodox church exposed Christians to common religious languages and rituals, which further enhanced the feeling of community for the majority who accepted the tradition. There were also those who secretly rejected many aspects of the church's tradition, but they were usually in the minority and ran great risks.

The secular clergy consisted of two groups: an upper and a lower clergy. The upper clergy was made up of priests and bishops. By the Renaissance, deacons and subdeacons were considered steps towards the priesthood. The lower clergy, or those in minor orders, consisted of doorkeepers, acolytes, lectors, and exorcists. The lower clergy were not often scrutinized carefully upon entrance and not bound by a permanent commitment to celibacy. Many in fact were married. They were set off from the world by their haircut (tonsure), which was short with a bald spot at the back of their heads. Members of the lower clergy could leave minor orders simply by growing their hair out. If they stayed in the service of the church, they shared in many of the clergy's privileges, such as the right to be tried for crimes in church rather than secular courts.

Much more was expected of the higher grades of the secular clergy than from those in the lower ranks. They were to be recognized by their tonsure and sober clothing. Since the eleventh century the church frowned upon sexual activity carried out by members of the higher clergy. Candidates for the priesthood were to be at least twenty-five years old, unmarried, of good moral character, educated, and have a reliable means of support. Those who lacked a church job of sufficient income could earn additional revenue in an "honorable profession" such as that of teacher or chaplain. All

these requirements could be waived or ignored by securing a papal dispensation. Married priests or priests with concubines could still be found, especially in rural parishes.

The regular clergy followed such monastic rules as poverty, chastity, obedience, and humility. Some lived in cloistered religious communities behind walls, away from the hustle and bustle of the workaday world. There they could experience lives of quiet devotion with usually seven occasions for prayer throughout the day, from early in the morning to sunset. There was also time for study and manual work. This life was open to both men and women, although male houses always outnumbered female, and convents required male clerics to say Mass. Monks and friars were tonsured and wore distinctive clothing, from the black robes of the Augustinian friars to the white robes of the Cistercian monks. Nuns also had short hair and wore distinctive habits and head coverings, which visibly separated them from their lay sisters. Convents were the only places where European women in significant numbers could utilize fully their intellectual and administrative gifts. Intellectually inclined male clerics not only had their monasteries, but also the universities, which excluded women with only a few rare exceptions.

Although membership in the religious orders was theoretically open to all, men and women from rich families dominated their ranks. Most monastic houses for women required a form of dowry or deposit. In fifteenth-century Florence, the average deposit for future nuns was 435 florins (more than sixteen times what the average journeyman made in a year). While it was still usually less expensive to become "a bride of Christ" than to marry a mortal man, convents were havens for the daughters of the privileged. Male clergy also came predominantly from the ranks of the nobility and the patriciate. Some came by choice, whereas others were sent into the church in order to avoid dividing inheritances or straining family resources.

Most clerics seemed to have kept their vows despite the popularity of stories of lascivious monks, friars, nuns, and priests written by writers such as Giovanni Boccaccio (1313–1375) in his *Decameron Tales,* Geoffrey Chaucer (c. 1340–1400) in his *Canterbury Tales,* or Marguerite of Navarre (1492–1549) in her *Heptameron.* Regional studies have indicated that 80 to 90 percent of the clergy in 1500 remained continent. The lifestyles of the clergy varied enormously, from begging

friars and monastic houses that practiced severe discipline and where food was modest, to Chaucer's drawn-from-life "regal" prioress, who ate "so primly and so well." Those at the top of the clerical hierarchy such as bishops, cardinals, and popes lived in splendor comparable to the great secular lords whose refined manners they emulated. The princes of the church were also waited upon by hosts of servants. Although the church had its share of problems, as we shall see, the surviving records indicate that the overwhelming majority of the sixteenth-century clergy lived lives of relative holiness despite the envy of some laity, who were all too willing to believe the worst of the first estate.

Further Reading

GENERAL SOCIAL HISTORY

Peter Burke, *Popular Culture in Early Modern Europe* (1978).

Roger Chartier, ed., *Passions of the Renaissance* (1989).

Natalie Davis, *Society and Culture in Early Modern France* (1975). A collection of her essays.

Lucien Febvre, *Life in Renaissance France.* Ed. and trans. by Marian Rothstein (1977).

Carlo Ginzburg, *The Cheese and the Worms: The Cosmos of a Sixteenth-Century Miller.* Tr. by John and Anne Tedeschi (1982).

George Huppert, *After the Black Death: A Social History of Early Modern Europe* (1986). An extremely valuable synthesis.

Henry Kamen, *The Iron Century: Social Change in Europe, 1550–1660* (1971). Still a valuable survey.

THE PEASANTRY

Andrew Appleby, *Famine in Tudor and Stuart England* (1978).

Natalie Davis, *The Return of Martin Guerre* (1983). A fascinating true story of a peasant imposter.

Jan de Vries, *The Dutch Rural Economy in the Golden Age, 1500–1700* (1974).

Emmanuel Le Roy Ladurie, *The French Peasantry, 1450–1660* (1987).

———, *Montaillou: The Promised Land of Error* (1978). An intriguing account of life and heresy in a fourteenth-century French village.

———, *The Peasants of Languedoc* (1969).

Thomas Robisheaux, *Rural Society and the Search for Order in Early Modern Germany* (1989).

Warren Sabean, *Power in the Blood: Popular Culture and Village Discourse in Early Modern Germany* (1984).

Richard Wunderli, *Peasant Fires: The Drummer of Niklashausen* (1991).

WOMEN AND GENDER

Bonnie Anderson and Judith Zinsser, *A History of Their Own: Women in Europe from Prehistory to the Present.* 2 vols. (1988). Although a general survey, it has a great deal to say about women in the Renaissance period.

Natalie Zemon Davis and Arlette Farge, eds., *A History of Women in the West,* vol. 3, *Renais-*

sance and Enlightenment Paradoxes (1993). Seventeen very important essays.

Barbara Hanawalt, ed., *Women and Work in Preindustrial Europe* (1986). Ten significant essays.

Constance Jordan, *Renaissance Feminism: Literary Texts and Political Models* (1990).

Margaret King, *The Death of the Child Valerio Marcello* (1994).

———, *Women of the Renaissance* (1991). A very important overview with particular attention given to women in Italy.

Thomas Kuehn, *Law, Family, and Women: Toward a Legal Anthropology of Renaissance Italy* (1991).

Gerda Lerner, *The Creation of Feminist Consciousness* (1993).

Ian MacLean, *The Renaissance Notion of Woman* (1980).

Marilyn Migiel and Julianna Schiesa, eds., *Refiguring Woman: Perspectives on Gender and the Italian Renaissance* (1991). A collection of diverse essays.

Merry Wiesner, *Women and Gender in Early Modern Europe* (1993). A fine survey.

———, *Women in the Sixteenth Century: A Bibliography* (1983).

———, *Working Women in Renaissance Germany* (1986).

JEWS

Salo Baron, *A Social and Religious History of the Jews,* 2nd ed. 14 vols. (1952–1969).

Robert Bonfil, *Jewish Life in Renaissance Italy* (1994).

R. Po-chia Hsia, *The Myth of Ritual Murder: Jews and Magic in Reformation Germany* (1988).

———, *Trent 1475: Stories of a Ritual Murder Trial* (1992).

——— and Hartmut Lehman, *In and Out of the Ghetto: Jewish-Gentile Relations in Late Medieval and Early Modern Germany* (1994).

Jonathan Israel, *European Jewry in the Age of Mercantilism, 1550–1750* (1985).

Heiko Oberman, *The Roots of Anti-Semitism* (1981).

Brian Pullan, *The Jews of Europe and the Inquisition of Venice, 1550–1670* (1983).

Raymond Waddington and Arthur Williamson, eds., *The Expulsion of the Jews: 1492 and After* (1994). Important essays.

AFRICANS AND OTTOMANS

Franz Babinger, *Mehmed the Conqueror and His Time* (1992).

Stanford Shaw, *Empire of the Gazis: The Rise and Decline of the Ottoman Empire, 1280–1808* (1976).

John Thornton, *Africa and Africans in the Making of the Atlantic World, 1400–1680* (1992).

Andrew Wheatcroft, *The Ottomans* (1994).

URBAN LIFE

Robin Briggs, *Communities of Belief: Cultural and Social Tensions in Early Modern France* (1989).

James Farr, *Hands of Honor: Artisans and Their World in Dijon, 1550–1650* (1988).

Barbara Hanawalt, *Growing Up in Medieval London: The Experience of Childhood in History* (1993).

Lewis Mumford, *The City in History* (1961).

Gerald Strauss, *Nuremberg in the Sixteenth Century* (1976).

Lee Palmer Wandel, *Always Among Us: Images of the Poor in Zwingli's Zurich* (1990).

THE CAPITALISTS

Janet Abu-Lughad, *Before European Hegemony: The World System 1250–1350* (1989).

Felix Gilbert, *The Pope, His Banker, and Venice* (1980).

Harry Miskimim, *The Economy of Early Renaissance Europe, 1300–1460* (1975).

Richard de Roover, *The Rise and Decline of the Medici Bank, 1397–1494* (1966).

THE NOBILITY

Davis Bitton, *The French Nobility in Crisis, 1560–1640* (1969).

Kristin Neuschal, *Word of Honor: Interpreting Noble Culture in Sixteenth-Century France* (1989).

Ellery Schalk, *From Valor to Pedigree: Ideas of Nobility in France in the Sixteenth and Seventeenth Centuries* (1986).

Lawrence Stone, *The Crisis of the Aristocracy, 1558–1641* (1965).

THE CLERGY

John Bossy, *Christianity in the West: 1400–1700* (1985).

K. J. P. Lowe, *Church and Politics in Renaissance Italy: The Life and Career of Cardinal Francesco Soderini (1453–1524)* (1993).

Joseph Lynch, *The Medieval Church: A Brief History* (1992).

Francis Oakley, *The Western Church in the Late Middle Ages* (1979).

Paolo Prodi, *The Papal Princes. One Body and Two Souls: The Papal Monarchy in Early Modern Europe* (1982).

R. W. Swanson, *Religion and Devotion in Europe, c. 1215–c. 1515* (1995).

Larissa Taylor, *Soldiers of Christ: Preaching in Late Medieval and Reformation France* (1992).

Thomas Tentler, *Sin and Confession on the Eve of the Reformation* (1977).

John Thomson, *Politics and Princes 1417–1517: Politics and Polity in the Late Medieval Church* (1980).

Notes

1. Cited in Bonnie Anderson and Judith Zinsser, *A History of Their Own: Women in Europe from Prehistory to the Present*, 2 vols. (New York: Harper, 1988), vol. 1, p. 88.
2. Cited in Jonathan W. Zophy, *Patriarchal Politics and Christoph Kress (1484–1535) of Nuremberg* (Lewiston, N.Y.: Edwin Mellen Press, 1992), p. 41.
3. Ibid., p. 39.
4. Castiglione, *The Book of the Courtier*, tr. by George Bull (Baltimore, Md.: Penguin, 1967), p. 216.

3

AN AGE OF DISASTERS

The Renaissance was born against the background of one of the most catastrophic periods in all of human history. It was an age of almost incessant warfare, most notably the so-called Hundred Years' War between the English and French kingdoms, which actually dragged on for 116 years (1337–1453). That frequently horrific conflict was followed for the English by a civil war—the so-called War of the Roses (1455–1485). As if these wars were not enough tragedy, Europe also witnessed the even greater catastrophe of the Black Death (1347–1350). For nearly three years highly contagious and often fatal plagues ravaged the entire Continent and killed almost a third of the European people. Although bubonic and pneumonic plagues would continue to afflict the Europeans until well into the eighteenth century, the worst of them hit the Europeans in the fourteenth century. Warfare and plague were accompanied by widespread outbreaks of famine and large-scale peasant rebellions in Flanders (1323–1328), France (1358), and England (1381).

Some viewed the plagues as God's judgment on a sinful world; others, however, were more concerned with the troubles in the Western church, particularly those involving what the early humanist Francesco Petrarca dubbed the "Babylonian Captivity of the Church of God" (1305–1376). This was the period when the headquarters of the Roman Catholic church were moved from Rome to Avignon, a smaller town near the French kingdom. The Captivity was followed by the Great Western Schism (1378–1417) in which the Catholic church had two and sometimes three popes: Usually one pope sat in Rome and another sat in Avignon. These difficulties helped fuel an increase in questioning of church doctrine and practice and led to what some viewed as *heresy* (the denial of accepted doctrine, which was considered a form of treason against God). The ideas and lives of such fourteenth-century thinkers as John Wycliffe in England, Jan Hus in Bohemia, and Marsilius of Padua presented a serious challenge to the authorities of the Western church. The beginnings of the Renaissance as a cultural movement, indeed, took place during one of the most difficult periods in Western history.

The Black Death, 1347–1350

Of all the disasters to afflict Europe in the fourteenth century, the most lethal was the widespread outbreak of plague in Europe between 1347 and 1350. Called the Black Death by later historians, the era of plague epidemics began in the winter of 1347 and

Albrecht Dürer, *Knight, Death, and the Devil* (1513). Engraving. Foto Marburg/Art Resource.

plague spread rapidly from the Mediterranean ports throughout much of Europe. A series of mild, damp winters also helped keep the fleas and their host animals active. Congested urban centers such as Florence were particularly vulnerable, especially if they were involved in the rat-infested grain trade. Some areas were completely bypassed by the plagues, whereas others lost as many as half their populations in less than three years. All told, the population of Europe declined by a third during the peak period of the Black Death.

Young children, the elderly, the sickly, and the undernourished were the hardest hit, but even some among the rich and powerful fell victim to the plagues that ravaged Europe. Those courageous priests who administered last rites to plague victims and medical personnel were also at special risk. Towns and families were ripped apart by the plague. The chronicler Agnolo di Tura described the horrors of the plague which ravaged his hometown in 1348 as follows:

1348 with the arrival of rat-infested merchant ships from the East. Those ships appear to have carried infected black rats, who in turn hosted parasitic fleas. The newly arrived rats mixed with local rodent populations. Fleas would then jump onto humans and animals and infect them with *bubonic plague*. When persons with respiratory infections contracted bubonic plague, they often became ill with a form of *pneumonic plague* as well. Recently some scholars have argued that anthrax, a highly contagious and lethal disease caused by spore-forming bacterium, was a major contributor to the Black Death. Anthrax can easily be transmitted from warm-blooded animals such as rats to humans.

Although no exact diagnosis is possible, it is quite clear that the various forms of

> ... the victims died almost immediately. They would swell beneath their armpits and in their groins, and fall over while talking. Father abandoned child, wife husband, one brother another.... And none could be found to bury the dead for money or friendship.... And in many places in Siena great pits were dug and piled deep with the multitude of the dead.... I buried my five children with my own hands.[1]

Europeans were overwhelmed by the magnitude of the disaster. Many attributed the plagues to the anger of God, who was punishing his children for their sins. Some went around in bands flagellating themselves and each other. Others used such traditional scapegoats as the Jews, who were thought to have spread the plague by poisoning wells. Still others blamed cats, dogs, and pigs and ordered their destruction.

Ironically, these creatures were enemies of the real culprits, the flea-infested black rats.

Gradually more and more surviving Europeans built up their immunities to the plague germs and instances of the plague died out by 1350, but returned in 1361–1362, hitting children born after the first wave of plague especially hard. The plague struck again in 1369, 1374–1375, 1379, 1390, 1407, and throughout much of the remainder of the Renaissance period. Although later outbreaks were never as lethal as the first waves of the plague in 1348 and 1349, Europe would not be free of the plague until the introduction of brown rats into Europe in the eighteenth century. Short nosed, short tailed, and ferocious, the brown rats waged war on the black rats and virtually wiped them out. Since brown rats do not provide suitable hosts for the plague bearing fleas and lice, the contagion lost its chief means of spreading. In addition, over time immunities had been built up in the human population; therefore, plague stopped being a widespread problem in Europe after the eighteenth century.

During the Renaissance, however, the repeated bouts of plague left indelible scars on the minds of Europeans. Their grief at losing so many people and expensive farm animals in so short a time was overwhelming. Instead of having a surplus of laborers, many villages were deserted; parts of cities were abandoned for almost a century. Some peasants attempted to take advantage of the situation to claim abandoned lands and to have their wages increased. Landlords attempted to artificially hold down wages. In England, for example, the Statute of Laborers of 1351 tried to freeze wages to pre-Plague levels. Such measures angered peasants, and were not always effective because some landlords were willing to pay wages above those dictated by law. Some of the landlords were proceeded against by the newly created chancellor's court, designed to close loopholes in the common law and compel obedience by the lower orders. The upper classes banded together to protect their privileges in the great crisis produced by the Black Death in England.

Some English landowners also decided to convert their fields to sheep runs and enter the lucrative wool trade. Since sheep farming is not as labor intensive as farming, such enclosures resulted in many peasant families in England being driven off the land, a situation that worsened during the late Renaissance. Enclosures only added to the unrest of people in the English countryside who were still trying to recover from the ravages of the Black Death. In other parts of Europe, some rural workers were displaced because of an increased shift to cash crops such as honey and wine production.

Peasant and Artisan Revolts

The Black Death also contributed to the rise of rural and urban violence. Ravaged by plague, depression, and mercenary marauders unleashed by the Hundred Years' War between France and England, elements of the French peasantry rebelled in 1358. Since so many peasant males were named Jacques, the insurrection in northern France was dubbed the "Jacquerie." For two weeks French peasants struck at the ruling elite. During one particularly savage episode, a noblewoman was forced to eat her roasted husband before being raped and killed. The nobility and urban elites then crushed the uprising with ferocious brutality.

Similar peasant rebellions also took place in parts of the Holy Roman Empire, Flanders, Italy, the Iberian peninsula, the Netherlands, and England. During the English Peasants' Revolt of 1381, an attempt was made to cast aside the last vestiges of serfdom. Some blamed the Oxford professor and church reformer John Wycliffe for contributing to the unrest by challenging the authority and wealth of the church. Some of his followers, called Lollards, insisted on using Wycliffe's English translation of the Bible and questioning injustices in both the church and the state. At one point in the 1381 rebellion, rebels paraded around London with the severed head of the archbishop of Canterbury. This rebellion, called the Wat Tyler Revolt after one of its leaders, was also put down with great savagery.

The plagues added to the considerable social tensions already present in some towns. People from plague-ravaged villages drifted into towns, but were not always able to find work. Because the Black Death disrupted trade in many parts of Europe, unemployment levels were higher than usual. Guilds often overreacted to the crisis by making even greater than normal restrictions on employment and more jealously guarding their monopolies. Many guilds now made inheritance the only avenue to shop ownership. Recession, unemployment, poverty, tensions between factions, guild rivalries, struggles for power, and sometimes petty jealousies all contributed to outbreaks of urban violence in places such as Nuremberg (1348–1349), Lucca (1369), Siena (1371), Perugia (1370–1371, 1375), Florence (1378), and Bologna (1411).

Troubles in the Church

No segment of European society or institution was safe from unrest in the fourteenth century, not even the great papal monarchy that was the Roman Catholic church. In the course of the Middle Ages the Western church had become one of the grandest monarchies in Europe. Talented canon-

lawyer popes such as Gregory VII (r. 1073–1085) and Innocent III (r. 1198–1216) had developed a doctrine known as the "fullness of power" (*plenitudo potestatis*) according to which the bishop of Rome had absolute authority over the church. The pope was not only the successor to Christ's great disciple St. Peter as the supreme spiritual head of the church and the representative (vicar) of Christ on earth, but also the supreme administrator, lawgiver, and judge. These pretensions had, of course, been challenged by Holy Roman emperors, among others, during the reigns of Pope Gregory VII and Pope Innocent III. Still, aggressive popes had come to be recognized as formidable monarchs who, in some cases, could overawe secular kings and emperors.

THE BABYLONIAN CAPTIVITY, 1305–1376

In 1294 the sacred college of cardinals found itself deadlocked between rival candidates for the papacy from the influential Roman families of the Colonna and the Orsini. Indeed, the cardinals had been deadlocked for eighteen months since the death of Pope Nicholas IV in 1292. Neither faction would agree to support the opposition's candidate. A division of the church (schism) seemed imminent. Peter Morone, a well-known Benedictine hermit in his eighties, sent the cardinals a stern letter warning them that divine vengeance would soon fall upon them if they did not elect a pope soon. In desperation the ailing and aged dean of the college of cardinals, Latino Malabranca, cried out, "In the name of the Father, the Son, and the Holy Ghost, I elect brother Peter of Morone!"[2]

The exhausted cardinals ratified Malabranca's inspired decision, and the venerable hermit became Pope Celestine V. Unfortunately, Celestine soon found that life as pope was not conducive to the quiet, spiritual life he craved. Even though he refused to move to congested Rome, at the papal castle in Naples, Celestine ordered a special wooden cell to be built so he could attempt to hide from the worldly cardinals, papal officials, and hordes of office seekers who made up the papal court. Miserable as pope, Celestine turned for advice to Benedict Gaetani, an accomplished canonist at the papal court and one of the cardinals who had elected him. The ambitious and oily Gaetani suggested that Celestine resign, which he agreed to do a mere fifteen weeks after his coronation.

Ten days after Celestine's abdication of December 13, the college of cardinals met again in Naples and elected Benedict Gaetani as pope. He took the name of Boniface VIII (r. 1294–1303), moved the papacy back to Rome, tried to increase papal revenues, and attempted to further develop the doctrine of the "fullness of power." In 1296 he found himself in a quarrel with King Philip IV, "the Handsome," of France (r. 1285–1314) and King Edward I (r. 1272–1307) of England. Philip and Edward had begun to tax their clergy without papal consent in order to pay for a war against each other. Incensed, Pope Boniface issued the bull *Clericis laicos*, which forbade taxation of the clergy without papal approval and threatened both kings with excommunication. To be excommunicated was to be deprived of the sacraments and guaranteed eternal damnation. It was a threat that his heroes Gregory VII and Innocent III had used to force several medieval monarchs to change their policies.

However, since the heyday of papal power in the high Middle Ages (eleventh through thirteenth centuries), things had changed, most notably in the rise of power of the early Renaissance state. Both Philip and Edward refused to submit to Boniface's threats and were supported in that refusal

by their nobles. Efforts to mediate the situation failed and Boniface was forced to back down when King Philip stopped all papal revenues gathered in France from leaving the kingdom for Rome. Bolstered by the enormous success of a church jubilee for the year 1300, which brought hordes of pilgrims to Rome and swelled the papal coffers, Boniface in 1302 issued the papal bull *Unam Sanctam* in which he asserted "that all human creation be subject to the pope of Rome."[3]

The iron-willed and wily Philip the Handsome now summoned his estates and accused Boniface of such crimes as practicing black magic, sodomy, murder, and keeping a demon as a pet. Philip's agents had been spreading similar stories about Boniface for years, so it was not surprising that the representatives of the French estates should have agreed to support their king in his struggle with the "evil pope." Philip dispatched armed men to Italy to confront Boniface at his villa at Anagni. Philip's troops pillaged the papal residence of "utensils, and clothing, fixtures, gold and silver, and everything" they found.[4] They also tried to force the aging pontiff to return with them to France to stand trial. Although Boniface was rescued from French hands three days later, he died a few weeks later in a state of shock and humiliation. The vicar of Christ was not used to such rude treatment.

What grief the wily Philip IV may have felt at the unexpected death of his papal rival was soon assuaged by the election of a Frenchman, Clement V (r. 1305–1314). Two years later Clement V moved the papal headquarters from faction-ridden Rome to Avignon, a papal town on the Rhone river, where his holiness could gaze out at the border of his native France. Needless to say, the French pope and his successors got along quite nicely for the most part with the

French monarchy and they stayed in Avignon for the next seventy years. Since Avignon did not have a sufficient set of palaces and churches to accommodate the transplanted papal court, an enormous building boom commenced. At the same time, the papacy had to find funds for armies in order to reassert its control over central Italy and compensate for lost revenues in the Papal States. This put enormous pressure on the Avignon popes to raise money and contributed to such long-standing church problems as *simony* (the selling of offices). One Avignon pope, the prodigal Clement VI (r. 1342–1352), bellowed, "I would sell a bishopric to a donkey if the donkey had enough money."[5]

Some of the other popes at Avignon such as John XXII (r. 1313–1334) showed great skills in administration and as fundraisers, but they had lost some of that spiritual authority and an aura of impartiality which had gone with being located in Rome, the city where St. Peter, the first "pope," had allegedly been crucified upside down. With the papacy in Avignon, it was too easy to think of it as captive to the interests of the nearby French monarchy.

For the poet and cleric Francesco Petrarca, who had grown up in Avignon and returned there in 1326, it was the "Babylon of the West," where "instead of soberness, licentious banquets; instead of pious pilgrimages, unnatural and foul sloth."[6] Although we must make allowances for Petrarca's rhetoric and recognize that other critics have said much the same thing about the late medieval papacy when it was still at Rome, it was clear from the widespread circulation of his diatribe in intellectual circles that many prominent Catholics had real concerns about the papacy's presence at Avignon, its lifestyle, and some of its fund-raising methods. As King Edward III of England (1327–1377) observed: "The successors of the Apostles

were ordered to lead the Lord's sheep to pasture; not to fleece them."[7]

Despite these criticisms, many of the popes who ruled at Avignon were among the most talented in the long history of the church and were not always subservient to the interests of the French crown. There were several efforts during the Captivity to return the papacy to Rome, but factional violence in the city on the Tiber frustrated attempts to make the return.

Finally in 1376 Pope Gregory XI (r. 1370–1378) returned the papacy to Rome. By so doing he was responding to growing public pressure, including the urging of the visionary Catherine of Siena (c. 1347–1380), who was later canonized for her holiness and her many contributions to the welfare of the poor. As for Pope Gregory, he was soon appalled by the turbulent conditions in Rome, "the holy City," and made plans for a return to Avignon. His death in 1378 prevented him from carrying out those plans. Under severe pressure from Roman mobs, the college of cardinals elected an Italian to serve as pope. Pope Urban VI (r. 1378–1389), a previously colorless bureaucrat, surprised everyone by turning into a zealous reformer who sought to curb the power and wealth of the cardinals.

THE WESTERN SCHISM OF 1378–1417

Alarmed by Urban's efforts at reform, the homesick French cardinals ruled his election invalid because of mob duress and elected Robert, cardinal of French-speaking Geneva, as pope and returned with him to Avignon. Urban VI refused to recognize the validity of the new election, excommunicated the rebel cardinals and their new pope, and appointed new cardinals to replace those who had fled to Avignon. For the next thirty-seven years, the Catholic church was torn between a succession of rival popes each claiming to be the lawful successor to St. Peter while damning his rival as the anti-Christ. Excommunications were hurled back and forth between Rome and Avignon for decades.

Such unseemly behavior only added to the confusion of many prominent Europeans. Choices had to be made about which pope to support. France backed the French popes of Avignon, as did Castile, Aragon, Navarre, Naples, Sicily, Portugal, and Scotland. Since England was still fighting France in the Hundred Years' War, it stayed loyal to the popes in Rome, as did parts of the Holy Roman Empire, Ireland, Flanders, and northern and central Italy. Some states shifted from one side to another as it suited their particular interests. Individual Christians wondered if their immortal souls were in danger should the sacraments be performed by a false priest ordained by a false bishop loyal to a false pope.

As the schism dragged on, thoughtful Christians began to suggest that the only solution was for a general council of the church's leaders to meet and settle the matter. Neither the pope in Avignon nor the one in Rome would agree to be judged by their "inferiors," even when in convocation. The situation got worse in 1409 when 500 prelates meeting in council at Pisa decided to depose both popes and elect a new one. Both the Roman pontiff and the one in Avignon refused to accept their deposition, so for a while Europe had three living popes, each claiming to be the true supreme head of the church on earth. Three such popes, obviously, were not three times better than one.

Finally, the Holy Roman Emperor Sigismund of Luxembourg (r. 1411–1437) decided to break the impasse by playing the role that the Roman Emperor Constantine (r. 306–337) had played in calling the Council of Nicaea in 325 in order to settle a quarrel over the nature of Jesus which threatened to rip apart the Christian community. Sigismund was well aware of the arguments made seventy years earlier by a physician and philosopher immersed in Roman legal traditions, Marsilius of Padua (c. 1280–1342). Marsilius argued in his *Defender of the Peace* (1324) that the church must be subject to the state, which had the greater responsibility for maintaining law and order. He also asserted that a general church council, rather than the pope, should govern the church because councils represented the body of the faithful better than a single man. Since these ideas were considered by leading papal supporters to be subversive, Marsilius was forced to flee from his university position in Paris and ended his days in the service of Holy Roman Emperor Lewis IV (r. 1314–1347), who was pleased to have such a prominent intellectual tell him that he was superior to the pope.

Emperor Sigismund had no intention of asserting his own authority over the church on a lasting basis, but he did think he could use his power to help settle the crisis if supported by a sufficient number of powerful prelates, some of whom were sympathetic to the notions of sharing governance between pope and council. In 1414 Sigismund summoned important churchmen from all across Europe to come to the Swiss town of Constance for a great council that lasted until 1418. At Constance, the churchmen voted to depose all of the existing popes and elect a new pope, Martin V (r. 1417–1431). Although the three deposed popes were not eager to step down, none of them had the support necessary to stay in power. The Western Schism had at last ended, but what should be the nature of the governance of the church in the future? Should papal monarchs rule with the guidance of regular meetings of male church leaders meeting in council?

THE CHALLENGE OF JOHN WYCLIFFE
(c. 1320–1384)

During the crisis period of the fourteenth century, challenges to the theology and practices of the Catholic church came from a number of sources. One of the most influential was the English intellectual John Wycliffe. Wycliffe came from a modest landed family in Yorkshire and pursued a distinguished career as a scholar at Oxford University. He earned a B.A. in divinity in 1368, and then a doctorate in 1372. Although granted a number of church positions, Wycliffe was a frequently absent cleric. His true passion was scholarship and Oxford remained his real home as he lived the life of a university professor.

Wycliffe's intensive studies of the Bible and scholastic literature led him to a number of the same conclusions as Marsilius of Padua and the controversial English Franciscan William of Ockham (c. 1290–1349). He agreed with William that religious belief had to be based largely on faith and that God's will is inscrutable and His power limitless. Wycliffe also argued that the lawful exercise of lordship, or dominion over men and women, depends on the righteousness of the person who exercises it. Like Marsilius of Padua, he appealed to the authority of Scripture and secular authority rather than to canon law and papal power. Pope Gregory XI complained that Wycliffe was attempting "to overthrow the status of the whole church" by teaching the "opinions and ignorant doctrine of Marsilius of Padua."[8]

Wycliffe's disenchantment with the papacy had only been increased by the outbreak of the Western Schism in 1378 and the financial demands that Pope Gregory made upon the English clergy to support him in his war with the Milanese. In his published work from Oxford, Wycliffe attacked the wealth and worldliness of the church, thus tapping into English anticlericalism. In his tract *On Simony*, the Oxford don argued that the church is essentially spiritual in nature and therefore has no right to wealth and secular power. Wycliffe asserted that the church has grown rich at the expense of the poor and that the sale of offices (simony) was the root cause of church corruption. He also objected to church ceremonies, rites, and rituals as unnecessary. For Wycliffe, salvation comes not through the sacraments, but through divine grace alone.

From the point of view of the church leadership, Wycliffe failed to appreciate the church's need for income if it was to render necessary services and maintain its independence. The Oxford don was seen as a dangerous heretic and a threat to social order. Wycliffe's heretical ideas were condemned by the English bishops, but he found protection for a while from John of Gaunt, the duke of Lancaster and brother of King Edward III (r. 1327–1377). The unscrupulous Gaunt had his own interests in attacking the wealth and power of the English church.

John of Gaunt later deserted Wycliffe when he began to publish his view that the church was a community of true believers and to question transubstantiation (which asserts that the bread and wine are transformed into the body and blood of Christ in the Eucharist, while retaining their outward appearance). Wycliffe's reputation was tarnished by the English Peasants' Revolt of 1381, which some unfairly blamed him for because of his attacks on authority. He was placed under house arrest at the rectory at Luttersworth in 1382, where he died and was buried in 1384. In 1428, after additional condemnations at the Council of Constance and elsewhere, the bishop of Lincoln had Wycliffe's bones dug up and cast into the river Swift.

Despite these efforts to eradicate his memory and his writings, Wycliffe continued to exert an influence on English church life. His English translation of the Bible proved popular even after his death. Wycliffe's followers, called Lollards for their use of English in church services, managed to survive as an underground movement despite persecutions sanctioned by King Henry IV after 1401. Although it is difficult to assess the impact of Lollardy on the sixteenth-century Reformation, there is no question that many of Wycliffe's ideas were similar to those raised by Martin Luther and others.

THE BURNING OF JAN HUS (c. 1372–1415)

Wycliffe's most influential immediate disciple proved to be a Czech cleric named Jan Hus. At age forty-three, Hus found himself before the Council of Constance as an accused heretic. He had been invited to the council by Emperor Sigismund to answer charges of heresy. The emperor had promised Hus he would not be harmed, but shortly after his arrival at Constance in October 1414 he was imprisoned. He languished there until June 1415 when he was finally brought before the council meeting in the great cathedral at Constance and allowed to defend himself. When he tried to explain his views about the nature of the church, outraged churchmen shouted him down. Hus complained to no avail, "In such a council as this, I had expected to find more propriety, piety, and order."[9]

For the next four weeks, enormous pressure was placed on the condemned Czech to recant or deny his teachings. Brought to the cathedral of Constance for a final time on July 15, 1415, Hus was given one last chance to save his life if he would recant. Refusing, he was stripped of his clerical vestments and a paper crown with three

demons painted on it was put on his head with the words "We commit thy soul to the devil." Hus was then led to the town market square and burned alive. Fire was thought of as a cleansing element and to burn an unrepentant heretic like Hus was the only way to clean his soul and stop the spread of his contagious "infection." Shortly before his death, Hus was heard to say, "In the truth of that Gospel which I have written about, taught, and preached, I now die."[10] The churchmen at Constance had literally cooked the goose, which is what Hus means in Czech.

What had Hus done to deserve such a death? Why were the assembled churchmen and the emperor at Constance so determined to see him die? The search for answers goes back to Hus's youth as a poor peasant lad encouraged by his mother and a local priest to escape from a life of rural poverty in southern Bohemia by entering the service of the church. The boy had excelled in school; his intelligence was obvious. In 1390 he enrolled in the recently founded Charles University in Prague, the capital of Bohemia. There he again proved a superior student, earning his B.A. three years later and an appointment to the faculty, where the handsome Hus became an exceptionally eloquent and popular lecturer.

Partly in order to advance his career, Hus had become a priest in 1400. In studying for the priesthood, he had become a serious student of the Bible. "When the Lord gave me knowledge of the Scriptures, I discarded from my mind all foolish funmaking," he wrote.[11] Already well-known as an eloquent university lecturer, Hus now gained additional fame as a preacher. In 1401 he became the confessor of Queen Sophia of Bohemia. She also came to hear him preach at the new Bethlehem Chapel in the heart of Prague.

His talent, fame, and influential patrons should have made him eventually a great man in the church, but Hus's mind became increasingly troubled by the anticlerical ideas of John Wycliffe, especially the idea that all church doctrine should be based on the Bible. He said of the controversial Wycliffe:

> I am attracted by his writings, in which he makes every effort to lead all men back to the law of Christ, and especially the clergy, inviting them to abandon pomp and dominion of the world, and live, like the apostles, according to the law of Christ.[12]

However, many of Hus's German colleagues on the faculty were appalled by Wycliffe's call for church reform. The dispute over reform threatened to tear apart the university, particularly as it also began to touch on the subject of who was to control the university and the church in Bohemia. Hus was the most prominent spokesperson for the cause of the Czech-speaking students.

Finally, in January 1409 King Wenceslaus IV, Emperor Sigismund's brother and a supporter of Hus and moderate reform, issued a decree that gave the Czech-speaking student "nation" at the university three votes for every German one, a complete reversal of the previous situation. Several thousand students and professors, mostly Germans, left Prague and founded a new university 150 miles away at Leipzig. On October 17, 1409, the new Czech national hero, Jan Hus, was elected rector of the university, its highest administrative office.

Despite his new honors Hus still had his enemies among the local clergy, and they urged Archbishop Zbynek to proceed against him as a dangerous heretic in the Wycliffite mold. Hus had spoken and written in favor of Wycliffe's notion of the universal priesthood of all believers, the idea that each person has a direct, spiritual relationship with Christ, the sole head of the church. This threatened the power of the priests as intercessors between the laity and God and made the hierarchy of church office holders seem unnecessary.

Hus also preached against the sale of *indulgences,* which were relaxations for some of the penalties in purgatory for sin. The church taught that most people are not ready for heaven or not sinful enough for hell when they die. Instead, a truly penitent sinner goes to a cleansing place known as purgatory to have the soul purified in preparation for admission to heaven. Indulgences were being sold to finance a crusade against the Christian king of Naples, a political rival of one of the schismatic popes. Hus's preaching against indulgences not only threatened one of the papal pocketbooks, but also that of King Wenceslaus, who had been assured a percentage of the profits for the indulgences sold in Bohemia. The king's support of Hus evaporated rapidly. In July 1410, Zbynek ordered Wycliffe's books burned and excommunicated Hus.

Hus continued to preach his call for reform. Zbynek retaliated by placing the whole city under an interdict on June 20, 1411. The interdict was a general excommunication which closed all churches and stopped all baptisms, marriages, and burials. Everyone in Prague was threatened with eternal damnation. Not wishing to cause such great harm to Prague, Hus left the city in October 1412 at the suggestion of King Wenceslaus. For the next year and a half, he preached and wrote in his homeland of southern Bohemia, winning many new friends and followers to the cause of church reform.

Then Hus was summoned to the great reform council at Constance by his king's brother. After his trial and execution of 1415, 452 Bohemian nobles sent an indignant protest to the council and the emperor. Sigismund angrily and foolishly replied that he would very soon "drown all Wycliffites and

Hussites." This was the final insult from an emperor who was seen as responsible for the death of a Czech national hero. Rebellion soon spread throughout Bohemia, and King Wenceslaus was powerless to calm the storm.

THE HUSSITE REVOLT

Emperor Sigismund and Pope Martin V proclaimed a crusade against the Hussites, who found excellent military leadership in the person of Jan Zizka (1376–1424). Amazingly bold and resourceful, Zizka continued to direct artillery in battle even after being blinded. With such valiant officers and soldiers, the Hussite rebels managed to repel three successive waves of invasion led by an emperor increasingly obsessed with maintaining his imperial authority over Bohemia and encouraged by a papacy in Rome fearful that heresy might spread. Despite ferocious fighting and theological divisions among the Hussites, Sigismund could not crush Zizka's fighters. The Hussites had divided into two major groups: the *Utraquists*, a moderate group who believed in communion in both kinds (bread and wine), and the *Taborites*, who took their name from the town of Tabor, which became their capital. The Taborites recognized only the two biblically based sacraments of baptism and the Eucharist and wanted simple, early church-style ceremonies. Zizka was a Taborite and less willing to compromise with Sigismund and the church than the Utraquists. A civil war between the Hussite factions raged on until the Utraquists scored a decisive victory over the Taborites at the Battle of Lipan in 1434, ten years after the death of Zizka.

After gaining control of Bohemia and having beaten the forces of Sigismund on four major occasions, the Utraquists moved to achieve peace and official recognition from the church. In 1436 the Council of Basel wisely allowed the Utraquists to continue their unique practice of celebrating the Eucharist with the laity receiving both the bread and the wine. Having been unable to enforce uniformity of practice by the sword, the leadership of the church shrewdly knew that keeping Bohemia nominally Catholic was better than losing the Hussites altogether. Even Emperor Sigismund was forgiven by the Czechs and allowed to visit Prague for the first time in sixteen years.

The Council of Basel (1431–1449) in Switzerland, which achieved a measure of reconciliation with the Hussites, proved to be the last of the important medieval councils. Enthusiasm was waning for the theories of the conciliarists. Even though the Council of Constance had decreed that a general church council derived its authority directly from Christ, and therefore the entire church was bound by its decisions, the pope (Martin V) elected by that council believed in papal supremacy and did his best to undermine the theories of Marsilius of Padua and other conciliar thinkers. The Council of Constance had also declared in 1417 that the general council should meet frequently (*Frequens*), but popes stopped calling councils for the most part after Basel. They also ignored most of the reform measures advocated at Constance and elsewhere. Councils met at Florence (1439–1442) and at the Lateran (1503–1513), but not until the Council of Trent of 1545–1563 would a major church council succeed in making fundamental and lasting reforms.

The Hundred Years' War

The Latin church was not the only segment of society in deep trouble during the fourteenth and fifteenth centuries. The monarchies of England and France fought a terrible war in 1337, a conflict that was waged on and off for the next 116 years. The Hundred Years' War began in a sense with the Nor-

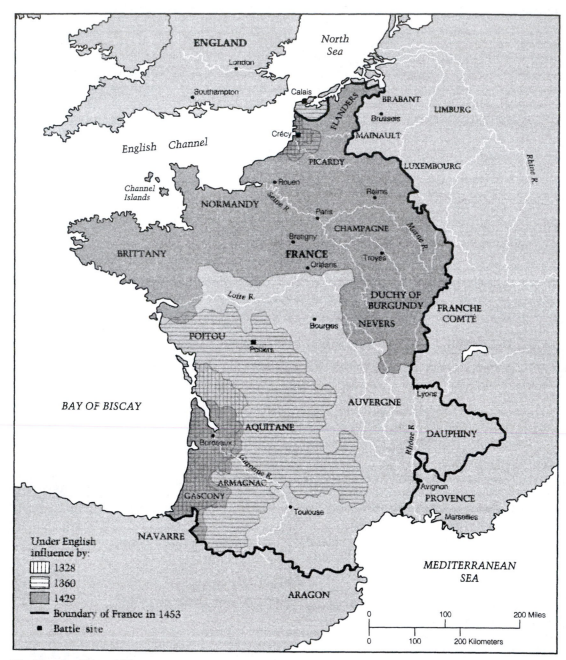

The Hundred Years' War.

man French conquest of England in 1066. Since the time of William the Conqueror, the affairs of France and England were thoroughly intertwined. Things had become even more entangled when the former wife of the French King Louis VII, Eleanor of Aquitaine (1122–1204), married the red-haired Henry of Anjou, who became King Henry II of England (r. 1154–1189). Henry had title to land in France and Eleanor had control of even more French land than did the French monarchy.

During the course of the thirteenth century and early fourteenth century, French monarchs such as Philip II (r. 1180–1223) and Philip IV, the Handsome, had been working assiduously to recover land from the English and had clashed with their English rivals on a number of occasions. France and England also quarreled over Flanders, which the French claimed and with which England was intimately connected in the wool trade. Tensions between England and France escalated in 1328 when the last Capetian king of France died without sons. King Edward III of England decided to "pick the French lily" or claim the French crown. His mother was a daughter of Philip the Handsome. Philip of Valois challenged Edward's claim. He was the son of Philip IV's younger brother. Deeply disturbed by the possibility of an English king sitting on the throne of France, the French nobility argued unhistorically that the right to inherit in France cannot pass through a woman (Salic law), even though no such impediment existed among the English. They then declared Philip of Valois to be their sovereign. His Valois dynasty would rule France until 1589, but not without a challenge from England, where the Salic law traditions did not apply.

In 1337 Edward III decided to press his claim to the French throne. Both Edward and Philip VI (r. 1328–1350) had romantic, chivalrous notions of warfare and neither

Battle of Crécy, Chronicles of Froissart (second half of the fourteenth century). Folio with illumination miniature. Bibliotheque Nationale, Paris, France. Snark/Art Resource.

was willing to make the necessary conces-
sions to avoid war. They almost gleefully
dragged their kingdoms into a conflict that
went on for five generations and devastated
many parts of France. The French soon
learned at Crécy (1346) and at Poitiers (1356)
that mounted knights on horseback were no
match for longbowmen, whose arrows
could pierce armor. Although England won
the major battles of the war, subduing the
much larger France proved impossible, especially when the English were distracted
by the removal of Richard II, Edward III's
successor, in 1399. Later King Henry V
(r. 1413–1422) renewed hostilities and won a
major victory for England in the mud at Ag-
incourt in 1415. France seemed destined to
lose the war despite the premature death of
the seemingly robust Henry V in 1422.

JOAN OF ARC (1412–1431)

At this critical juncture, a sixteen-year-old
peasant girl named Joan of Arc appeared in
the spring of 1428 and claimed that God had
called her to join the French army, lift the
English siege of the town of Orléans, and see
the Dauphin (the Valois heir) crowned as
king at Rheims. Joan (Jeanne d'Arc in
French) claimed that since the age of thirteen she had been hearing the voices of
Saints Michael, Catherine, and Margaret.
The church had a long history of special,
mystical people who claimed to receive direct communications from God or His angels. Mystics such as St. Francis of Assisi
(c. 1182–1226) or Hildegard of Bingen (1098–
1179) had achieved great fame and even papal recognition.

There were, of course, also those who
claimed direct communication with God
only to be eventually shown to be more concerned with self-aggrandizement than spiritual growth. Was Joan one of those fake
mystics? Her voices had not spoken about a

life of contemplation, which seemed to be
the usual message given to mystics. Rather
Joan's divine voices called her to a life of action, action considered impossible for a
woman in the fifteenth century where military armor was officially defined as "male
clothing." This tradition obviously helped
men maintain a virtual monopoly on military power. Initially Joan's efforts to be recognized were rejected by her local lord,
Robert de Baudricourt, but eventually he re-
lented and sent her with six of his men-at-
arms to the court of the Dauphin Charles at
Chinon.

There the seventeen-year-old, dressed
in men's clothing, managed to convince the
religious and secular elite of France that she
was God's chosen instrument of their salvation. The Dauphin authorized "the maid"
to go with 4,000 troops to Orléans, which
was besieged by the English. Her very presence inspired the French soldiers and
alarmed the English. The French lifted the
siege of Orléans in May 1429. Although
twice wounded, Joan fought bravely in at
least seven military engagements and advised the French military commanders on a
number of occasions. Her presence changed
the course of the war and in July 1429, the
dauphin was crowned as King Charles VII
of France (r. 1422–1461).

As for Joan, she continued to fight and
was captured at Compiègne by the Burgundians, who sold her to the English. Joan was
forced to endure a harsh imprisonment and
a grueling series of cross-examinations by
unsympathetic clergy with vested interests
in discrediting her. Chained to a block of
wood at night, she was questioned several
times a day from January 9 to May 30, 1431.
Unable to make her deny her visions or give
up her wearing of men's clothes, French
churchmen in the service of the English
tried Joan as a heretic and a witch. Joan was
accused of having been trained by some

Henri Scheffer, *Entry of Joan of Arc into Orléans, 8 May 1429*. Chateau Versailles, France. Giraudon/Art Resource.

"old women" in "the use of sorcery, divination, and other superstitious works or magic arts." Faced with death, she recanted briefly before changing her mind. Joan of Arc was then convicted of being "a relapsed heretic" and burned at the stake on May 30, 1431.

King Charles VII and his government made no effort to rescue her. The brave young woman had served her purpose. The French were revitalized; her king saw no reason to allow her to become an even greater heroine, whose fame might outstrip his own. She was best forgotten. Others such as the courtier and writer Christine de Pizan disagreed. In her last known poem, Pizan hailed Joan as a heroine in the tradition of such biblical heroines as Esther, Judith, and Deborah:

> Ah, what honor to the feminine sex!
> Which God so loved that he showed
> A way to this great people
> By which the kingdom once lost,
> Was recovered by a woman,
> A thing men could not do.[13]

Following the death of Joan, French armies went from victory to victory. By 1453, the English were completely driven out of France, with the exception of the well-fortified port city of Calais on the channel, twenty-six miles across from the English port of Dover. Large sections of France had been devastated by the war, plague, famine, and a ferocious peasant revolt in 1358. King Charles VII was able to devote himself to the rebuilding of his ravished country. During the war he had gained a standing army, secure tax revenues, and an expanded royal administrative structure. Charles used these tools to strengthen the monarchy, as did his successors, most notably the "Spider King" Louis XI (r. 1461–1483). The crafty Louis loved plotting and removed several of his rivals by treachery and murder. In 1477 he confiscated the duchy of Burgundy when its last duke died fighting against Louis' allies, the Swiss. France, now disentangled from England, was well on the road to becoming an even greater power in Europe.

The War of the Roses, 1455–1485

The English, though humbled by their defeat in the Hundred Years' War, soon found themselves in a nasty struggle for the throne between the rival houses of York and Lancaster. Hostilities began in 1455 when Richard, the duke of York, attempted to overthrow the inept and mentally troubled Lancastrian King Henry VI (1422–1461), who was blamed for the humiliating defeat in France by many among the English nobility. King Henry's able and assertive wife, Margaret of Anjou (1429–1482), rallied those loyal to the house of Lancaster, whose emblem was the red rose. Although Richard of York was defeated and killed at Wakefield in 1460, the Yorkist (white rose) cause was ably championed by Richard's son, Edward IV

Unknown, *Edward IV*. Courtesy of the National Portrait Gallery, London, United Kingdom.

(r. 1461–1483), whom the English Parliament declared king in 1461 after his great victory at Mortimer's Cross. The deposed King Henry and Queen Margaret fled to Scotland, where she continued to struggle against Edward.

King Edward IV was a brilliant military leader, but could at times be lazy and cruel. He also had autocratic tendencies and called Parliament as seldom as possible. Things took an ugly turn when Edward's ally, the earl of Warwick, and his royal brother, Clarence, switched allegiances and sided with the Lancastrians. Supported by the Spider King, Louis XI of France, in 1470 they succeeded for a time in restoring Henry VI and Margaret to the throne. Six months later, however, Edward IV killed Warwick in battle at Barnet and then crushed Margaret and her army at Tewkesbury. Margaret was exiled to France; her husband and the treacherous Clarence ended their days in the Tower of London. Edward IV ruled England for the next twelve years before his sudden death in May 1483. The elder of his two infant sons was declared to be his successor as King Edward V (b. 1470).

Edward IV's younger brother, Richard, duke of Gloucester, who was the king's lieutenant in the north and protector of the child king, outfoxed his rivals and in less than three months mounted the throne as Richard III. The deposed young king was declared illegitimate and placed in the Tower along with his brother. Opposition leaders were executed and the king was widely suspected of murdering the two young princes in the Tower. Henry Tudor, earl of Richmond, now appeared as the champion of all those who considered Richard an evil usurper. In 1485 during a showdown battle at Bosworth Field, Henry's forces overwhelmed those of Richard, who died in the battle. The able Henry, now King Henry VII (r. 1485–1509) of Lancastrian descent, married Elizabeth of York, ended the War of the Roses, and established the remarkable Tudor dynasty.

Chronology

1294	Election of hermit Pope Celestine V; replacement of Celestine with Boniface VIII.	1303	Humiliation and death of Boniface VIII at the hands of agents of Philip the Handsome.
1302	Boniface VIII issues *Unam Sanctam*.	1304–1374	Life of Petrarca.

1305	Beginning of the Babylonian Captivity (popes at Avignon).
1324	Marsilius of Padua publishes *The Defender of the Peace*.
1337	Hundred Years' War begins.
1340–1400	Life of Geoffrey Chaucer.
1346	English win the battle of Crécy.
1347	Beginning of the Black Death.
1348–1349	Artisans' Revolt in Nuremberg.
1356	The Jacquerie Peasant Revolt in France.
1364–1430	Life of Christine de Pizan.
1376	Papacy returns to Rome.
1378	Cloth workers revolt in Florence; the Great Western Schism begins.
1381	Wat Tyler Peasants' Revolt in England.

1384	Death of John Wycliffe.
1409	Council of Pisa (three popes).
1414–1418	Council of Constance.
1415	Death of Jan Hus at Constance; English under Henry V win the battle of Agincourt.
1417	End of the Great Western Schism.
1429	French lift the siege of Orléans.
1431	Death of Joan of Arc.
1432–1442	Council of Florence.
1436	Council of Basel and the end of the Hussite Wars.
1453	End of the Hundred Years' War.
1455–1485	The War of the Roses in England.
1461–1483	Reign of Louis XI (Spider King) in France.
1485–1509	Reign of Henry VII (Tudor) in England.

Further Reading

GENERAL WORKS

C. Warren Hollister, *Medieval Europe: A Short History*, 7th ed. (1994). A highly readable textbook.

Johan Huizinga, *The Waning of the Middle Ages* (1954).

Robert Lerner, *The Age of Adversity: The Fourteenth Century* (1968).

Barbara Tuchman, *A Distant Mirror: The Calamitous 14th Century* (1968). To be used with care since she was not a medievalist, but very well written and lively.

Daniel Waley, *Later Medieval Europe*, 2nd ed. (1985).

THE BLACK DEATH

William Bowsky, ed., *The Black Death: A Turning Point in History?*, 2nd ed. (1978).

Ann Carmichael, *Plague and the Poor in Early Renaissance Florence* (1986).

Carlo Cipolla, *Public Health and the Medical Profession in the Renaissance* (1976).

Samuel Cohn, *The Cult of Remembrance and the Black Death: Six Renaissance Cities in Central Italy* (1992).

William Dohar, *The Black Death and Pastoral Leadership: The Diocese of Hereford in the Fourteenth Century* (1995).

Robert Gottfried, *The Black Death: Natural Human Disaster in Medieval Europe* (1983).

Rosemary Horrox, ed. and tr., *The Black Death* (1994). A useful collection of documents.

William McNeill, *Plagues and Peoples* (1978).

Robert Palmer, *English Law in the Age of the Black Death, 1348–1381: A Transformation of Governance and Law* (1993).

Nancy Siraisi, *Medieval and Early Renaissance Medicine* (1990).

Paul Slack, *The Impact of the Plague in Tudor and Stuart England* (1991).

Sharon Strocchia, *Death and Ritual in Renaissance Florence* (1992).

Graham Twigg, *The Black Death: A Biological Reappraisal* (1984).

Philip Ziegler, *The Black Death* (1969).

POPULAR REVOLTS

R. H. Hilton and Trevor Aston, eds., *The English Rising of 1381* (1984). This collection also has materials on the Ciompi Revolt and the Jacquerie.

Michel Mollat and Philippe Wolff, *The Popular Revolutions of the Late Middle Ages* (1973).

William TeBrake, *A Plague of Insurrection: Popular Politics and Peasant Revolts in Flanders, 1323–1328* (1993).

TROUBLES IN THE CHURCH

Anthony Black, *Council and Commune: The Conciliar Movement and the Fifteenth-Century Heritage* (1979).

C. M. D. Crowder, ed., *Unity, Heresy, and Reform, 1378–1460* (1977). Valuable collection of sources.

Denys Hay, *The Church in Italy in the Fifteenth Century* (1977).

Howard Kaminsky, *A History of the Hussite Revolution* (1967).

Anthony Kenny, *Wyclif* (1985).

Richard Kieckhefer, *Unquiet Souls: Fourteenth-Century Saints and Their Religious Milieu* (1984).

Gordon Leff, *Heresy in the Later Middle Ages: The Relation of Heterodoxy to Dissent, c. 1250–1450* (1967).

Louise Ropes Loomis, *The Council of Constance* (1961).

Francis Oakley, *The Western Church in the Later Middle Ages* (1979).

Yves Renouard, *The Avignon Papacy, 1305–1403* (1970).

Matthew Spinka, *Jan Hus* (1968).

Joachim Stieber, *Pope Eugenius IV, the Council of Basel, and the Secular and Ecclesiastical Authorities of the Empire* (1978).

Phillip Stump, *The Reforms of the Council of Constance, 1414–18* (1994).

J. F. A. Thompson, *Popes and Princes, 1417–1517* (1980).

Brian Tierney, *Foundations of the Conciliar Theory* (1955).

Donald Weinstein and Rudolf Bell, *Saints and Society: The Two Worlds of Western Christendom, 1000–1700* (1986).

THE HUNDRED YEARS' WAR

Christopher Allmand, *Henry V* (1992).

———, *The Hundred Years' War* (1988).

Anne Curry, *The Hundred Years' War* (1993).

Marina Warner, *Joan of Arc: The Image of Female Heroism* (1981).

THE WAR OF THE ROSES

Michael Bennett, *The Battle of Bosworth* (1985).

S. B. Chrimes, *Henry VII* (1973).

John Gillingham, *The War of the Roses* (1981).

E. F. Jacob, *The Fifteenth Century, 1399–1485* (1993).

Charles Ross, *Edward IV* (1974).

Notes

1. Cited in William Bowsky, ed., *The Black Death: A Turning Point?* (New York: Holt, Rinehart, and Winston, 1971), p. 13.
2. Cited in E. R. Chamberlin, *The Bad Popes* (New York: Dial Press, 1969), p. 80.
3. Cited in Warren Hollister, et al., eds., *Medieval Europe: A Short Sourcebook*, 2nd. ed. (New York: McGraw-Hill, 1992), p. 216.
4. Ibid., p. 217.
5. See Joseph Lynch, *The Medieval Church: A Brief History* (New York: Longman, 1992), p. 176.
6. Cited in Hollister, *Sourcebook*, p. 240.
7. Cited in John Harrison and Richard Sullivan, *A Short History of Western Civilization* (New York: Alfred Knopf, 1961), p. 127.
8. Cited in William Estep, *Renaissance and Reformation* (Grand Rapids, Mich.: William Eerdmans, 1986), p. 62.

9. Cited in J. W. Zophy, "Hus," in his *The Holy Roman Empire: A Dictionary Handbook* (Westport, Conn.: Greenwood Press, 1980), p. 228.

10. Ibid.

11. Cited in Theodore Rabb, *Renaissance Lives: Portraits of an Age* (New York: Pantheon Books, 1993), p. 20.

12. Ibid., p. 22.

13. Cited in Bonnie Anderson and Judith Zinsser, *A History of Their Own: Women in Europe from Prehistory to the Present*, 2 vols. (New York: Harper and Row, 1988), vol. 1, p. 161. Copyright © by Bonnie Anderson and Judith Zinsser. Reprinted by permission of HarperCollins Publishers, Inc.

4

ITALY:
HOME OF THE RENAISSANCE

Despite the great series of disasters which afflicted Europe beginning in the fourteenth century, Renaissance culture developed and took root in Italy and then eventually spread to the rest of Europe and the world. Why did the cultural movement known as the Renaissance first begin in the Italian peninsula? What was so special about Italy? What kind of places and people made up Italy during the Renaissance?

The nineteenth-century Swiss historian Jacob Burckhardt argued that "Italy began to teem with personalities; the interdict which had lain on personalities was here completely broken . . . the rest of Europe still lay under the spell of the community."[1] Although modern historians may be less inclined to view the Renaissance as the "triumph of individualism" as did Burckhardt, there is much to be said for his admiration of the great heroes of Renaissance culture. But what other factors help account for the spectacular accomplishments of outstanding Renaissance individuals such as Cosimo de' Medici, Isabella d'Este, Lorenzo Valla, Machiavelli, Michelangelo, Titian, or Artemisia Gentileschi? What did their Italian world have to do with shaping them and the larger cultural movement of which they were a part? To find partial answers to these questions, let us begin by looking at the setting of the Renaissance.

In the fourteenth and fifteenth centuries, Italy was just a geographical expression for an enchanting land of lovely hills and valleys, dotted with remains of an ancient past. The Italian peninsula was made up of a series of independent city-states and principalities of varying size and power. Economically, Italy had taken advantage of its location between the well-developed markets of the eastern Mediterranean and the underdeveloped principalities of Europe north of the Alps. Italians had forged ahead of other Europeans in banking, trade, and cloth manufacturing to become the most urbanized and prosperous people of Europe, even during the long depression of the fifteenth century. The wealth of the Italian elites would help stimulate a Renaissance in the arts.

Culturally, Italy was still the leading heir to the grandeur of the Roman Empire in the West, even though most of that grandeur had long since faded. Italy was the home and headquarters of the Roman Catholic church once again after the Avignon papacy ended in 1417. As such it occupied a special place in the minds of many Europeans. Italy's stature as a cultural center would grow because of the intellectual and artistic creations of several generations of highly talented producers of art, literature, and scholarship.

Italy in the Fifteenth Century.

Rome and the Papal States

Renaissance Rome, filled with the crumbled remains of ancient buildings, was no longer the center of a vast world empire nor was it even one of Italy's great trade centers. Ancient Rome had been home to over a million people in the third century; only about a tenth of that number lived in Renaissance Rome. Cows now grazed amidst the ruins of the ancient Roman forum, where Julius Caesar and Cicero once debated. Except for the difficult period from 1305 to 1376 when the headquarters of the church was in Avignon, Renaissance Rome's economy was mostly sustained by the presence of the huge bureaucracy of the Roman Catholic church and tourism (pilgrimages). Rome was also the largest market town in the Papal States. Wealthy patrician families such as the Colonna, Gaetane, Frangipani, Orsini, Santa Croce, and others struggled with each other and the popes to control Rome's municipal government and to win favors from the papacy. These families also struggled repeatedly to gain control of the papacy itself.

COLA DI RIENZO (1313–1354)

In 1347 and again in 1354, Cola di Rienzo took advantage of the absent papacy to attempt to win Rome's independence from papal and feudal control. The son of a tavern keeper and a laundress, Rienzo was a student of Roman history and archaeology. An eloquent speaker, he managed to convince some of his followers that he was the illegitimate son of the Holy Roman Emperor Heinrich VII (r. 1308–1313) and as such could be the new Roman "tribune of the people," who would restore Rome to its lost glory. Wearing a toga, Rienzo urged his supporters to "die in freedom so that posterity may be born in freedom."[2] They managed to gain control of the city for seven months before being toppled from power by the combined forces of the major Roman families and the papacy, who were appalled at the pretensions of this upstart.

In 1350 Rienzo traveled to Prague to gain the support of the Holy Roman Emperor Charles IV (r. 1347–1378). The wily Charles found him interesting but unstable. The emperor declined to support Rienzo's bid for power in Rome. Instead, Charles had Rienzo imprisoned until Pope Innocent VI (r. 1352–1362) secured his release. The pope hoped that the still influential Rienzo might help pave the way for the return of the papacy from Avignon. In 1354 Rienzo led a second successful revolt in Rome and took over the city. Despite his pretensions of planning to restore the glories of the ancient Roman republic, Rienzo soon showed himself to be a petty tyrant and was killed less than a year later during a revolt of the common people, who felt betrayed by their erstwhile champion.

RENAISSANCE POPES

The papacy reasserted its full control over the impoverished and strife-torn city and its surrounding communities in the late 1350s. Then came the difficult period when the papacy moved back to Rome in 1376, only to be followed by the Great Western Schism with one pope in Rome and another in Avignon. Finally with the reign of Pope Martin V (r. 1417–1431), the papacy was back in Rome for good. It faced a considerable rebuilding task, but papal leadership during the Renaissance became dedicated to restoring the grandeur of Rome. Pope Nicholas V (r. 1447–1455) resumed the massive cleanup campaign begun by Martin V. He constructed a new Vatican palace, rebuilt the Trevi fountain, and began rebuilding St. Peter's Basilica. A true friend of learning, he brought in the renowned humanist Lorenzo Valla to help him create the superb Vatican Library.

Three years later, Aeneas Silvius Piccolimini, one of the leading humanists in Italy, succeeded to the throne of St. Peter. As Pope Pius II (r. 1458–1464), he supported artists and writers and tried to launch a crusade against the Ottomans. Sixtus IV (r. 1471–1484) initiated an ambitious program to establish the political power and prestige of the papacy. Completely ruthless, he plotted the death of his enemies in central Italy and Florence (the Pazzi Plot of 1478). As a patron, he was responsible for the building of the Sistine Chapel in St. Peter's.

Political corruption and immorality in the Vatican reached their all-time peak during the reign of Rodrigo Borgia as Alexander VI (r. 1492–1503). Borgia was the nephew of Pope Calixtus III (r. 1455–1458) and as such rose rapidly in church preferment. Even as an up-and-coming young churchman, he gave signs of things to come. In June 1460, Pope Pius II wrote a letter of reproach to the young cardinal and vice-chancellor in which he admonished Borgia for indulging in "licentious dances" and an "orgy" in Siena with several married women. Despite this reprimand, the Spaniard, who was also a skilled administrator, managed to bribe and cajole his way onto St. Peter's throne.

As pope, Borgia continued to indulge both his political and sensual appetites. He continued to live an extravagant lifestyle that included lavish parties, weddings, receptions, and even bullfights. Gangsterism flourished in Alexander's Rome and according to his master of ceremonies, Johannes Burchardus, the pope had "full knowledge" of more than 250 murders.[3] Although little was done to improve the plight of the Roman poor, Pope Alexander used the power and wealth of the papacy to foster the careers of his four children by his beloved mistress, the inn-keeper Vanozza Catanei, who lived like a queen.

The worst of the papal brood was the ambitious and vicious Cesare (1476–1507), who was made a cardinal of the church at age fourteen. Cesare fascinated the diplomat and political theorist Niccolò Machiavelli and others by his ruthlessness, which extended to murdering his older brother as well as the second husband of his sister, Lucretia. With the support of his father, he attempted to carve out a large state for himself in the Romagna of central Italy. In 1498 an alliance with the French king Louis XII brought him a French bride and the title duke of Valentinois. Taking advantage of the French invasions, Cesare made progress in creating his new state until his father's death in 1503 seriously reduced his revenues. Alexander VI's successor was his bitter enemy Giuliano della Rovere, Pope Julius II (r. 1503–1513), who wanted to expand the papal state in central Italy. Cesare's empire quickly collapsed around him and he was imprisoned in a castle at Ischia. He died three years later in Spain.

Julius II became known as "Papa Terrible" because of his relentless energy, love of war, and the fear and awe he inspired. Contemporaries said that he "loved the smell of smoke and the blood of battle."[4] Papa Terrible attempted to strengthen the

Unknown, *Portrait of Cesare Borgia.* Accademia Carra, Bergamo, Italy. Alinari/Art Resource.

papacy by expanding papal land holdings in central Italy. In 1505 he marched through the Romagna and Emilia, territories formerly ruled by Cesare Borgia. In November 1506 the warrior-pope forced the proud city of Bologna to surrender. He also masterminded a coalition of forces determined to weaken the French and drive them out of Italy. In between diplomatic negotiations and military campaigns, the energetic pope found time to commission spectacular works of art by the great Michelangelo, Bramante, and others before dying of fever.

It was the Renaissance papacy, through its patronage of artists, that managed to rekindle some of the greatness of the city on the Tiber. Rome endured even after being horribly sacked by rebellious troops of the Holy Roman Emperor Charles V in the summer of 1527. The popes of the Catholic reform continued their interests in the arts while seriously raising the spiritual tone of the papacy. In fact, Rome became one of the fastest growing cities in Europe in the second half of the sixteenth century. The papacy helped encourage the development of such important Roman artists as Bernini, Caravaggio, and Artemisia Gentileschi, plus many others who were attracted to the city for its abundant patronage and stimulating cultural and religious life. The eternal city would live on through its rich artistic and spiritual heritage.

Naples and Sicily

South of the Papal States lay the kingdoms of Naples and Sicily, both of which were surrounded by a mountainous countryside with relatively poor soil. Like the Papal States, power was concentrated at the top. How much power was shared with chancellors and other officials depended to a large extent on the whim of the sovereigns. Naples was one of the great port cities in Europe at the beginning of the Renaissance and would become one of the largest cities in Europe in the course of the sixteenth century. Ships from all over the Mediterranean—including Sicily, which had been the major granary of the ancient Roman Empire in the West—used the deep harbor of Naples. Palermo on Sicily was another major economic and cultural center early in the period. While surrounded by feuding nobles, other coastal towns in south Italy also flourished as market centers.

Unfortunately, the region suffered from a turbulent political history caused in part by its vulnerability to outside invasion. Southern Italy had been overrun by Muslim and then Norman invaders in the Middle Ages. The Holy Roman Emperor Frederick II (1197–1250) attempted to rule his vast empire north of the Alps from his base in Sicily. After his death, ties to the Holy Roman Empire gradually weakened until Charles of Anjou, third son of King Louis IX of France, seized the thrones of Naples and Sicily in 1266. Cruel, glum, and reckless, Charles of Anjou managed to hang onto power until a bloody uprising against the French broke out on Easter of 1282.

The Sicilian revolt began when a French soldier molested a young married woman on her way to evening Vesper services in Palermo. Outraged Sicilians struck down the Frenchman and raised the cry, "Death to the French!" A long, indecisive struggle ensued between the French monarchy supported by the papacy against the Sicilians and the kings of Aragon from Spain, who saw this as a good time to gain a toehold in southern Italy. This twenty-year conflict, known as the War of the Sicilian Vespers, separated Naples from Sicily, which came to be ruled by the house of Aragon for the remainder of the fourteenth century and into the fifteenth century.

Naples was dominated by the French house of Anjou, whose brightest light was Duke Robert (1309–1343), a friend and admirer of Petrarca. He had given the city on the bay a short period of cultural splendor. His granddaughter, the beautiful Joanna I (1343–1382), brought Naples into great disrepute. She had been married at age five to her seventeen-year-old cousin, Andrew of Hungary. Andrew was a dull, lumpish fellow, whom the intellectually inclined Joanna grew to despise. One of her lovers murdered him and Joanna had to journey to Avignon to plead her innocence before the pope. Although judged innocent, a cloud of suspicion hung over Joanna and finally in the summer of 1381 another relative, Charles of Durazzo (r. 1382–1384), led a campaign with the support of the Roman pope to overthrow the sensual Joanna. Charles succeeded in capturing Joanna and had her strangled with a silken cord and her body exposed in the marketplace. His power over Naples was challenged by Louis of Anjou, brother of the king of France.

THE REIGNS OF JOANNA II (1414–1435), ALFONSO V (1416–1458), AND FERRANTE I (1458–1494)

At the start of the fifteenth century, Naples was ruled by the aggressive Ladislaus (r. 1386–1414). He occupied Rome in 1408 and then threatened Florence. Naples and Florence finally agreed to peace in 1411. Ladislaus was succeeded by the cultivated but dissolute Joanna II, who was corrupted by her power and wealth and fully indulged all her appetites. Joanna's reign was marked by a series of adulteries, intrigues, and assassinations. In July 1421 one of her lovers, King Alfonso V, agreed to support her against the French in return for being named her heir.

Because Alfonso was already king of Aragon and Sicily, when he finally drove out the French in 1442 he was able to unite all three crowns and provide a measure of stability for war-torn southern Italy. King Alfonso was also a major patron of the arts. A friend of learning, Alfonso the Magnanimous founded a university at Catania and helped support important scholars such as Lorenzo Valla.

His son, Ferrante I (r. 1458–1494), reverted back to the old ways of cruelty and caprice. In 1479 he had joined Pope Sixtus IV (r. 1471–1484) and the duchy of Milan in making war against the republic of Florence led by Lorenzo de' Medici (1449–1492). He so alienated his subjects that many preferred Muslim invaders to him. Ferrante, in vivid contrast with his father, did little to stimulate the arts and learning. His death in 1494 gave King Charles VIII of France (r. 1483–1498) an opportunity to invade Italy and assert old French claims to the crown of

Naples and Sicily. Following the defeat of the French, Naples reverted to the control of the Spanish and underwent a period of growth, becoming one of the most populous cities in Europe by the end of the sixteenth century and a major center of cloth manufacture and trade. Nobles crowded into squalid but beautiful Naples to escape an increasingly impoverished countryside.

The Power of Milan

To the north of the Papal States in the center of the rich Po River Valley lay the bustling city of Milan, whose rulers exerted a great deal of power in Italy. Milan was dominated by the house of Visconti. Holy Roman Emperor Heinrich VII, whose ancestors had long claimed "overlordship" of Milan, designated Matteo Visconti imperial vicar in 1311. After a series of bloody family feuds, including the murder of his co-ruler and uncle, Giangaleazzo Visconti (1352–1402) took supreme power in 1385. Ten years later he purchased the title of duke of Milan from Emperor Wenceslaus (r. 1378–1400). Not only did Duke Giangaleazzo start the construction of the gigantic, white, many-spired Gothic cathedral of Milan, he dreamed of making himself king of Italy. Toward that end, he conquered the city-states of Bologna, Perugia, Pisa, Siena, and Verona. All this was a prelude to his assault on the republic of Florence, which was encircled by Milanese power. It was a classic confrontation between a principality and a republic, where governance was shared at least among an elite.

Then in July 1402, as Florence seemed ready to fall to the Goliath of the north, Giangaleazzo died of the plague. His kingdom of northern Italy dissolved as his two dissipated young sons, Giovanni Maria (r. 1402–1412) and Filippo Maria (r.

1412–1447), failed to hold what their father had conquered. Giovanni was a vicious psychopath who kept a menagerie of leopards, English hounds, and falcons, which cost a fortune to maintain. His reign ended with assassination. His younger, more able brother, Filippo, succeeded in restoring Milan and expanding its territory into Lombardy before degenerating into a self-indulgent recluse. His aggression provoked a war with Florence and Venice, which lasted, on and off, until Filippo's death in 1447.

THE RISE AND FALL
OF THE SFORZA, 1450–1499

During the last stages of this war, Filippo gave his only child, an illegitimate daughter, Bianca Maria, in marriage to the ambitious mercenary general (*condottieri*) Francesco Sforza (r. 1450–1466). The son of a peasant, Sforza had risen to power as a skillful military man and leader of soldiers of fortune. A sometimes unscrupulous opportunist, he was capable of taking money from both sides in the same conflict, as he did when he offered his services to Venice in 1446 while still in the pay of its enemy Milan. In 1450, claiming that Milan had not adequately compensated him for his military services, Francesco Sforza overthrew the republic that had been established following the death of Filippo Visconti and declared himself duke and Bianca Maria duchess of Milan.

Four years after taking power, Sforza succeeded through clever diplomacy in securing peace with Venice and making a new alliance with Florence, Milan's old rival. Francesco and Bianca Sforza ruled Milan from a massive redbrick fortress they had reconstructed in the heart of the city, and which still stands today. A symbol of princely power, the Sforza Castle housed several thousand of Francesco's best sol-

diers. It was quite clear on what his power as duke was based.

The Sforza dynasty continued through the coldly efficient reign of their son, Galeazzo (r. 1466–1476), and grandson, Giangaleazzo II (1476–1494), whose dark-skinned uncle Ludovico il Moro (the Moor) usurped the throne as regent for his seventeen-year-old nephew. In 1491 the ambitious Ludovico married Beatrice d' Este (b. 1475), the fifteen-year-old daughter of the duke of Ferrara. Despite her youth, the fashionable and cultivated Beatrice had a profound influence on the Milanese court during her six years there as duchess. She died shortly after giving birth to a stillborn son in January 1497. The Sforza court had attracted the services of marvelous artists such as Leonardo da Vinci, who had come to Milan as a military engineer and court painter in 1481, and the architect and painter Bramante.

Beatrice's life had been complicated by her husband's infidelities, extravagances, and political intrigues. In 1494 Ludovico il Moro encouraged the twenty-four-year-old French king, Charles VIII, to claim the throne of Naples as a prelude to a crusade against the Ottomans. Ludovico wanted French help against Duke Louis of Orléans, Pope Alexander VI, and the Florentine republic, who were determined to remove Ludovico from power. Sforza calculated that the French king could save him from his enemies. He and Beatrice greeted the young French king with open arms at Pavia in October 1494. Delighted by Beatrice's charms, King Charles headed south on his way to an easy conquest of Naples with 30,000 troops, the largest army anyone had ever seen in Italy since the time of the ancient Romans. The French force also included the largest artillery train ever in Europe, about seventy large guns.

While the French were moving through the peninsula in what became a virtual military parade, the ailing Giangaleazzo II finally succumbed to tuberculosis. Ludovico had himself proclaimed master of Milan by his fellow citizens and persuaded Holy Roman Emperor Maximilian I (r. 1493–1519) to declare him and his heirs dukes of Milan, disregarding a surviving son of Giangaleazzo II. Duke Ludovico and his duchess, Beatrice, celebrated their new titles with a sumptuous coronation, including imaginative displays and fireworks designed by the ingenuity of Leonardo da Vinci.

As news of Charles VIII's easy conquest of Naples reached Milan, Ludovico began to worry that the successful French might make good on their own claim to his duchy. He soon joined an anti-French "Holy League" with Venice, Mantua, the papacy, Emperor Maximilian, and the king of Aragon. The French had taken Naples without fighting a single battle, but holding the prize proved more difficult than anyone could have imagined. The arrogance and corruption of the conquerors soon alienated the people of Naples, who found the French as bothersome as the Aragonese. An epidemic of syphilis, brought to Europe by returning sailors from Christopher Columbus's first voyage to the Americas, soon decimated the ranks of the French army.

Realizing he was overextended, King Charles soon led a hasty retreat toward France. On July 6, 1495, he fought a brief and bitter battle at Fornova with the forces of the Holy League, led by Ludovico's brother-in-law, Francesco Gonzaga of Mantua. Both sides claimed victory, but Charles was able to withdraw to France with most of his surviving army. He died three years later still dreaming of glory and adventure. His successor, King Louis XII (r. 1498–1515), the former duke of Orléans, invaded Italy in 1499 and claimed both Milan and Naples. The spendthrift Ludovico, who had made an

elaborate display at the death of his wife, Beatrice, in 1497 by burning thousands of candles in her honor and wrapping her corpse in gold, was soon driven from Milan. Although he managed to hire Swiss mercenaries in the Tyrol, he was captured by the French in 1500 and died imprisoned in a French castle in 1508. Milan remained relatively prosperous, although dominated by the French until 1535 and then by the Spanish until 1714.

The Mantua of Isabella d'Este

Although Beatrice d'Este was unfortunate in her parents' choice of a husband, her older sister, Isabella (b. 1474), married the leader of the Italian forces at the battle of Fornova against the retreating French army of Charles VIII. She became the wife of Francesco Gonzaga, marquis of Mantua (r. 1494–1519), in 1490 after a ten-year engagement. At first it seemed Isabella had married below her younger sister, who had gained the hand of Ludovico il Moro, the real power of the great duchy of Milan. Mantua, which bordered Beatrice's family duchy of Ferrara, was a much smaller principality. Both Ferrara and Mantua, however, were major centers of Renaissance learning, thanks in part to the establishment of humanistic court schools by Guarino da Verona and Vittorino de Feltre, two of the leading lights in Renaissance education.

Both d'Este daughters received an excellent classical and linguistic education in Ferrara and at their grandmother's court in Naples, where they spent eight years. The lovely Isabella was especially adept and while still a teenager had mastered Greek and Latin grammar, could quote large sections of Virgil and other Roman poets from memory, played the lute well, danced skillfully, embroidered faultlessly, and could converse with great political sophistication with anybody. She became the model of the intellectually well-rounded, politically astute Renaissance woman. Her soldier-husband shared her interests in the arts and learning and their court soon became a great center of literary and artistic life, attracting important talent from all over Italy.

Isabella not only became a focal point of the intellectual life of the court, she also worked to gather one of the finest libraries in Italy and was a demanding patron of the arts who knew exactly what she wanted. For example, in one of her letters to the artist Perugino, she wrote:

> Our poetic invention, which we greatly want to see painted by you, is a battle of Chastity against Lasciviousness, that is to say, Pallas and Diana fighting vigorously against Venus and Cupid. And Pallas should seem almost to have vanquished Cupid, having broken his golden arrow and cast his silver bow underfoot; with one hand she is holding him by the bandage which the blind boy has before his eyes, with the other she is lifting her lance and about to kill him.[5]

The marchioness also carried on an extensive correspondence with family, friends, nobles, artists, merchants, and intellectuals all over Europe.

Relations with her sister, Beatrice, became strained when she aided and abetted her husband's scheme to bring the French into Italy in 1494. Isabella's husband, in contrast, became the hero of Italy's liberation. Mantua's security was enhanced not only by Francesco's skills as a soldier, but also by Isabella's talents as a diplomat. When, for example, her brother, Duke Alfonso d'Este of Ferrara, married the cultivated Lucretia Borgia (1480–1519) of the unsavory papal family in 1501, Isabella secured her good will and that of her malevolent brother, Ce-

sare, to keep him from attacking her small principality.

When her husband was captured in a war against Venice in 1509, Isabella became sole regent of Mantua. She ruled so well in his absence that Francesco became jealous of her success as an administrator. He was also frustrated by the slowness of the process for obtaining his release, for which he blamed his wife. Francesco wrote her from prison in 1512: "We are ashamed that it is our fate to have as a wife a woman who is always ruled by her head." Isabella responded with firmness and pride, "Your excellency is indebted to me as never a husband was to a wife."[6]

After Francesco's release from captivity, relations between the two were frosty until his death in 1519. Isabella then governed six years for her nineteen-year-old son, Federigo, who was in awe of her abilities. Her skills as a diplomat secured him the title of duke from Holy Roman Emperor Charles V (r. 1519–1556) and a cardinalate for her second son, Ercole. She died on February 13, 1539, honored by her contemporaries as "the first lady of the world."

Duke Federigo's Urbino

Located in central Italy, southeast of Florence in the northern Marches, lay the small hill town of Urbino. During the Renaissance, this principality also became a leading center of art and culture under the leadership of the great *condottieri* Duke Federigo da Montrefeltro (1422–1482). As a boy he had studied under Vittorino de Feltre in Mantua, where he learned "all human excellence."[7] Although he made his career as a mercenary soldier, Federigo never lost his taste for art, learning, and piety. In 1444 he succeeded his assassinated half brother as ruler of Urbino. Duke Federigo continued to sell his services as one of Italy's most successful soldiers, winning a great reputation for honesty and benevolence.

Federigo da Montefeltro's greatest legacy was his contribution to Renaissance patronage. A competent Latinist, he attempted to create in Urbino the greatest library since antiquity. Virtually the whole corpus of known classics was in his library, as well as important works by the great Muslim scholars Avicenna and Averroës. The duke also had a great taste in architecture and his palace was considered one of the most tasteful in Italy. His cultural activities were supplemented by those of his second wife, Battista Sforza, who was celebrated for her Greek, Latin, and remarkable memory. The duke praised her as "the delight of my public and private hours."[8] She ruled Urbino for him during his frequent absences while campaigning.

Their son Guidobaldo (1472–1508) continued to promote culture after he became duke in 1482. Less skilled than his father as a soldier, he was overshadowed by his remarkable wife, Elisabetta Gonzaga (1471–1526). She was the daughter of Federigo Gonzaga, marquis of Mantua, whose court was another lively center of art and learning. Elisabetta married Guidobaldo in 1488 and earned a great reputation during twenty years of childless married life for her fortitude and virtue. She set the tone for the court life in Urbino and is immortalized in Castiglione's *Book of the Courtier*.

Venice: The Queen of the Adriatic

As important as princely patronage was to the development of Renaissance culture, city-states such as Venice and Florence played crucial roles in stimulating and supporting the arts and learning. Venice, known as the queen of the Adriatic and the hinge of Europe, was the busiest of all the Italian maritime ports. Its share of Mediterranean commerce surpassed even Naples and the bustling sometime republic of Genoa on the northwest coast of Italy. Venice was also a major producer of books, glass, saddles, soap, metalwork, and other luxury goods. Added to Venice's strategic location and well-defended port was the stability of its government. From 1297 to 1797, an oligarchy of wealthy merchant families controlled the beautiful city of bridges, canals, and islands situated on a lagoon. Venice was in an ideal spot to dominate the trade of the Adriatic Sea and the eastern Mediterranean.

VENETIAN POLITICS AND SOCIETY

As a republic, Venice had a more complex form of government than many of its neighboring principalities. The Venetian state was headed ceremonially by an official, the *doge*, who was elected for life by the male members of the richest families. The doge, with his six councilors and three chief judicial magistrates, made up the ducal council. It set the agenda for the Great Council and presided over the Venetian Senate of 300 men. The doge was the head of state for ceremonial purposes and was also responsible for watching over the functioning of government. The Senate was the real center of power; it had the responsibility for making laws, directing foreign policy, and managing the finances of the state.

In times of emergency, actual authority rested with the Council of Ten, chosen from among the wealthiest and most influential patrician families. Meeting in secret, the Ten dealt with urgent matters of state security and could exercise judicial power. Underneath all of the Venetian organs of government was the Great Council, which served as an electoral body. Since 1297 its ranks had been closed to all except males twenty-five years of age or older who came from 200

Giovanni Bellini, *Portrait of the Doge Leonardo Loredano.* National Gallery, London, Great Britain. Alinari/Art Resource.

elite families. The various organs of Venetian government tended to work well together, for the most part, and the interests of the rich merchant families were well protected.

Because its internal history and lifestyle seemed relatively calm compared to many of the less affluent city-states in Italy, Venice was also known in the Renaissance as the "most serene one." Beneath the sometimes placid surface lurked social and political tensions, but they were seldom as disruptive as in other Italian communes. Aristocratic families vied with each other for power; gangs of artisans fought mock battles on bridges with fists and sticks; and incidental violence sometimes broke out during Venice's famous and licentious carnival season. Yet compared to the often stormy political life of Florence or Naples, Venice seemed specially blessed by fortune despite her frequent involvement in wars to protect the commune's robust commercial life and expanding territory.

Venice's closed oligarchy wanted to maintain not only a vast trading empire, but also to hold a great deal of the territory surrounding the city for security and economic reasons. In order to survive as a great commercial power, Venice had fought rival maritime power Genoa for much of the fourteenth century. Venice finally emerged victorious from that long struggle. During the fifteenth century, Venice reached its peak of military strength, defeating the Turks at Gallipoli in 1414. The Venetians went on to secure the Morea, Cyprus, and Crete between 1414 and 1428. In Italy they captured Verona, Vicenza, Padua, Udine, Brescia, and Bergamo. For much of the second half of the fifteenth century, Venice dueled the Ottomans for control of the Adriatic Sea. In the sixteenth century, as trade shifted to the Atlantic, Venice gradually declined as an economic and military force. Its role in helping defeat the Ottomans at the major naval battle of Lepanto in 1571 in some ways marked the republic's "last hurrah" as a great political power.

VENICE AND THE ARTS

Even in gradual decline, Venice's enormous commercial prosperity helped support a host of celebrated Renaissance artists, including Jacopo Bellini and his sons Gentile and Giovanni, Giorgione, Tintoretto, Titian, and Veronese. The gifted Florentine sculptor Andrea del Verrocchio created his last and greatest sculpture, the giant equestrian statue of the mercenary general Colleoni, in Venice. Pietro Aretino, famous for his satirical *Lewd Sonnets,* and Veronica Franco, a courtesan and one of Italy's leading female poets, were established residents of Venice and drew inspiration from its vibrant and

Andrea del Verrocchio, *Monument to Bartolommeo Colleoni* (c. 1481–1496). Campo SS Giovanni e Paolo, Venice, Italy. Alinari/Art Resource.

cosmopolitan economic and social life. Cardinal Pietro Bembo (1470–1547), a native Venetian noble, was a great arbiter of literary taste and a skilled historian, poet, and humanist.

Venice's churches and stately mansions were filled with art and craft goods. Their construction also afforded Renaissance architects and builders with a great deal of employment. Venice was renowned throughout Europe for the glories of its architecture, both domestic and public. Even skilled Jewish persons were welcomed to cosmopolitan Venice as the city prized their talents. Only Sicily had a larger Jewish population in Italy. Venice's public pageantry at civic and religious festivals was remarkable. Such was its prosperity that the government in 1512 felt compelled to limit the size of banquets. Renaissance Venice was, indeed, a place of marvels, which continued to inspire great art long after its political eclipse.

Florence: "The Most Beautiful of Cities"

The perceptive English poet Elizabeth Barret Browning (b. 1806), who spent fifteen years living in Italy, hailed Florence as the "most beautiful of cities." Given the stunning beauty of places like Pisa, Siena, and Venice, this was quite a compliment, but one which Florence deserves. The trade and cloth manufacturing town on the Arno River became known as "queen city of the Renaissance." Artists of the stature of Giotto, Masaccio, Brunelleschi, Donatello, Fra Angelico, Boticelli, Fra Filippo Lippi, Leonardo da Vinci, Michelangelo, Cellini, and a host of others flourished. The city on the Arno was also the home of the poets Dante, Petrarca, and Boccaccio, who helped to make their Tuscan dialect into a superb literary vehicle. Historians such as Machiavelli and Guicciardini were native Florentines, as was the philosopher Marsilio Ficino. Florentine humanism was graced by the likes of Poggio Bracciolini, Leonardo Bruni, Francesco Filelfo, Niccolò Niccoli, and Coluccio Salutati.

Arts and letters thrived there almost in spite of the city's troubled political history. In the twelfth and thirteenth centuries, the commune was torn between rival factions loyal to the Holy Roman emperors (Ghibellines) or the popes (Guelfs). In 1283 the wealthy merchants of Florence initiated constitutional changes that would give them supremacy over the often unruly Florentine nobility. Only male members of the seven great guilds of cloth importers, dealers in wool, silk manufacturers, furriers, bankers, judges and notaries, and doctors and apothecaries were allowed to hold public office. That monopoly was challenged by members of some of the less powerful guilds (blacksmiths, shoemakers, butchers, carpenters, bakers, cloth sellers, etc.), who were given a minority share in the government. Noblemen were specifically excluded from public office.

The patriarchal government of Florence was headed by a board of nine guildsmen (the *Signoria*), one of whom was known as the "Standard Bearer of Justice" and was responsible for maintaining law and order throughout the town. The members of the *Signoria* were chosen by lot and served a two-month term. They met daily and lived in the great fortress-like town hall in the heart of the city during their two months in office. Any legislation proposed by the *Signoria* had to be approved by two other bodies with rotating membership—the Twelve Good Men and the Sixteen Standard Bearers. Major laws had to gain the additional approval of the 300 member Council of the People and the 200 member Council of the Commune. On rare occasions, an assembly of all male citizens could be convened by the *Signoria* for the purpose of altering the governmental structure.

The political wisdom of the elite Florentine guildsmen was severely challenged during the calamitous fourteenth century. Its greatest banking houses—the Bardi and the Perruzi—had loaned too much money to King Edward III of England and others at the start of the Hundred Years' War. In 1339 King Edward suspended payment on his loans to the Florentines and then in 1346 repudiated them altogether. Already overextended, the Bardi and Peruzzi banks collapsed and never recovered fully from this blow. Three years later the Black Death hit Florence and killed almost half of its citizens. Periodic famines in the countryside also troubled the Florentines, as did a series of wars with Lucca, Milan, Pisa, and the Papal States. In 1378 the unskilled cloth work-

Arnolfo di Cambio, Palazzo Vecchio (Town Hall), Florence, Italy. Alinari/Art Resource.

ers known as *Ciompi* revolted, demanding a more popular form of government and burning some of the houses of the rich. Not until 1382 was order restored after the lesser guilds were granted political representation in the *Signoria*.

At the start of the fifteenth century, Florence was almost conquered by Duke Giangaleazzo of Milan before his premature death in July 1402. The republic had triumphed over the principality. Florence now identified itself as the biblical hero David, having defeated the mighty Goliath of the north with the aid of God, as many Florentines believed. Having escaped conquest by Milan, the Florentines now assumed the of-

fensive and captured Pisa in 1406. The city now had a port fifty miles away on the west coast of Italy at the mouth of the Arno River, which flowed through the heart of Florence. The Florentines had to fight off Naples between 1409 and 1411, Milan again in 1421, and Lucca in 1429 to 1433. The fight with the nearby silk-producing republic of Lucca eventually drew in Milan as well and almost resulted in disaster for the Florentines.

THE MEDICI IN FLORENCE

Although Florence had many prominent families striving for economic and political power, one family—the Medici—came to

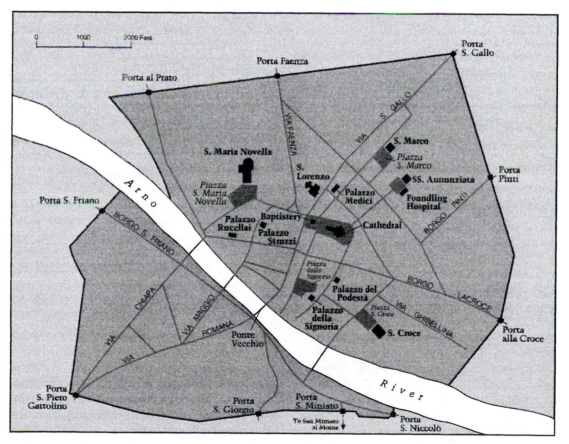

Renaissance Florence.

dominate the city for 300 years. The rise of the Medici to political prominence began with Cosimo de' Medici's (1389–1464) opposition to the war with Milan and Lucca, which was championed by the politically dominant Albizzi family. The Medici were a well-established banking and cloth manufacturing family. Cosimo de' Medici was married to Contissena Bardi, the daughter of one of his father's old banking partners. The Bardi were no longer rich, but they were still respected, as were the Medici, who had shown sympathy to the working people during the crisis of the Ciompi Revolt. The public criticisms of the war and tax policies of the ruling oligarchy by this popular member of a prominent family threatened the Albizzi hold on power in Florence. Under some pressure Cosimo moved to the relative safety of Verona.

Much to the consternation of the Albizzi, a new *Signoria* favorable to the Medici was chosen in the fall of 1434, and Cosimo was recalled from exile. An Albizzi plot to overthrow the government failed, and they and their mostly aristocratic followers were sent into exile. For the next 300 years, the house of Medici dominated the political history of Florence. They had a wide circle of business and political friends and married into many other prominent families who identified their business and political interests with that of the Medici.

Cosimo de' Medici consulted often with his political support groups and remained accessible to a wide range of people during his thirty years in power. He respected the forms of republican government, only serving as Standard Bearer of Justice for a total of six months, and always supported moderate policies. The newly created executive council (*balia*), which had broad powers to scrutinize voter lists, pass tax bills, and appoint ministers, often met in his palace. Working to keep taxes low,

Cosimo made huge personal loans to the city in times of crisis. He also loaned money to other prominent Florentines, making them personally obligated to him. As the owner of three textile factories and a leading banker, Cosimo de' Medici was one of Florence's major employers, something he seldom let his employees forget. He was often present when wages were paid to Medici workers.

THE RISE OF THE MEDICI BANKING EMPIRE

Cosimo de' Medici knew that ultimately his political power rested upon the financial success of his business empire. His father, Giovanni (d. 1429), had carefully studied the example of the Bardi when he set up his own banking network. To avoid becoming overly centralized and overextended, the Medici shared risks with their local partners. Local managers were allowed to make independent decisions, but they had to make considerable investments of their own capital to ensure their caution. If need be, the Medici in Florence could exercise control over their subsidiaries because they always held at least 50 percent of the branch bank's stock.

Better guarantees for loans were also demanded from royal clients than those obtained by the Bardi and the Peruzzi. Even when banking for the papacy, the Medici demanded and received a controlling interest in the lucrative papal alum mines at Tolfa in northeastern Italy. Cosimo's father had established branch banks in Naples, Rome, Venice, and Geneva in Switzerland. Cosimo added branches in Avignon, Bruges, London, Milan, and Pisa. They dealt in all forms of credit and loans. Money deposited in the Medici banks was then invested in a wide variety of business activities, further extending the family's influence.

COSIMO DE' MEDICI AS A PATRON

Many of the early capitalists of the Renaissance made a great deal of money. Why did the Medici give so much more back to their community in the form of cultural patronage? Why did they worship the florin less than some of their business rivals? The answers lie partly in the background and wide-ranging interests of Cosimo himself. Educated at a monastic school and "grave in temperament," Cosimo had learned German, French, Latin, and some Hebrew, Greek, and Arabic. His active mind found business and politics to be insufficiently stimulating to absorb all his considerable mental energies and to enrich his spirit. Therefore, he continued to attend humanist discussion groups throughout his life as he found philosophy challenged him as nothing else did in the world of affairs. Cosimo even "adopted" the Neoplatonic philosopher Marsilio Ficino (1433–1499), the son of his physician, and helped establish the Platonic Academy, a group of scholars dedicated to the thought of the Greek philosopher.

Cosimo also developed an interest in art and architecture, which he found could be used to enhance his family's "honor," as well as that of his city. A good friend to the sculptor Donatello, Cosimo was supportive of many artists and architects. The fortress-like Medici Palace, which Cosimo had built in the heart of the city, provided his family and friends with comfort, aesthetically pleasing surroundings, privacy, and security. Although the Medici Palace made an impressive show of power and wealth, it was not as excessive as the Pitti Palace. Influenced as well by the Ciceronian notion that the rich must give something back to their communities, Cosimo was directly or indirectly responsible for erecting many other structures in Florence, including the church of San Lorenzo, the monastery of San Marco, and several villas in the countryside. Given the title "father of the state," Cosimo growled, "in a few years, they will remember me only for my buildings."[9]

The Medici dynasty in Florence was continued by Cosimo's son, Piero "the Gouty." A skilled financier, Piero did not have his father's political sophistication and was limited by his poor health. He did continue Cosimo's alliances with Milan and the papacy and kept the Venetians at bay. Piero's position was enhanced by the abilities of his poet-wife, Lucretia, who came from a prosperous, venerable Florentine family. She helped her husband dispense abundant patronage to artists and produced five well-educated children. Their children were all married into prominent families.

Michelozzi, Palazzo Medici Riccardi, Florence, Italy. Alinari/Art Resource.

Piero's five years of dominance ended in 1469, but he was able to pass a great deal of power to his more talented sons, Lorenzo and Giuliano.

THE MAGNIFICENT LORENZO (1449–1492)

Lorenzo de' Medici was a talented and complex individual who became renowned for his generous support of the arts. Many talented artists, musicians, and philosophers were directly supported or encouraged by the sensual Lorenzo, known as "the Magnificent." Filippo Lippi, Domenico Ghirlandaio, Sandro Botticelli, Verrocchio, Michelangelo, and others received commissions from Lorenzo. The Medici library expanded under his patronage and he continued to support the Platonic Academy of Marsilio Ficino, his intimate friend. A sensual man of many interests and abilities, Lorenzo also wrote provocative and often ribald poetry and staged elaborate annual festivals.

As the political leader of Florence, Lorenzo de' Medici attempted to defend aggressively the financial interests of the city. Unfortunately for him, his family's friend Pope Paul II (r. 1464–1471) was succeeded by Francesco della Rovere as Pope Sixtus IV. Sixtus IV distrusted and disliked Lorenzo, who had attacked Volterra in 1472 for its rich alum mines. Alum, a very valuable sulfate, was absolutely essential in the dyeing of textiles. Both the pope and the banker wanted to control this important asset. Sixtus also had his own family ambitions and wanted to bestow strategic Imola in the Romagna on one of his nephews. Lorenzo opposed this and also the appointment of Francesco Salviati as archbishop of Pisa.

THE PAZZI PLOT OF 1478

As relations with the papacy cooled, enemies of the Medici flocked to Rome and found a sympathetic papal ear. Foremost among them were members of a rival Florentine banking family, the Pazzi, who replaced the Medici as papal bankers. With the blessing of the pope, Francesco de Pazzi, Archbishop Francesco Salviati, and others attempted to assassinate Lorenzo and Giuliano de' Medici during the celebration of High Mass at the cathedral of Florence on April 26, 1478. Giuliano was stabbed to death, but Lorenzo escaped with only a shoulder wound.

The Pazzi conspirators also failed to seize the town hall or to rally the people against the Medici. Instead, the people of Florence joined Lorenzo in severely punishing the conspirators. Francesco de Pazzi and Archbishop Salviati were hanged from the windows of the Florentine town hall. Other

Andrea del Verrocchio, *Lorenzo de' Medici*. Photo courtesy of the National Gallery of Art, Samuel H. Kress Collection, Washington, D.C.

plotters were brutally murdered by angry mobs. Pope Sixtus retaliated by excommunicating Lorenzo de' Medici, imposing an interdict on Florence, and then invading Tuscany with his ally Naples. Abandoned by its ally Venice, Florence struggled for two desperate years to hold off its enemies.

During the course of the war, Lorenzo de' Medici risked his life on a secret diplomatic mission to the court of the capricious and often cruel Ferrante I of Naples. He finally managed to persuade Ferrante that it would not be in Naples' interest to increase the power of the Papal States at the expense of Florence. Without the support of Naples, Sixtus IV had to agree to a separate peace with Florence.

THE FALL OF THE MEDICI

Having survived the great crisis of the Pazzi Plot, Lorenzo de' Medici continued to dominate Florentine politics for the rest of his life. He helped create a new executive committee, the Council of Seventy, which controlled most of the executive powers of government through its subcommittees. Lorenzo was a permanent member of the Seventy and had his representatives serve on the other important organs of power. He also fused his personal fortune with that of the state, probably to his own advantage.

His generous expenditures continued throughout his life, although not to the same extent as in an earlier time. Between 1434 and 1471, the Medici spent 663,755 gold florins on architectural and artistic commissions, charity, and taxes. Lorenzo said of this astounding sum: "I think it casts a brilliant light on our estate, and it seems to me that the monies were well spent and I am very well pleased with this."[10] Indeed, Medici's preoccupation with artistic and political matters caused him to neglect his family's business affairs. Ignoring one of the key lessons of the Bardi experience, he made an overly generous loan to a fellow art collector, Charles the Bold, duke of Burgundy, which was never repaid. Medici banks were already closing before Lorenzo's death in 1492 and the invasion of the French two years later.

The French invasion caused the Medici to close the Rome branch and finally the home bank in Florence itself. There was still enough wealth left to secure the futures of his children if competently managed. His second son, Giovanni, had become a cardinal at age thirteen and later became Pope Leo X (r. 1513–1521). Lorenzo de' Medici was succeeded in Florence by his oldest son, the wastrel Piero. The incompetent Piero was blamed for losing territory to the invading French and was exiled from Florence for life in November 1494. The unthinkable had happened: the Medici of Florence had fallen.

Chronology

1254	Coining of the first Florin.	1347	Outbreak of the Black Death; Cola di Rienzo seizes control of Rome.
1282–1302	War of the Sicilian Vespers.		
1295	Marco Polo returns to Venice from Asia.	1354	Fall of Cola di Rienzo.
1297	Founding of the Venetian republic.	1376	Papacy returns to Rome.
1346	Collapse of the Bardi and Peruzzi banks.	1378	Cloth workers revolt in Florence.

1385–1402	Reign of Giangaleazzo I in Milan.	**1478**	Pazzi Plot in Florence.
1389–1464	Life of Cosimo de' Medici.	**1492**	Reign of Pope Alexander VI (Borgia).
1414–1435	Reign of Joanna II in Naples.	**1494**	Invasion of King Charles VIII of France; closing of Medici banks in Rome and Florence.
1416–1458	Reign of Alfonso V of Aragon and South Italy.		
1417–1431	Reign of Pope Nicholas V; rebuilding of Rome.	**1495**	Battle of Fornova.
1444–1482	Reign of Federigo da Montefeltro in Urbino.	**1496**	Burning of the vanities in Florence.
1449–1492	Life of Lorenzo de' Medici.	**1498**	Death of Savonarola.
1450–1466	Reign of Francesco and Bianca Sforza in Milan.	**1499**	Invasion of King Louis XII of France.
1458–1464	Reign of Pope Pius II (Aeneas Silvius).	**1503–1513**	Reign of Pope Julius II (Papa Terrible).
1458–1494	Reign of Ferrante I in Naples.	**1507**	Death of Cesare Borgia.
1471–1484	Reign of Pope Sixtus IV.	**1508**	Death of Ludovico il Moro.
1474	Birth of Isabella d'Este.	**1527**	Sack of Rome.
1476	Ludovico il Moro takes power in Milan as regent; birth of Cesare Borgia.	**1535**	Death of Isabella d'Este.

Further Reading

THE ITALIAN RENAISSANCE: GENERAL STUDIES

Peter Burke, *The Historical Anthropology of Early Modern Italy* (1987).

Denys Hay and John Law, *Italy in the Age of the Renaissance* (1989).

Michael Mallett, *Mercenaries and Their Masters: Warfare in Renaissance Italy* (1984).

Lauro Martines, *Power and Imagination: City-States in Renaissance Italy* (1979).

Garrett Mattingly, *Renaissance Diplomacy* (1955).

John Stephens, *The Italian Renaissance: The Origins of Intellectual and Artistic Change Before the Reformation* (1990).

Giovanni Tobacco, *The Struggle for Power in Medieval Italy* (1990).

David Waley, *The Italian City Republics*, 3rd ed. (1988).

PAPAL ROME

Anthony Grafton, ed., *Rome Reborn: The Vatican Library and Renaissance Culture* (1993). Important collection of essays by various scholars.

Egmont Lee, *Sixtus IV and Men of Letters* (1978).

Michael Mallett, *The Borgias* (1987).

Rosamond Mitchell, *The Laurels and the Tiara: Pope Pius II* (1962).

Laurie Nussdorfer, *Civic Politics in the Rome of Urban VIII* (1992).

Peter Partner, *The Pope's Men: The Papal Civil Service in the Renaissance* (1990).

Kenneth Setton, *The Papacy and the Levant, 1204–1571*, 4 vols. (1976–1984).

Christine Shaw, *Julius II, The Warrior Pope* (1993).

Charles Stinger, *The Renaissance in Rome* (1985).

VENICE

David Chambers, *The Imperial Age of Venice, 1380–1580* (1970).

—— and Brian Pullan, eds., *Venice: A Documentary History, 1450–1630* (1993). 250 wide-ranging documents.

Robert Davis, *The War of the Fists: Popular Culture and Public Violence in Late Renaissance Venice* (1994).

Robert Finlay, *Politics in Renaissance Venice* (1980).

Paul Grendler, *The Roman Inquisition and the Venetian Press, 1540–1605* (1977).

Margaret King, *Venetian Humanism in an Age of Patrician Dominance* (1986).

Frederic Lane, *Venice, A Maritime Republic* (1973).

Richard Mackenney, *Tradesmen and Traders: The World of Guilds in Venice and Europe* (1987).

John Martin, *Venice's Hidden Enemies: Italian Heretics in a Renaissance City* (1994).

Ruth Martin, *Witchcraft and the Inquisition in Venice* (1989).

Edward Muir, *Civic Ritual in Renaissance Venice* (1981).

John Norwich, *A History of Venice* (1989).

Brian Pullan, *Rich and Poor in Renaissance Venice* (1971).

Donald Queller, *The Venetian Patriciate: Myth vs. Reality* (1986).

Dennis Romano, *Patricians and Popolani: The Social Foundations of the Venetian Renaissance State* (1987).

Guido Ruggiero, *Binding Passions: Tales of Magic, Marriage, and Power at the End of the Renaissance* (1993).

FLORENCE

Marvin Becker, *Florence in Transition*, 2 vols. (1967–1968).

Gene Brucker, *The Civic World of Early Renaissance Florence*, 2nd ed. (1985).

——, *Renaissance Florence* (1969).

Samuel Cohn, *The Laboring Poor in Renaissance Florence* (1980).

Christopher Hibbert. *Florence* (1990).

Dale and F. W. Kent, *Neighbors and Neighborhoods in Renaissance Florence* (1982).

Carol Lansing, *The Florentine Magnates: Lineage and Factions in a Medieval Commune* (1991).

Anthony Molho, *Marriage Alliance in Late Medieval Florence* (1994).

John Najemy, *Corporation and Consensus in Florentine Electoral Politics* (1982).

Ferdinand Schevill, *A History of Florence* (1936).

Laura Stern, *The Criminal Law System of Medieval and Renaissance Florence* (1994).

Richard Trexler, *Public Life in Renaissance Florence* (1980).

Ronald Weissman, *Ritual Brotherhood in Renaissance Florence* (1982).

THE MEDICI

C. M. Ady, *Lorenzo de' Medici and Renaissance Italy* (1955).

Frances Ames-Lewis, ed., *Cosimo "il Vecchio" de' Medici, 1389–1464* (1992).

Alison Brown, *The Medici in Florence: The Exercise of Language and Power* (1992).

Melissa Bullard, *Lorenzo il Magnifico: Image and Anxiety, Politics and Finance* (1994).

J. R. Hale, *Florence and the Medici* (1977).

Dale Kent, *The Rise of the Medici: Faction in Florence* (1978).

Nicolai Rubenstein, *The Government of Florence Under the Medici (1434–94)* (1966).

OTHER STATES

Jerry Bentley, *Politics and Culture in Renaissance Naples* (1987).

William Bowsky, *A Medieval Italian Commune: Siena* (1981).

M. E. Bratchel, *Lucca: The Reconstruction of an Italian City-Republic, 1430–1494* (1995).

Judith Brown, *In the Shadow of Renaissance Florence: Pescia* (1982).

Trevor Dean, *Land and Power in Late Medieval Ferrara: The Rule of the Este* (1988).

Joanne Ferraro, *Family and Public Life in Brescia, 1580–1650: The Foundations of Power in the Venetian State* (1993).

James Grubb, *Firstborn of Venice: Vicenza in the Early Renaissance State* (1988).

Werner Gundersheimer, *Ferrara: The Style of a Renaissance Despotism* (1973).

David Herlihy, *Medieval and Renaissance Pistoia* (1967).

———, *Pisa in the Early Renaissance* (1958).

P. J. Jones, *The Malatesta of Rimini and the Papal State* (1972).

John Larner, *The Lords of the Romagna* (1965).

Gregory Lubkin, *A Renaissance Court: Milan under Galezzo Maria Sforza* (1994).

Edward Muir, *Mad Blood Stirring: Vendetta and Factions in Friuli during the Renaissance* (1993).

Alan Ryder, *Alfonso the Magnanimous, King of Aragon, Naples, and Sicily, 1396–1458* (1990).

Kate Simon, *A Renaissance Tapestry: The Gonzaga of Mantua* (1988).

Nicholas Terpstra, *Confraternities and Civic Religion in Renaissance Bologna* (1993).

Notes

1. Cited in G. R. Elton, ed., *Renaissance and Reformation 1300–1600*, 3rd ed. (New York: Macmillan, 1976), p. 94.
2. Cited in Lewis Spitz, *The Renaissance and Reformation Movements* (Chicago: Rand McNally, 1971), p. 94.
3. Cited in Kenneth Bartlett, ed., *The Civilization of the Italian Renaissance: A Sourcebook* (Lexington, Mass.: D. C. Heath, 1992), p. 316.
4. Cited in De Lamar Jensen, *Renaissance Europe: Age of Recovery and Reconciliation*, 2nd ed. (Lexington, Mass.: D. C. Heath, 1992), p. 305.
5. Cited in D. S. Chambers, ed., *Patrons and Artists in the Italian Renaissance* (Columbia, S.C.: University of South Carolina Press, 1971), p. 136.
6. Cited in Maria Bellonci, "Beatrice and Isabella d'Este," in *Renaissance Profiles*, J. H. Plumb, ed. (New York: Harper and Row, 1961), p. 151.
7. Cited in Denis Mack Smith, "Federigo da Montefeltro," in Ibid., p. 125.
8. Cited in Jensen, *Renaissance*, p. 71.
9. Cited in Spitz, *Renaissance and Reformation*, p. 108.
10. Cited in Lauro Martines, *Power and Imagination: City-States in Renaissance Italy* (New York: Alfred Knopf, 1979), p. 243.

5

THE CULTURE
OF RENAISSANCE HUMANISM
IN ITALY

The city-states and principalities of Renaissance Italy produced artistic masterpieces in abundance throughout the period. Seldom has so much talent appeared at one time and place and achieved such comparatively high levels of sophisticated public and private support. Underlying the achievements of the Renaissance artists was the culture of Renaissance humanism. *Humanism* can be defined as a movement that encouraged the study of the form and content of classical learning. Renaissance humanists were obsessed with the recovery, study, interpretation, and transmission of the intellectual heritage of ancient Greece and Rome. They were particularly interested in what the Roman philosopher and statesman Cicero (106–43 B.C.) defined as "humane studies" or the liberal arts. Cicero favored those subjects such as grammar, rhetoric, poetry, literature, and moral philosophy (ethics) which help us to become more eloquent, thoughtful, and virtuous human beings. The fundamental agenda of the humanists was to use what they called the study of humanity (*humanitas*) to make people more civilized and more humane.

The humanists of the Renaissance, whether businessmen such as Cosimo de' Medici, politicians such as Isabella d'Este, or professional scholars such as Lorenzo Valla, had a tremendous faith in the power of language. They urged the study of classical languages such as Greek and Latin and the return to the original source materials whenever possible. Some of the humanists also hoped to transform the use of Latin in their own day, to purge it of what they thought were barbarisms and return it to the glories of Cicero's day. Inspired by classical models, Renaissance humanists made rich contributions to the development of history and philosophy. In literature, many of the humanists contributed to the flowering of Italian vernacular drama and poetry.

Setting the Agenda:
Early Renaissance Humanists

Much of the agenda of early Renaissance humanism came from the lives and thoughts of Francesco Petrarca and Giovanni Boccaccio. Both were men of formidable literary talents, whose Italian writings, along with those of Dante, helped to shape the development of that language as a literary vehicle. They became good friends and came to share a passion for the ancient Greek and Latin classics that greatly influenced the development of Renaissance humanism in Italy and elsewhere.

FRANCESCO PETRARCA (1304–1374)

Petrarca was born in Arezzo near Florence in 1304. His notary father had been exiled from Florence for his involvement in a long-standing political dispute between different factions of the Guelf (papal) movement. When Francesco was seven years old his family moved to Pisa and then a year later to a small village near Avignon, where the papacy had moved during the period of what he would later call the "Babylonian Captivity of the church of God." His father, Pietro, worked in the papal bureaucracy. Young Francesco picked up his interest in the classics from his father, who was fond of reading Cicero's letters aloud at home.

At age twelve Petrarca was sent fifty miles away to the University of Montpellier in France to begin the study of law, which he hated. Instead of concentrating on his legal studies, he immersed himself in the Latin classics. His mother died while he was away from home at Montpellier. At age sixteen, he was dispatched by his father to the University of Bologna, the foremost law school in Europe. When his father died in 1326, the handsome and vain Petrarca returned to Avignon and lived the life of a young dandy. As he wrote later, "I could not face making a merchandise of my mind."[1] Indeed, he seemed more worried about his reddish-brown hair, which had turned prematurely gray. To support himself and his growing interest in poetry, he took minor orders in the church, but was never ordained.

His career as a poet was bolstered after he first laid eyes on the lovely "Laura" at a church in Avignon on April 6, 1326. She was married to someone else and they had no significant personal contact. Nevertheless, Petrarca immortalized her charms in his increasingly popular Italian sonnets. He called her "the candid rose, thorn-compassed and shy, and yet our age's glory and despair."[2] In 1330 he became a chaplain in the house of a cardinal, but insisted on having ample time for his writing and scholarship. Francesco Petrarca was quickly recognized as the greatest Italian poet since Dante. Occasional diplomatic missions, church benefices, gifts, prizes, and his writings gave him sufficient income for a life of travel, a bit of art patronage, and retirement to a modest villa. Petrarca made it all the way to the Netherlands, traveling through the forested lands of the Holy Roman Empire in central Europe. Back in Italy he was crowned "Poet Laureate" by the Roman senate in a magnificent ceremony in Rome in April 1341.

Italy's incessant wars almost did him in as he traveled about seeking inspiration and hospitality. Petrarca was nearly killed in 1344 during a siege of Parma. He survived the Black Death, but many of his friends perished, as did the inspiration of his sonnets, Laura. The poet was also a friend of Cola di Rienzo, who shared his love for the ancient Romans. After Cola's second effort to restore the grandeur of Rome ended in petty tyranny in 1354, the disappointed Petrarca made the long journey from Milan to Prague in order to beg Holy Roman Emperor Charles IV to bring peace to troubled Italy. After a number of years of inner turmoil caused partly by his guilt over his battles with lust, Petrarca found increasing need for quiet contemplation and spiritual comfort. He wrote in his *Secretum* of 1358, "I am very sorry I was not born without feelings. I would rather be a senseless rock than to be troubled by so many urges of my body."[3] Petrarca spent the last years of life in quiet solitude tended by his illegitimate daughter, Francesca, at his retirement villa near Venice.

Before his death, Petrarca had done a great deal to help revive the study of antiquity. He had even imitated the Roman poet

Virgil by producing his own epic poem, *Africa,* in honor of Scipio Africanus, who defeated the Carthaginian Hannibal in 202 B.C. The modern historian Lewis Spitz, Jr., has called it an "epic bore." Petrarca also edited a version of the writings of the Roman historian Livy. He even published a collection of *Letters to the Ancient Dead* in which he informed the ancient Cicero, Seneca, Horace, Virgil, Homer, and others how bad things were in his own day and how much he wished he was living with them. To get to know the ancients better, Petrarca tried to learn classical Greek and began searching for ancient manuscripts.

Increasingly religious as he grew older, Petrarca also found great solace in the writings of St. Augustine (d. 430). His own love of the classics never diminished and he continued to urge others to make their own discovery of the rich heritage of ancient Greece and Rome. He passed on to later humanists the idea of the active and contemplative lives, the Stoic notion of virtue as "greatness of soul," a hostility to speculative knowledge, and a strong faith in human rationality. Petrarca developed many of the fundamental ideas of Renaissance humanism and influenced generations of thinkers, both men and women. As the later humanist Leonardo Bruni wrote of him, "Francesco Petrarca was the first who had such grace of talent and who recognized and restored to light the ancient elegance of style which was lost and dead by recovering the works of Cicero."[4]

GIOVANNI BOCCACCIO (1313–1375)

In his own lifetime. Petrarca had a profound impact on one of the most gifted literary men of the early Renaissance, Giovanni Boccaccio. Boccaccio was born in Paris, the illegitimate son of a Florentine merchant and a French woman. His father intended him to pursue a career in business and sent him to Naples to learn the profession. He worked for a branch of the Bardi bank and also tried his hand at studying canon law. The collapse of the Bardi bank and the disorders connected with the Black Death forced his return to Florence to assist his father.

In the stimulating atmosphere of disaster-plagued Florence, Giovanni Boccaccio found time to pursue his literary interests and wrote some of the most important works of the Renaissance. Out of the catastrophe of the Black Death came Boccaccio's finest literary accomplishment, the *Decameron,* 100 folk tales, some of them irreverent and lascivious, but told with great elegance of style. Written in Italian, the *Decameron* also contains the best surviving derivative account we have of the Black

Andrea del Castagno, *Portrait of Giovanni Boccaccio.* S. Apollonia, Florence, Italy. Alinari/Art Resource.

Death. The tales, written in an essentially medieval style, became extremely popular and established Boccaccio's literary fame. They provided a world still stunned by grief with some badly needed comic relief of high quality. Few have matched his gifts as a storyteller.

Under the influence of Francesco Petrarca, whom he called his "illustrious teacher," Boccaccio began to write more in Latin and to devote more attention to classical and religious subjects. Like his mentor, he tried to learn Greek and was instrumental in having a chair in that language established at the University of Florence. Boccaccio also loved collecting ancient manuscripts and managed to find texts of the Roman satirist Martial, the poet Ovid, and the historian Tacitus. His classical studies also resulted in a *Genealogy of the Gods*, a manual of ancient geography, and a collection of essays on famous men and women from antiquity. Boccaccio's *Concerning Famous Women* treats 106 women from the Old Testament through medieval times. Although filled with misogynistic assumptions, it did a great deal to make his readers aware of a gender normally forgotten in a period of male-dominated letters and scholarship. His legacy includes a biography of the great Florentine poet Dante and a commentary on his *Divine Comedy*. Boccaccio was particularly incensed that Florence should have ever banished the illustrious Dante, who hardly merited such treatment because of "his virtue, learning, and good services."[5]

Boccaccio's love of poetry, as well as his inherent sexism, is reflected in the following excerpt from his "In Praise of Poetry":

> This poetry, which ignorant triflers cast aside, is a sort of fervid and exquisite invention, with fervid expression, in speech or writing, of that which the mind has in-

vented. It proceeds from the bosom of God, and few, I find, are the souls in whom this gift was born; indeed, so wonderful a gift that true poets have always been the rarest of men.[6]

Despite the limitations of his worldview, Giovanni Boccaccio was one of the rarest and most talented of men to appear during the early Renaissance. One wonders what he would have made of the talented women poets who came after him.

Civic Humanists

Although Francesco Petrarca and his associate Giovanni Boccaccio pursued their classical studies for their own sake and that of their souls, some later humanists chose to become more involved in the affairs of their communities. They chose to live more active and public lives as had their hero Cicero, the ancient Roman lawyer, statesman, and philosopher. Coluccio Salutati, Leonardo Bruni, and Poggio Bracciolini were three of the many civic humanists who chose to put their knowledge of the classics to practical use in the service of their communities. Once again, a grounding in the humanities proved to be the best training for careers as well as life.

COLUCCIO SALUTATI (1331–1400)

Coluccio Salutati was yet another Florentine humanist influenced by Petrarca. Salutati studied law at Bologna and became a notary. He held bureaucratic positions in Rome and at various places in Tuscany before becoming chancellor of the republic of Lucca. In 1375 he became chancellor of the Florentine government, a position he held for the rest of his life. Although he thought that "the active life is inferior" to the contemplative life, "many times it is to be preferred . . . as it concerns necessary things."[7] Salutati used his position to promote the growth of humanism and was an elegant Latin stylist. Giangaleazzo I of Milan said that a letter from Salutati was "worth a contingent of cavalry."[8]

Salutati helped guide Florence through the great crisis of the Cloth Workers (*Ciompi*) Revolt of 1378 and counseled the ruling elite to avoid harsh reprisals against the rebels. During outbreaks of plague, he refused to leave his post or to allow his family to leave. His reading of the Roman Stoics had convinced him that no one could die before his appointed time. When the Milanese threatened Florence, Salutati's rally of its defenders so infuriated Giangaleazzo that he sent assassins to kill him; when that failed he sent forged letters implicating the chancellor in treason. Giangaleazzo had used a similar ruse to get the marquis of Mantua to behead his own wife. Fortunately for Salutati, the Florentine *Signoria* did not fall for the trick.

In addition to his numerous civic duties, Salutati found time to write on the classics and religion and to locate lost manuscripts, including Cicero's *Familiar Letters*. Devoted to ancient learning, the chancellor also brought Manuel Chrysoloras (c. 1350–1415), a leading Greek scholar, from Constantinople to Florence in 1396. Chrysoloras became a municipally paid public lecturer and helped further spread classical learning among the Florentine elite, including Leonardo Bruni, Salutati's civic humanist successor as chancellor.

LEONARDO BRUNI (1370–1444)

Bruni was born in Arezzo near Florence to a family of modest means. An obviously gifted and determined youth, he was helped by Salutati and taught Greek by Manuel Chrysoloras. He became a language tutor in the Medici household. His celebrated skill as a Latinist won him a position in 1405 as a secretary in the papal chancery in Rome. Bruni returned to Florence for good in 1415 as a member of the Florentine bureaucracy, rising to the position of chancellor in 1427, an office he held to his death in 1444.

Leonardo Bruni continued Salutati's tradition of civic humanism, using his intellectual skills for the good of his community. He urged others to "read authors who can help you not only by their subject matter, but also by the splendor of their style and their skill in writing; that is to say, the works of Cicero and of any who may possibly approach his level." On the other hand, Bruni found nothing except boredom in the study of law, which he called "the yawning science," and found no honor in "the mercenary traffic in law-suits."[9]

His own writings were extremely important to the development of the discipline of history. He is best known for his influential *History of the Florentine People*, on which he labored for three decades. Bruni's *History* was modeled after the classic work of the Roman historian Livy. Bruni argued that events were the result of human not divine activity and that even recent history was a worthwhile enterprise because of the moral lessons it taught. He also translated Aristotle's *Ethics* and *Politics* and much of Plato into Latin. His attitudes toward women seemed more in keeping with the spirit of Aristotle, who viewed women as "defective men," than Plato, who had to concede that women could be admitted to the highest (guardian) class in his ideal *Republic* because in essence equal potential for reasoning is found in both sexes. A great Florentine patriot, the Florentine chancellor also wrote *In Praise of the City of Florence*, a book which lauded the freedom of the republican form of government, its capitalistic business practices, and praised the beauty of the city. In his life and in his work, Leonardo Bruni affords us a significant example of the humanist in the service of his community.

POGGIO BRACCIOLINI (1380–1459)

Poggio Bracciolini was not only one of the more colorful of the civic humanists, but also one of the greatest finders of lost classical manuscripts. A native of a village near Florence, Poggio studied with the Greek scholar Manuel Chrysoloras and was a friend of the humanist merchant Niccolò Niccoli (1363–1437). A fine Latinist, he was a member of the humanist circle of Salutati, the Florentine chancellor. Bracciolini then found employment in Rome as a papal secretary. Poggio attended the Council of Constance (1414–1418) in the service of Pope John XXIII (r. 1410–1415). When John was deposed, Poggio was free to search for classical manuscripts in the rich but underutilized monastic libraries of northern Europe.

Poggio Bracciolini became one of the most successful collectors of manuscripts among the Renaissance humanists. He found several of Cicero's orations in the summer of 1415 at the well-known monastery at Cluny. His greatest discovery came the next year in the Swiss monastery of St. Gall where he discovered the complete text of the Roman rhetorician Quintilian's *Institutes of Oratory*. These texts laid the foundations for the humanists' doctrine on rhetoric. In later years Bracciolini also located important works by a number of Roman authors, including Apuleius's *The Golden Ass*, the Roman poet Lucretius's *The Nature of Things*, writings by the historian Ammianus Marcellinus, the full text of Vitruvius's *On Architecture*, nine comedies by Plautus, and several histories by Tacitus, including his *Germania*, which created a sensation among German humanists starved for information about their ancestors.

In addition to his manuscript collecting, Poggio continued in the services of several popes for nearly fifty years. Despite his work for the papacy, his personal life was hardly exemplary. He fathered at least twelve illegitimate children and at the age of fifty-five dropped their mother and his mistress in favor of marriage to a young woman of a good family. Poggio was also known for his cutting wit. Francesco Filelfo (1398–1481), a rival humanist and manuscript collector, referred to Poggio's tongue as "the herald of malicious lies that sheds its venom on the good and the wise."[10]

Even with Poggio's acerbic personality, he found favor in the eyes of the powerful Cosimo de' Medici, who admired his wit and his scholarship. In addition to his manuscript collecting, Poggio had written an important description of Roman ruins (*De varietate fortunae*) and a popular collection of Boccaccion tales, the *Facetiae*. Poggio returned to Florence to serve for a while as chancellor. In his last years, he worked on his *History of the People of Florence*, which continued the work of Leonardo Bruni and covered the century of the Florentine-Milanese wars, 1352–1455. Like Bruni, Poggio used his sources critically and helped advance the study of history.

The Illustrious Lorenzo Valla (c. 1407–1457)

Fifteenth-century Renaissance humanism hit its peak in the life and work of Lorenzo Valla. Valla was arguably the most brilliant of the humanists of the Italian Renaissance. A native of Rome, his father was an ecclesiastical advocate. Lorenzo studied under Vittorino da Feltre, the foremost schoolmaster of the Italian Renaissance. Excelling in Latin and Greek, Valla served as a professor of eloquence at the University of Pavia beginning in 1429. In 1433 he was forced to flee Pavia after a controversy over his spirited attacks on the legal theories of the popular Bartolus of Sassoferato. He then resumed his life as a wandering scholar with stops in Milan, Genoa, and Mantua, among other places. He made the acquaintance of most of the leading humanists in Italy, including Leonardo Bruni and Poggio Bracciolini. In 1437 Valla took a position as secretary to King Alfonso the Magnanimous of Naples, whom he advised on cultural matters.

Lorenzo Valla parted company with other humanists in preferring the Latin style of Quintillian to Cicero and Epicureanism to Stoicism. In his *On Pleasure*, he argued that while the ethical doctrines of Christianity were superior to those of the Epicureans, it was better to pursue happiness than pain. His own pleasure was found chiefly in scholarship despite the attacks of his critics. Undaunted by his foes, Valla wrote, "I have published many books, a great many, in almost every branch of learning. Inasmuch as there are those who are shocked that in these I disagree with certain great writers already approved by long usage, and charge me with rashness and sacrilege, what must we suppose some of them will do now!"[11]

More controversy followed with his *On the False Donation of Constantine* of 1440 in which Valla demonstrated through historical, linguistic, and logical analysis that the first Christian emperor could not possibly have been the author of the document which allegedly transferred the territorial sovereignty over the Western Roman Empire to the papacy. Valla showed that a number of terms used in the "Donation" were not in use until at least a century after the time of Constantine. He wondered: would Constantine give up the best part of his empire? If the emperor did so, why is there no proof that it was received? Although summoned to Rome in 1444 by Pope Felix V

(r. 1439–1449), Valla stayed in Naples under the protection of the pope's enemy, King Alfonso.

His *On the Elegances of the Latin Language* (1444) became the standard textbook throughout Europe for all those interested in philological precision and a graceful writing style. Valla asserted that even though we have lost ancient Rome's "power and dominion," yet through the power of Latin "we continue to rule, even now in a great part of the world."[12] Valla's own scholarship did a great deal to preserve the linguistic legacy of ancient Rome.

Applying his critical methods to the Bible, Valla produced his highly influential *Annotations on the New Testament*, which demonstrated many errors in the Vulgate translation of the Bible, the official Bible of the medieval Roman Catholic church. This work was known only in manuscript form to a limited circle until published by the Dutch humanist Erasmus in 1505. Erasmus then used Valla's work in producing his own remarkable translation of the New Testament in 1516, which in turn influenced the German translation by the reformer Martin Luther.

Valla also entered into some of the other great intellectual debates of the age. In his treatise *On Free Will*, he argued faith and reason can be reconciled, even if love and faith must be emphasized. Valla also rendered a great service to history by his translations of the classical Greek historians Herodotus and Thucydides, as well as writing his own history of the reign of King Ferrante I of Naples. In 1448 he became secretary to Pope Nicholas V (r. 1447–1455) and a professor at the University of Rome. In Rome, Valla spent the last years of his life helping the humanist pope collect rare Greek editions and establishing the papal library. It was a fine ending to a life of controversy and scholarship, which illustrated so many of the finer qualities of Renaissance humanism.

Women Humanists

Scholarship, like most public activities, was considered a man's field during the Renaissance and the centuries that had preceded it. With only a few rare exceptions, women were not admitted to the universities or allowed to practice the learned professions. Opportunities for learning were severely restricted for women outside the walls of convents and elite courts. Indeed, only 186 European laywomen have been identified as book owners during the fourteenth and fifteenth centuries. Those who tried to enter the world of the male humanists found mostly ridicule and suspicion. Despite all this discouragement, several women did manage to make contributions to the humanist movement. We shall offer brief sketches of two of these female Renaissance humanists, whose lives reveal many of the challenges intellectual women faced in the period.

ISOTTA NOGAROLA (1418–1466)

One of the most talented of the women humanists was Isotta Nogarola of Verona. She was born to a noble family with a tradition of learning that included her aunt, Angela. Isotta's widowed mother insisted that both her daughters have the finest education possible for girls in the Renaissance, which was not a typical attitude for mothers in an age that assumed females to be lesser creatures than males. Isotta and her talented sister, Ginevra, were tutored by Martino Rizzoni, a student of the great humanist pedagogue Guarino da Verona.

The Nogarola sisters became quite well known for their learning in northern Italian humanist circles. Even among the humanists, however, learned women were considered threatening. The usual mode of attack was to impugn their character. Anonymous letters were circulated accusing Isotta of making "her body generally available for promiscuous intercourse." Snubbed by Guarino da Verona, Isotta lamented, "Why then was I born a woman, to be scorned by men in words and deeds?" When Guarino finally replied, he praised her learning. He then told her that she should set her gender aside and create "a man within the woman." That is, if she were going to enter into what he considered "masculine pursuits," she must become like a man in her mind.[13]

In 1438 Ginevra married a Brescian nobleman and was forced to give up her studies completely, as so often happened to the few young, educated women of the period. Duties as a wife and mother were expected to take almost all the time of even a noblewoman. Most Renaissance wives did not have parents or husbands who encouraged them to use their minds. Few could defy the society's insistence on submission to the absolute authority of husbands.

Distressed by the loss of her sister to marriage and the scorn she received from some of her humanist correspondents, Isotta moved to more cosmopolitan Venice, but returned to Verona in 1441. She vowed never to marry and instead retreated to her "book-lined cell" in her mother's house to pursue religious rather than classical studies. In the 1450s she drew close to the civic humanist and diplomat Ludovico Foscarini, whom she had known earlier when he was the Venetian governor of Verona. Out of their correspondence grew her two most important writings, *Dialogue on Adam and Eve* and *Oration on the Life of St. Jerome*, both of which revealed a sophisticated understanding of theological issues. The Venetian scholar Lauro Quirini praised her for overcoming her "own nature. For that true virtue, which is essentially male, you have sought with singular zeal."[14]

LAURA CERETA (1469–1499)

Like Isotta Nogarola, Laura Cereta was a talented scholar who also found it difficult to find acceptance from male humanists. She began life as the daughter of a noble in Brescia and received some of her early education in a convent. At the age of nine, Laura returned home to be tutored by her supportive father in Latin, Greek, and mathematics. Inspired by the example of Petrarca, she began an active correspondence and showed a fine Latin style. Cereta was married to a Brescian merchant at age fifteen but was widowed eighteen months later when he died of the plague. In little more than a year, she had been "a girl, bride, widow, and pauper."

Her humanist studies helped her recover from the death of her beloved and supportive husband. She plunged more deeply than ever into mathematics, philosophy, and theology, where she found knowledge not "shadowy and vaporous," but "perpetually secure and perfect." "I care more for letters than for flashy clothes," she wrote. "Moreover, I have committed myself absolutely to that cultivation of virtue which can profit me not only when alive but also after death."[15] Cereta was attacked for her learning and outspoken opinions. A prominent Dominican, Thomas of Milan, advised her to "blunt your pen and temper it with the file of modesty" and give up classical studies as "things unworthy of her." Before lapsing into obscurity, Laura Cereta wrote a wide range of Latin works, including her letters to fellow humanists and an important defense of humanist learning for women. She died at age thirty and is only now being rediscovered as an important Renaissance thinker, whose full potential was never realized.

Humanists as Educators

Although women of intellect such as Isotta Nogarola and Laura Cereta were seldom allowed to develop fully their scholarly interests, bright young men of prosperous circumstances had expanded opportunities to pursue lives of learning and to make valuable contributions to many areas of inquiry during the Renaissance. Fifteenth-century humanists were deeply concerned with education, especially for males. The need for improvements in education was staggering. The Florentine chronicler Giovanni Villani reported that in 1338, 8,000 to 10,000 boys and girls between ages six to thirteen learned rudimentary skills in reading, writing, and arithmetic. Only an all-male elite of from 1,000 to 1,200 went on to learn advanced mathematics and business practices. Less than half of that group of boys would learn sufficient Latin, logic, and rhetoric to enter a university. Other communities had even less opportunities for learning.

There were a number of humanists in the Renaissance who thought that this situation needed to be changed. Not only was more schooling needed, but the quality needed to be enhanced. For Pier Paolo Vergerio (1370–1444), court tutor and a professor of logic and rhetoric at Padua, humanism was primarily a system of education for the sons of the ruling classes. A friend of Salutati and Bruni, Vergerio argued for the importance of a broad, well-rounded education in such "Liberal Studies" as history, literature, grammar, logic, rhetoric, music, arithmetic, geometry, and natural science. "Among these I accord the first place to History, on grounds both of its attractiveness and its utility, qualities which appeal equally to the scholar and the statesman."[16]

In his treatise *On the Manners of a Gentleman and on Liberal Studies,* he recommended adapting the amount of subject matter to the age and abilities of each individual student:

> The choice of studies will depend to some extent upon the character of individual minds. For whilst one boy seizes rapidly the point of which he is in search and states it ably, another, working far more slowly, has yet the sounder judgment and so detects the weak spot in his rival's conclusions."[17]

Vergerio's ideas on education received additional support from Poggio Bracciolini's discovery of Quintilian's *Institutes of Oratory* in 1416, which Vergerio published. This made available to an important audience the educational wisdom of one of ancient Rome's greatest teachers. Quintilian's ideas reinforced the Ciceronian notion of educating the whole person, which had long appealed to Renaissance humanists beginning with Petrarca and extending down to Leonardo Bruni, another powerful advocate of the liberal arts.

Humanists such as Vittorino da Feltre (1378–1446) and Guarino da Verona (1374–1460) set out to infuse education at all levels with new attitudes about and methods of learning. Both had studied at Padua, where Vergerio taught, and were impressed with his educational theories. Vittorino established a court academy at Mantua in 1423 that attempted to achieve the classical Greek ideal of a sound mind in a sound body. Therefore, his students studied the writings of Plutarch, Tacitus, and the church fathers along with lessons in swimming, riding, fencing, and military style drill. The classical texts were read, translated, and imitated. Vittorino's school was called the "Happy House," even though the diet was Spartan and discipline was strictly enforced. Music was played at meals to give pupils a sense of harmony.

To make the experience more multicultural and to provide a means of social mobility, Vittorino insisted that a number of bright youngsters from poor families be taught at no charge alongside the sons of Mantuan courtiers. His pupils included Federigo da Montefeltro, duke of Urbino, Lorenzo Valla, and Cecilia Gonzaga, the pious daughter of his princely patron. As the fame of his school spread, other princes wanted humanist schools like Vittorino's for their own courts.

In 1429 Niccolo d'Este, duke of Ferrara, hired Guarino da Verona to set up a school where his son could be educated. Guarino was also considered one of the greatest teachers of the Renaissance. Guarino had studied at Padua and been impressed with the ideas of Vergerio. A native of Verona, he came to Florence to study with the Greek scholar Manuel Chrysoloras and then returned with him to Constantinople, where he remained for five years. Guarino brought back a rich haul of fifty-four Greek manuscripts to Florence in 1408. After a period as a teacher in Florence and his hometown, he established a famous boarding school in Ferrara that stressed the classics of Greek and Latin literature. Guarino's school at the elementary level stressed proper pronunciation and basic grammar. Using his own manual of Latin grammar, Guarino's students worked on oral composition through classroom conversations and recitations of memorized classical texts. In the final stage of his school, his students began composing their own works in imitation of Latin masters such as Cicero and Quintilian. Like his contemporary Vittorino da Feltre, Guarino also encouraged his students to develop social graces, good manners, and sound character. He is also known as the author of a number of educational treatises and the translator of works by Plutarch, Strabo, Isocrates, and other ancients.

Few of these pedagogues had a real sense of what could be achieved by women. As we have seen, Guarino da Verona had advised Isotta Nogarola to set aside her gender if she was going to attempt such "masculine pursuits" as learning. Vittorino da Feltre had taught Cecilia Gonzaga to become a skilled Latinist, but she, like Isabella d'Este, was seen as a rare exception to what could be expected of females. Most Renaissance girls outside of convents were instructed solely in piety and how to manage a household, spin, and weave. A few learned how to read and write in basic Italian, but few outside the cloisters and some of the courts ever achieved a high degree of proficiency in languages. There were a few literate women who taught and tutored, but for the most part education remained a largely male activity.

Humanism also had an impact upon the universities, although not as immediate as its impact upon elementary schooling. Universities remained bulwarks of scholasticism throughout the Renaissance, but they also experienced an increasing emphasis on language, literature, and rhetoric. Humanists eventually joined university arts faculties in good numbers. Guarino da Verona, for example, became a professor of rhetoric at the newly founded University of Ferrara in 1442, the only university in Europe devoted exclusively to the arts. His inspired teaching helped it rival the much older universities of Bologna and Padua. Lorenzo Valla ended up on the faculty of the University of Rome as well as working for the Vatican. In the advanced disciplines of theology, medicine, and law, medieval methods continued to dominate until the sixteenth

century. Universities also continued to be all-male monopolies.

Humanists as Philosophers

The Renaissance inherited a great philosophical heritage from ancient Greece and Rome. Philosophy had long been recognized as one of the best ways to train and exercise the mind. Even though Greek philosophers such as Aristotle continued to be important, especially for medieval theologians such as Thomas Aquinas, the Renaissance witnessed a renewed interest in him as well as a revival of interest in his great rival Plato. The discoveries of texts of some of the writings of ancient philosophers as well as new Latin translations of Plato's *Laws*, the *Gorgia*, and the *Republic* helped stimulate a revived interest in philosophy. Although the thought of Aristotle continued to dominate philosophy throughout the fifteenth and sixteenth centuries, two Italian humanists, Marsilio Ficino and Giovanni Pico della Mirandola, were on the cutting edge of the renewed enthusiasm for the thought of Plato.

MARSILIO FICINO (1433–1499)

Marsilio Ficino was the foremost Italian Neoplatonist of the Renaissance. He was the son of Cosimo de' Medici's personal physician and was intended for a career as a doctor. After a thorough grounding in Latin and Greek, Marsilio studied medicine at the University of Florence. It became apparent that his wide interests and soaring intellect qualified him for a different path than his father's. His intellectual abilities aroused the interest of the Medici patriarch, who informed him that as his father had cared for his body, so Marsilio would become "the curer of his soul."[18]

Cosimo allowed Ficino the use of his

summer home outside Florence at Careggi for his "Platonic Academy." Although he did not offer formal instruction or take in boarding students, Ficino presided over scholarly conversations with friends and visitors from a variety of backgrounds. Jurists, musicians, physicians, poets, politicians, priests, rhetoricians, philosophers, and a few businessmen were all drawn to the academy. Ficino took a lively interest in all of his conversation partners' activities and kept up a lively correspondence with many of them. In addition to spirited philosophical discussions and tutorials, the academicians also observed the anniversary of Plato's death every year with a banquet in the tradition of Plato's *Symposium.*

In 1463 Cosimo de' Medici hired the small and hunchbacked Ficino to translate all the known works of Plato into Latin, a task he completed by 1469. Then Ficino turned his attention to the completion of his own masterwork, *Platonic Theology,* which he published in 1474. The *Platonic Theology* was an important synthesis of Christian and Platonic thought. For Ficino, God is immanent or inherent in human personality and all are linked to God through love. As he wrote, "In loving bodies we shall really be loving the shadow of God; in souls, the likeness of God; in angels, the image of God. Thus in this life we shall love God in all things so that in the next we may love all things in God."[19]

Ficino was able to find truth in a wide variety of sources, including astrology and magic. In 1471 he translated some of the occult Hermetic works from Greek into Latin. These writings were mistakenly believed to have originated with the Greek god Hermes, fused with several Egyptian deities, and to have been known to Plato. Some of them were also attributed to the legendary third-century writer Hermes Trigmegistus. Ficino found points of comparison between

the Hermetic writings and the biblical account of creation. Therefore, perhaps these materials could be used to shed light on Christian truth as well as improving the health of humans. Not all humanists agreed with Ficino's interest in the occult. Both Leonardo Bruni and Poggio Bracciolini were hostile to the belief in magic. Although humanists shared common assumptions about the importance of the classics for moral education, they disagreed with each other on many areas of thought.

Marsilio Ficino continued to find favor with the Medici. Lorenzo de' Medici continued to support the work of the academy, whose more illustrious members included the artist Michelangelo, the great humanist scholar and poet Angelo Poliziano (1454–1494), and the philosopher Giovanni Pico della Mirandola. Marsilio wrote of his admiration for the Medici:

> I speak the truth when I say that no one was dearer to me than the great Cosimo. I recognized in that old man not human virtue, but the virtue of a Hero. I now acknowledge within the young man all the qualities of the old man. . . . That splendor of Cosimo now shines daily from our Lorenzo in many forms, bringing light to the Latin people and glory to the Florentine republic.[20]

Ficino was not pleased to see the Medici expelled in 1494, but continued his work of translating the third-century Neoplatonist Plotinus and others into Latin. He remained immersed in the classics until his own death in 1499.

GIOVANNI PICO DELLA MIRANDOLA (1463–1494)

Ficino's disciple Giovanni Pico was one of the most attractive personalities and intellects of the Italian Renaissance. He was the son of the count of Mirandola and Concordia, a small principality just west of Ferrara in the Po Valley. At age fourteen, Giovanni began the study of canon law at the University of Bologna and then moved to Padua and Florence. In Florence, he became a close friend and pupil of the influential Neoplatonic philosopher Marsilio Ficino, who had a profound influence on the development of his thought.

Moving on to Paris, Giovanni Pico della Mirandola became engrossed with scholastic theology and languages. Blessed with a hunger for learning and a gift for languages, Pico mastered Greek, Latin, and Hebrew. He also studied Arabic and other Near Eastern languages. His Hebrew studies led him into the mystical texts of Jewish theology known as the *Cabala*. Believing that all knowledge could be reconciled, Pico also ventured into Arabic philosophy, mathematics, music, and physics. In defense of this thesis, the twenty-four-year-old Pico traveled to Rome in 1486 and attempted to publish his 900 *Conclusions*, a summary of his vast erudition. He dared any learned person to come to Rome to debate him in public and offered to pay their expenses if need be.

Officials of Pope Innocent VIII's court forbade Pico's debate after having found thirteen of his theses to be heretical and prohibited his book's distribution. He wrote a hasty defense of his *Conclusions*, which got him in more trouble with some church authorities fearful of his fascination with Jewish and Arabic materials. The tall and handsome Giovanni Pico fled to France, but was arrested by the order of a papal legate and imprisoned in a castle at Vincennes outside Paris. Friends arranged his escape and he returned to Florence in Italy. Lorenzo de' Medici used his influence to have Pico forgiven by the new pope, Alexander VI. In Florence he came under the hypnotic spell

of the preacher Savonarola and gave up his mistresses, renounced his love poetry, and distributed his wealth to the poor. Shortly before he could take up the life of a Dominican friar, Pico died of a fever at age thirty-one, just as King Charles VIII of France was entering the city.

Although his love poetry, written in both Latin and Italian, was quite well thought of, Pico's reputation rests primarily on his life and philosophical writings. His most famous work was his "Oration on the Dignity of Man," which was originally composed as a preface to his *Conclusions*. Pico argued that humans, created specially by God, are "the most fortunate of creatures," not merely a link in the "universal chain of Being." Humans have the ability to rise upward toward the angels by the use of reason or to sink downward to the level of beasts by indulging in their sensual appetites. In support of his argument, he quoted from a vast array of sources, ranging from the Koran to the Persian prophet Zoroaster to the Pythagoreans.

Similar syncretistic tendencies are found in his other works, such as his *Of Being and Unity* in which he discussed God and creation. Unlike many of his contemporary humanists, Pico made use of Plato, Aristotle, and many other thinkers from a diversity of backgrounds and religious traditions. Like Ficino he was interested in the occult Hermetic writings, but went beyond his master in his explorations of Jewish mystical writings found in the *Cabala*. As Pico declared, "And surely it is the part of a narrow mind to have confined itself with single Porch or Academy. Nor can one rightly choose what suits oneself from all of them who has not first come to be familiar with them all."[21] Although he continued to be fascinated by the occult, later in his life Giovanni Pico della Mirandola became one of the few Renaissance intellectuals to challenge the widely held beliefs in astrology. He had observed that astrological weather predictions were usually wrong and that astrology was not supported by Aristotle or Plato. That bold treatise, however, did not appear until after his death.

Chronology

1265–1321	Life of Dante.
1304–1374	Petrarca.
1313–1375	Boccaccio.
1331–1400	Coluccio Salutati
1349–1420	Pietro Paolo Vergerio.
1364–1437	Niccolò Niccoli.
1370–1444	Leonardo Bruni.
1374–1460	Guarino da Verona.
1378–1446	Vittorino da Feltre.
1380–1459	Poggio Bracciolini.
1396	Manuel Chrysoloras (1350–1415) comes to Florence to teach Greek.
1398–1481	Francesco Filelfo.
c. 1407–1457	Lorenzo Valla.
1418–1466	Isotta Nogarola.
1433–1499	Marsilio Ficino.
1454–1494	Angelo Poliziano.
1463–1494	Giovanni Pico della Mirandola.
1469–1499	Laura Cereta.

Further Reading

RENAISSANCE HUMANISM IN ITALY

Hans Baron, *The Crisis of the Early Italian Renaissance*, 2nd ed. (1966).

Eugenio Garin, ed., *Renaissance Characters* (1991).

Victoria Kahn, *Rhetoric, Prudence, and Skepticism in the Renaissance* (1980).

Donald Kelley, *Renaissance Humanism* (1993).

Margaret King and Albert Rabil, eds., *Her Immaculate Hand: Selected Works by and about the Women Humanists of 1400 Italy* (1983). An invaluable source collection.

Benjamin Kohl and Ronald Witt, eds., *The Earthly Republic: Italian Humanists on Government and Society* (1978).

Paul Oscar Kristeller, *Renaissance Thought and Its Sources* (1979).

———, *Renaissance Thought and the Arts* (1980). Important essays by a leading authority.

George McClure, *Sorrow and Consolation in Italian Humanism* (1992).

Albert Rabil, ed., *Renaissance Humanism*, 3 vols. (1988). A major collection of essays by modern scholars.

Jerrold Siegel, *Rhetoric and Philosophy in Renaissance Humanism* (1968).

Charles Trinkhaus, *In His Image and Likeness: Italian Humanists on God and Human Dignity*, 2 vols. (1971).

———, *The Scope of Renaissance Humanism* (1983). Challenging scholarship.

Roberto Weiss, *The Renaissance Discovery of Classical Antiquity*, 2nd ed. (1988).

Donald Wilcox, *In Search of God and Self: Renaissance and Reformation Thought* (1975). A very readable survey.

RENAISSANCE EDUCATION AND PHILOSOPHY

Ernst Cassirer, et al., eds. *The Renaissance Philosophy of Man* (1948). Important but difficult reading.

Brian Copenhaven and Charles Schmitt, *Renaissance Philosophy* (1992).

Arthur Field, *The Origins of the Platonic Academy of Florence* (1988).

Anthony Grafton and Lisa Jardine, *From Humanism to the Humanities: Education and the Liberal Arts in Fifteenth- and Sixteenth-Century Europe (1988).

Paul Grendler, *Schooling in Renaissance Italy: Literacy and Learning, 1300–1600* (1989).

Charles Schmitt, *The Cambridge History of Renaissance Philosophy* (1988). Important survey by an outstanding authority.

INDIVIDUAL HUMANISTS

Thomas Bergin, *Boccaccio* (1981).

Morris Bishop, *Petrarch and His World* (1963).

Vittore Branca, *Boccaccio: The Man and His Works* (1976).

Ardis Collins, *The Secular Is Sacred: Platonism and Thomism in Marsilio Ficino's Platonic Theology* (1974).

William Craven, *Giovanni Pico della Mirandola: Symbol of His Age* (1981).

Iiro Kajanto, *Poggio Bracciolini and Classicism: A Study in Early Italian Humanism* (1987).

Paul Kristeller, *The Philosophy of Marsilio Ficino*, tr. by V. Conant (1943).

Nicholas Mann, *Petrarch* (1984).

Albert Rabil, *Laura Cereta, Quattrocento Humanist* (1981).

Ronald Witt, *Hercules at the Crossroads: The Life, Works, and Thought of Coluccio Salutati* (1983).

Notes

1. Cited in Morris Bishop, "Petrarch," in *Renaissance Profiles*, J. H. Plumb, ed. (New York: Harper and Row, 1961), p. 3.
2. Ibid., p. 11.
3. Cited in Benjamin Kohl and Alison Andrews Smith, eds., *Major Problems in the History of the Italian Renaissance* (Lexington, Mass.: D. C. Heath, 1995), p. 250.
4. Cited in James Bruce Ross and Mary Martin McLaughlin, eds., *The Portable Renaissance Reader* (New York: Viking Press, 1970), p. 128.
5. Cited in Kenneth Bartlett, ed., *The Civilization of the Italian Renaissance: A Sourcebook* (Lexington, Mass.: D. C. Heath, 1992) p. 54.
6. Cited in Ross and McLaughlin, *Renaissance Reader*, p. 421.
7. Cited in Bartlett, *Italian Renaissance*, p.81.
8. Ibid., p. 73.
9. Cited in Elton, *Renaissance and Reformation*, p. 57.
10. Cited in Lewis Spitz, *The Renaissance and Reformation Movements* (Chicago: Rand McNally, 1971), p. 152.
11. Cited in Werner Gundersheimer, ed., *The Italian Renaissance* (Englewood Cliffs, N.J.: Prentice Hall, 1965), p. 56.
12. Cited in Kohl and Smith, *Italian Renaissance*, p. 311.
13. Cited in Margaret King, *Women of the Renaissance* (Chicago: University of Chicago Press, 1991), p. 196.
14. Ibid., p. 197.
15. Cited in Margaret King and Albert Rabil, eds., *Her Immaculate Hand: Selected Works by and about the Women Humanists of 1400 Italy* (Binghamton, N.Y.: Medieval and Renaissance Texts and Studies, 1983), p. 79.
16. Cited in Kohl and Smith, *Italian Renaissance*, p. 306.
17. Ibid., p. 308.
18. Cited in Spitz, *Renaissance and Reformation*, p. 175.
19. Cited in Bartlett, *Italian Renaissance*, p. 124.
20. Ibid., p. 128.
21. Cited in Gundersheimer, *Italian Renaissance*, pp. 110–111.

6

PAINTING
IN RENAISSANCE ITALY

The Renaissance in Italy was one of the most exciting periods in the history of the fine arts. It was an incredibly fortunate melding of artistic talent, patronage, and demand. The elite of Italy provided a lively market for both religious and secular art. The dramatic increase in the numbers of churches and confraternities (lay religious brotherhoods) in the period and the expansion and remodeling of existing facilities helped provide abundant opportunities for architects, artists, and craftspersons. Religious organizations increased their use of art to tell biblical stories to a largely illiterate public. Discriminating patrons such as Isabella d'Este, Lorenzo de' Medici, and many others filled their palaces with great works of art. They also supported art that was visible to the public in churches and town squares. Even city governments commissioned public art in an effort to beautify their communities and to display their wealth and power. The result is a rich legacy of artistic masterpieces that still inspires us and influences our sense of what is beautiful.

Renaissance architects, painters, sculptors, and musicians made striking departures from the conventions and styles of medieval artists. Influenced by the culture of humanism, painters began to seek a window into nature and made a concerted effort to capture what the human eye actually saw.

Sculptors, inspired by classical models, also sought greater naturalism. Although religious subject matter continued to dominate the art of the Renaissance, it was supplemented by greater use of classical themes and was presented in strikingly new ways. Architects also used and modified classical models, but felt free to make striking innovations. The Renaissance was also a great period of creativity in music. All in all, it was an age of extraordinary achievement in the arts.

Early Renaissance Painting:
Giotto

Giotto (c. 1266–1337) was one of the first great artists of the Italian Renaissance. He was born the son of a laborer in a little town fourteen miles from Florence. Even as a young boy Giotto showed a talent for drawing and may have studied with one of the greatest Florentine painters of his day, Giovanni Cimabue (c. 1240–1302). Like many artists of the time, Giotto was broadly trained as an architect, sculptor, and painter. However, it was as a painter that he achieved his greatest fame. In contrast to the flat, elongated, unnatural figures of "Greek or Byzantine art," Giotto attempted to draw every figure from nature. He was among the very first Western painters to capture actual human emotions in scenes of compelling realism and to add a third dimension—depth—to painting.

An example of Giotto's ability to capture emotion is his famous fresco painting for the Arena Chapel in Padua, *The Lamentation*. The dead Christ is stretched across the lap of Mary while Mary Magdalene gazes down at his feet. Mary stares intently at the face of her dead son as the apostles share her grief and anguish. The angels above twist and turn discordantly and all nature seems lost in deepest mourning. Giotto's concern for an organic whole is reflected in the geometric clustering of the figures.

Giotto's art was greatly influenced by the tradition of St. Francis of Assisi and his reverence for nature. Like Francis, Giotto recognized the intimate connections between all living things and the importance of living in harmony with all God's creations. The Franciscans in Giotto's day kept alive the tradition of their founder's interest in nature. They, like the rival order of the Dominicans, wanted to use art for religious instruction. Increasingly, artists such as Giotto were hired to paint murals on the walls of their churches and chapels.

Artists painted on moist plaster with pigments ground in water so that the paint was absorbed by the plaster and became part of the wall itself. Giotto became a master of this *fresco* (fresh) technique and was hired to paint the walls of numerous churches and chapels. He had a particular affinity for Saint Francis of Assisi, and his admiration for the legendary saint is readily apparent in the numerous depictions of various scenes from the life of Francis painted for his church in Assisi and for the Bardi and Peruzzi banking families' chapels in the church of Santa Croce in Florence. In wall paintings such as *St. Francis Receiving the Stigmata*, one of twenty-eight scenes from the life of Francis that Giotto and his associ-

Giotto, *Lamentation*. Scrovengni Chapel, Padua. Photo courtesy of Alinari/Art Resource.

ates painted for the church built above the saint's tomb, the artist captures the moment when the saint learns that he is to receive wounds (stigmata) identical to those of Christ. Francis can now fully identify with the Son of God.

Pronounced the greatest painter of his day by Dante, Boccaccio, and Petrarca, Giotto received commissions from patrons in Assisi, Florence, Milan, Padua, Naples, and Rimini primarily for church frescoes. Toward the end of his life, he was appointed master of public works and building supervisor of the Florentine cathedral, for which he designed a graceful bell tower. His efforts at greater naturalism in painting attracted a vast number of imitators, but no one was able to rival his skill and technique until the time of Masaccio seventy-five years later.

MASACCIO (1401–1428)

Masaccio (Tommaso Guidi) was born the son of a notary in a small town outside Florence. He joined the artists' guild of Florence in January 1422 and worked there except for part of 1426 when he accepted a commission in Pisa. In the summer of 1428, Masaccio moved to Rome, where he died a virtually penniless young man of twenty-eight. Before his death, Masaccio achieved fame as the greatest master of naturalism since Giotto. His painting had an influence on the work of his sculptor friends Brunelleschi and Donatello. Obsessed with "the things

Giotto and associates, *St. Francis Receiving the Stigmata.* S. Francesco, Assisi, Italy. Alinari / Art Resource.

of art," he was known for his indifference to money, clothes, and even food. His nickname, Masaccio, literally means "the messy one."

Masaccio's reputation as an artist rests primarily upon a celebrated series of frescoes of the life of St. Peter painted for the Brancacci Chapel in the church of Santa Maria del Carmine in Florence. His *The Tribute Money* dominates the chapel and depicts a group of disciples clustered around Jesus waiting to hear his answer to the question: "Is it lawful to pay tribute to Caesar?" Masaccio's depiction of this scene is unique and came at a time when Florence was introducing a new system of taxation (the *castato*). The artist appears to be celebrating God's sanctioning of taxation. To underscore contemporary application, it should be noted that the setting of *The Tribute Money* is the banks of the Arno; the apostles are depicted as Florentine men of the street.

On the left side of the painting, the artist shows Peter finding a fish in shallow water. Jesus told Peter that he would find the tax gatherer's money in the mouth of a fish. On the right side of the painting, Peter is paying off the tax collector. The center of the painting is dominated by Christ instructing his apostles on how to handle the tax gatherer. It is a confrontation between secular and spiritual power, and the faces of the apostles clearly reveal their surprise and concern. All the figures in the fresco are shown as uniquely individual rather than as medieval archetypes. *The Tribute Money* reveals that, like Giotto, Masaccio could capture great moments of psychological truth, as do his vivid depictions of the *Crucifixion of St. Peter and the Martyrdom of St. John the Baptist*. In the left panel Peter is shown according to tradition being nailed to a cross and hung upside down in a scene of great poignancy and power. Humanism with its emphasis on individuality has already begun to shape Renaissance art.

Luminaries of the high Renaissance such as Leonardo da Vinci, Michelangelo, and Raphael studied the works of Masaccio for their use of perspective, skill in composition, psychological insight, and use of *chiaroscuro* (the contrast of light and shade to enhance modeling). His work in the Brancacci Chapel also had a profound influ-

Masaccio, *The Tribute Money*. S. Maria del Carmine, Florence Italy. Alinari/Art Resource.

Masaccio, *Crucifixion of St. Peter and Martyrdom of St. John the Baptist.* Gemäldegalerie, Staatliche Museen, Berlin, Germany. Foto Marburg/Art Resource.

ence on the Umbrian painter Piero della Francesca (c. 1416–1492). Masaccio may have learned about linear perspective from his friend Filippo Brunelleschi. Brunelleschi discovered that by making figures in the background of a painting smaller than those in the foreground, the artist was able to give his or her painting an illusion of depth. Mathematical proportions and rationalized geometric patterns further enhanced the effect of three dimensionality. Masaccio also achieved the feeling of depth in his paintings by creating a physical quality of atmosphere, hence his attention to landscapes and backgrounds.

FRA ANGELICO (c. 1400–1469)
AND FRA FILIPPO LIPPI (c. 1406–1469)

Masaccio also had a great impact upon two leading contemporary artists: Fra Angelico and Fra Filippo Lippi. Fra Angelico began life as Guido di Pietro and had already been working as a painter before he entered a Dominican friary. He put his talents as a painter to the service of his order, first in Fiesole and then at San Marco in Florence. Achieving great fame, Fra Angelico became known as "the angelic painter." According to the artist and pioneer art historian Giorgio Vasari

(1511–1574), Fra Angelico would pray before he began a work and when he painted a crucifixion scene the tears ran down his cheeks. Eventually the pious Fra Angelico became the prior of San Marco.

In contrast, Fra Filippo Lippi was much less comfortable in his religious vocation and fathered two illegitimate children by a nun. Born into a large family of an impoverished butcher in Florence, he entered into a Carmelite monastery in Florence at an early age and took his vows in 1421. Vasari claims that Filippo decided to become a painter after watching Masaccio at work in the Brancacci Chapel. His great talent as an artist brought him to the attention of Cosimo de' Medici and he became one of his favorite artists. Later, Filippo became chaplain of a convent in Prato, where he became enamored of a young nun, Lucrezia Buti. They produced a son, the future painter Filippino Lippi (1458–1504), and a daughter. The Medici patriarch may have persuaded Pope Pius II to release Filippo and Lucrezia from their vows and legitimize their children.

Both artists painted primarily religious subjects. Fra Angelico is noted for his traditional, gentle piety and angelic spirituality. He was fully aware of Masaccio's techniques but chose to restrain his use of light and shade, as well as his portrayals of emotion. Fra Angelico is also praised for his strikingly original landscapes and his mastery of delicate color. Fra Filippo Lippi gave his religious subjects a new cheerful, earthly reality. Painted in brilliant colors, his many madonnas are real women and his children are equally human. Their traditional gold halos have become transparent crystal disks flecked with gold for the first time in the history of Italian painting. Fra Filippo also exerted a pronounced influence on the work of his best pupil, Sandro Botticelli, who surpassed even his talented son, Filippino.

A Distinctive Style: Sandro Botticelli (c. 1444–1510)

Renaissance art continued to develop in the decades following the death of Masaccio as a host of artists mastered the techniques of perspective and naturalism. Oil painting, imported from the Netherlands, also began to influence Italian painters. Among the greatest of them was the Florentine Sandro Botticelli. Sandro was raised by his brother, a successful broker, and received much of his artistic training from Fra Filippo Lippi. He worked with Lippi and they became so close that when Lippi died he entrusted Botticelli with the care of his son, Filippino. Filippino became a master painter and completed Masaccio's frescoes in the Brancacci Chapel, among other works.

Botticelli also worked along with the young Leonardo da Vinci in the workshop of Andrea del Verrocchio. Although immersed in all the great traditions of Florentine art, Botticelli developed his own highly individualized and uniquely poetic style and did not always adhere to the growing tradition of scientific naturalism which followed from Giotto and Masaccio. Botticelli

became the favorite painter of the circle of humanists and poets that surrounded Lorenzo de' Medici. For this circle, he produced his two most famous paintings: *The Birth of Spring (La Primavera)* and *The Birth of Venus.*

In *The Birth of Spring* Botticelli painted a mysterious, dreamlike allegory that has long fascinated viewers. It was painted for a cousin of Lorenzo de' Medici on the occasion of his marriage. Perhaps the artist was also celebrating the reign of Lorenzo the Magnificent as a new beginning for Florence. The painting is set in a grove of dark orange trees, thickly massed. On the right side is Zephyr, the west wind god, who is pursuing the virgin nymph Chloris, whose mouth is filled with flowers. He will rape and then marry her. She will then be transformed into the eerily placid Flora, the goddess of Spring, shown strewing flowers from her flower-embroidered garment.

On the left side of the painting, the messenger god Mercury pokes his staff up among storm clouds that are trying to gather. Next to him, Three Graces dance provocatively in transparent garments in a ring. Above, the blindfolded Cupid is ready to shoot a golden arrow in their direction. In the center is a chaste and demure Venus, the goddess of love and marriage. For Marsilio Ficino, Botticelli's Venus represented "Temperance and Honesty, Comeliness, and Modesty." In depicting so many changeable aspects of spring and marriage (sudden, violent changes of weather and emotion), Botticelli reminds us that both nature and love can be dangerous as well as beautiful.

Painted on canvas with oil, Botticelli's *The Birth of Venus* is another work of allegory and mystery. It depicts a nude but modest golden-haired goddess of love, standing on a sea shell while Zephyr and a nymph waft her to shore. On the right a waiting Grace stands ready to cover Venus with a flowing

Botticelli, *La Primavera*. Uffizi Gallery, Florence, Italy. Alinari/Art Resource.

cloak. Contemporaries thought Botticelli was showing them the birth of studies of humanity, a Neoplatonic triumph of the spirit (mind) of Venus over her body.

Later in life Botticelli also came under the influence of the preacher Savonarola and was quite affected by his overthrow and death. Always a deeply religious man, some of his best work uses religious subject matter. As he grew older, he withdrew more and more from the world. Botticelli seems to have painted little in the last decade of his life. Commissions went to the new stylists of the high Renaissance, artists such as Leonardo, Michelangelo, and Raphael. According to Giorgio Vasari, Botticelli "became old and useless and fell to walking with two canes."[1] If true, this was a sad ending for one of the most original and poetic painters of the Renaissance.

The High Renaissance

Building on the work of great talents such as Giotto, Masaccio, Fra Angelico, Fra Filippo Lippi, and Botticelli, the next generations of Renaissance artists were able to go even further in creating windows into nature. Inventive minds such as Leonardo da Vinci utilized oil painting techniques imported from the Netherlands, new ways of modeling figures and treating light and shade, and his own scientific studies to produce masterpieces of scientific realism. Talented as Leonardo was, Michelangelo, Raphael, and Titian vied with him for commissions and for a reputation as Italy's greatest artist. The High Renaissance also witnessed the emergence of extraordinarily accomplished women painters such as Sofonisba Anguissola and Artemisia Gentileschi, the first fe-

Botticelli, *The Birth of Venus.* Uffizi, Florence, Italy. Alinari/Art Resource.

male plastic artists in the West to be given public recognition for their artistic brilliance.

LEONARDO DA VINCI (1452–1519)

Of all the multitalented men and women of the Renaissance, no one could match Leonardo da Vinci's accomplishments in so many fields. Not only was he a great painter, sculptor, and architect, but he also made valuable contributions to art theory, engineering, military science, anatomy, botany, geology, geography, hydraulics, aerodynamics, and optics. This incredible polymath began life as the son of a notary and a servant near the fortified village of Vinci, west of Florence. Leonardo's father had seduced his mother, Caterina, a family servant, but refused to marry her. Leonardo

was raised by a stepmother at his father's home. His father married four times in all and had eleven children.

When he was fourteen, the left-handed Leonardo was apprenticed to the renowned Florentine artist Andrea del Verrocchio, with whom he studied from 1470 to 1477. Verrocchio recognized his pupil's precocious talent and employed him on a number of major projects. Young Leonardo also learned from his painter friends Botticelli and Perugino (the latter eventually became the teacher of another artistic legend, Raphael). At age twenty, Leonardo da Vinci was admitted to the painters' guild and began receiving commissions from Lorenzo de' Medici and religious institutions.

A keen student of nature with unusually excellent eyesight, Leonardo sought to "learn the causes of things." He filled his

Notebooks with observations of many things, including human anatomy, birds in flight, rock formations, rare plants, and the motion and power of water. A congenial, handsome, young, homosexual man, Leonardo was also a skilled horseman and musician. He had a wide circle of friends and seemingly sufficient patronage. Then suddenly at age thirty, he left Florence for the Milanese court of Ludovico il Moro, to whom he offered his services primarily as a military engineer.

In addition to military and scientific projects, Ludovico also commissioned Leonardo to sculpt a giant equestrian statue of his father to honor his own marriage to Beatrice d'Este in 1491. Although Leonardo finished dozens of drawings for a project that was to be even larger than the equestrian statues of Donatello and Verrocchio, the work was never completed in what became a familiar theme in Leonardo's life as his interests shifted from project to project. As da Vinci wrote over and over again in his notebooks: "Who will tell me if anything was ever finished?"[2]

During his first Milanese period, Leonardo did manage to complete a number of stunning paintings, including his first *Virgin of the Rocks*, which was painted for the chapel of the Confraternity of the Immaculate Conception. Here Leonardo showed his mastery of oil painting that had been introduced in the fifteenth century and allowed artists to work in much greater detail than ever before and freed paintings from their earlier dependence on architectural settings as parts of altarpieces or walls. Oil paintings were also less expensive than frescoes or panel paintings and made art more affordable. Leonardo also demonstrated a new technique, *sfumato* ("smoky"), which he developed for modeling figures by virtually imperceptible gradations from light to dark.

In the altar painting *The Virgin of the Rocks*, Leonardo portrayed the youthful Madonna kneeling on the ground, her arm around the kneeling John the Baptist. Her left hand is extended protectively over the seated Christ child, who acknowledges the worship of John by blessing him. A kneeling angel steadies the Christ child and completes the third side of a compositional triangle. The painting is filled with a full array of scientifically identifiable rocks and plants. The shadowy caves stand in contrast to the brilliant light coming from behind the Virgin, which gives "a grace to faces," as the artist wrote. Leonardo showed a mastery of *chiaroscuro*, *sfumato*, and the portrayal of nature that few others have ever been able to rival.

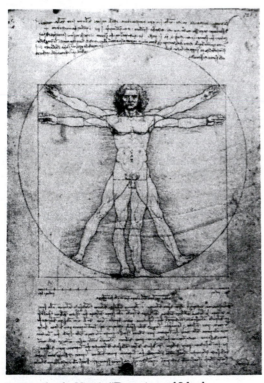

Leonardo da Vinci, "Drawing of Ideal Proportions of the Human Figure." Accademia, Venice, Italy. Alinari/Art Resource.

Leonardo da Vinci, *The Virgin of the Rocks.* Louvre, Paris, France. Alinari / Art Resource.

A dozen years later, da Vinci completed his *Last Supper* for a wall of the refectory of St. Mary's of Grace in Milan. Unhappy with the limitations of traditional fresco techniques, Leonardo experimented with an oil-tempera medium that did not adhere properly to the wall. By 1517 the painting began to deteriorate, but still earned great critical praise and several efforts at restoration. *The Last Supper* is a brilliant psychological study of the reactions of Christ's disciples to his charge that "one of you shall betray me." In dark profile and grasping a money bag, Judas is to the right of Christ with his hand defiantly stretched toward the bread on the table. In most traditional renderings of the scene, Judas is shown on the opposite side of the table from the disciples. Placing him with the other disciples emphasizes to a degree his common humanity with the other disciples, all of whom are asking "Lord, is it I?" Leonardo's *Last Supper* reveals his great skill in geometric and psychological composition. The dis-

Leonardo da Vinci, *The Last Supper.* S. Maria delle Grazie, Milan, Italy. Alinari / Art Resource.

ciples are clustered in four groups of three each, with the eyes of most of them focused on Christ in the exact center of the painting. Even the architectural lines of the room direct our eyes first to Christ and then out again to reveal the reactions of each of the disciples. Judas's shadowy profile contrasts with the lighted faces of the other disciples. He is one of them; yet he is different and certainly not worthy of the sacrament of the Eucharist.

With the fall of Milan to the French in 1499, Leonardo was forced to leave the employ of the Sforzas. After brief stays in Mantua and Venice, he returned to Florence, where he worked chiefly as an engineer and a surveyor. Even master artists like Leonardo, who "lived like a gentleman," had to worry about finances. Although socially slightly above the ranks of the artisans, masters like Leonardo were considered inferior to the nobles, rich merchants, and bankers, who dominated the economic and political scene. After a brief stint as a military engineer for Cesare Borgia, he returned to Florence to finish the great portrait of a young married woman, known to us as the *Mona Lisa*.

Leonardo worked for three years on this portrait, which has become famous for its mysterious expression. *Mona Lisa* appears to be a very self-confident young woman whose lips betray a hint of a smile. She dares to look directly at the viewer, in contrast to the advice of Renaissance etiquette books, which stressed that a woman must never look directly at a man. Her hands are gracefully poised and further reinforce the sense of calm that she exudes. Behind her is a harsh, possibly violent landscape of rocks and water, a striking contrast to this relaxed young woman of quiet resolve in the foreground. Is this a representation of the clash between *fortuna* (the background representing the forces of nature)

Leonardo da Vinci, *La Giaconda (Mona Lisa)*. Louvre, Paris. Giraudon/Art Resource.

and *virtù* (her face as a symbol of her qualities as a person)? Whatever the painting's real meaning, it is clear that da Vinci's contemporaries were shocked by this bold departure from traditional depictions of women and that moderns continue to be enthralled by the beauty and mystery of the painting.

In Florence Leonardo also competed with a younger rival, Michelangelo, for a commission to paint a mammoth battle scene fresco for the government. This work and several others were never completed because Leonardo returned to Milan in 1506 to work for the French king, Louis XII. He occupied himself mostly in scientific and anatomical studies until 1513 when he went to Rome to secure the support of Pope Leo X. In 1517 Leonardo accepted the invitation of King François I of France to live at the little chateau of Cloux near Amboise, where his only required duty was to talk to the king. He died there two years later at the age of sixty-seven. As the great polymath wrote in his *Notebooks*, "While I thought I was learning how to live, I have been learning how to die."[3]

Leonardo da Vinci left behind less than a dozen completed paintings, but his *Notebooks* are filled with wonderful philosophical musings and intriguing studies of anatomy, mathematics, and nature. "Let no one read me who is not a mathematician in my beginnings," he wrote. His notes are also filled with designs of airplanes, parachutes, helicopters, screw propellers, machine guns,

canal locks, and many other inventions that anticipated the modern world. His self-portrait reveals a man frustrated that he had not done more.

MICHELANGELO BUONARROTI (1475–1564) AS A PAINTER

Like his great rival Leonardo da Vinci, Michelangelo was also talented in many areas. Although his primary reputation is as a sculptor, Michelangelo was a fine painter, poet, engineer, and architect. He began life in Florence as the son of a minor shopkeeper and merchant, who claimed ancestors among the lesser nobility. His father had a would-be aristocrat's contempt for manual labor and was terribly disappointed when young Michelangelo showed nothing but a passion for art. Because Michelangelo was a sickly infant, his nineteen-year-old mother turned him over to a wet nurse, the wife of a stonecutter. He later claimed he had sucked in a love for art with this mother's milk in the fresh air "among the chisels and hammers of stonecutters."[4]

Despite the reluctance of his father and uncle, Michelangelo was apprenticed at age thirteen to the well-known Florentine artist Domenico Ghirlandaio (1449–1494). Already exhibiting a remarkable talent for drawing, Michelangelo was paid a salary by his teacher, which was most unusual for an apprentice. Ghirlandaio modestly confessed that "this youth understands more than I do myself." After barely a year with Ghirlandaio, Michelangelo was invited into the house of Lorenzo de' Medici and worked in an art school setting with other artists and humanist intellectuals. In the Medici circle, Michelangelo learned a great deal about art, humanism, and Neoplatonic philosophy, all of which had a profound effect upon his subsequent career.

With the death of Lorenzo the Magnif-

Leonardo da Vinci, *Self-Portrait*. Biblioteca Reale, Turin, Italy. Alinari / Art Resource.

icent in 1492, Michelangelo was forced to return to the house of his father. He later found work in Venice and Bologna before moving to Rome in June 1496, where he had a spectacular career as a sculptor, his favorite medium. In 1508, he was ordered by his powerful patron, Pope Julius II, to stop work on the pope's monumental but incredibly expensive tomb and instead to paint frescoes on the ceiling of the Sistine Chapel of St. Peter's Basilica. Michelangelo objected, "I am a sculptor, not a painter," but the pope insisted.

For the next four years, Michelangelo labored to cover the 6,300 square foot barrel-vaulted ceiling with nine huge panels depicting scenes from Genesis. Arranged out of chronological order, Michelangelo took his viewers on a Neoplatonic, allegorical journey from the "Drunkenness of Noah" to "The Creation of the World." Working by himself on a high scaffold, he was assisted only by paint mixers and plaster grinders. As the recent restoration efforts have shown us, Michelangelo used bright colors to paint over 300 figures in sumptuous detail. He portrayed the ascent of humans from the spiritual abyss of the drunkenness of Noah and the shameful nakedness of Adam and Eve through the purge of the flood upward to the final reunion with God. In his depiction of the "Creation of Adam," Michelangelo shows the cosmic moment when God reaches out his powerful, naked arm to touch a reclining Adam and give him life. This is a magnificent rendering of the greatness of God and the potential nobility of individual humans as God's special creations.

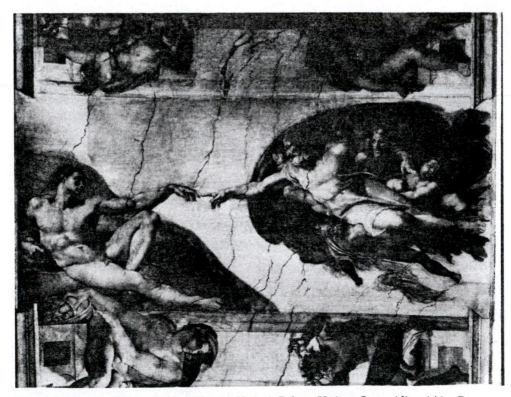

Michelangelo, *Creation of Adam*. Sistine Chapel, Vatican Palace, Vatican State. Alinari/Art Resource.

Completing the Sistine Chapel ceiling in spite of enormous discomfort, fatigue, illness, and fierce quarrels with his patron left Michelangelo partially crippled for life, but he managed to continue his career as a sculptor, architect, and poet in both Rome and Florence. In 1534, however, Pope Clement VII commissioned him to paint the altar wall of the Sistine Chapel. His *Last Judgment*, completed in 1541, is one of the monumental achievements of Renaissance painting. Medieval depictions of the last judgment generally showed figures dressed according to their social rank with Christ, the Virgin, and the Apostles enthroned in heaven.

Breaking sharply with medieval custom, Michelangelo's painting depicts a unified scene with 300 mostly undressed figures grouped around the central figure of a standing, muscular Christ as judge. The figures that surround Christ are part of an enormous wheel of fortune, where some rise from their graves, others gather round Christ, and still others sink downward toward Hell. The angels are shown without wings and halos. Christ is shown larger than any of the apostles who surround him, including an agonized self-portrait of Michelangelo as St. Bartholomew, who was flayed alive (to the lower right of Christ). The Virgin Mary is at Christ's side as he

Michelangelo, *Last Judgment*. Sistine Chapel, Vatican Palace, Vatican State. Alinari/Art Resource.

damns some and blesses others. Although influenced greatly by Dante's poetic visions, Michelangelo created his own special vision of the day when Christ comes again. It was an extraordinary achievement for a man in his fifties who was such a reluctant painter.

RAPHAEL SANZIO (1483–1520)

The sociable and calm Raphael stands in sharp contrast to the solitary and stormy genius of Michelangelo and the frustrated and aged Leonardo. He was born in the lively cultural center of Urbino in Umbria. His father was a mediocre painter and poet, who gave his son his earliest lessons before dying when Raphael was only eleven. In 1500 he moved to Perugia to study with the master artist Pietro Perugino (1446–1524), whose frescoes Michelangelo would later paint over for his rendering of *The Last Judgment*. Perugino was one of the favorite artists of Isabella d' Este, who commissioned a number of works from him. Raphael quickly absorbed the nuances of Perugino's graceful style and soon became the outstanding member of a busy workshop.

In 1504 he journeyed to Florence to find work and to learn from the brilliance of Leonardo da Vinci, Michelangelo, and others. The sister of the duke of Urbino recommended him as "a modest young man of distinguished manners." While learning the techniques of the Florentine masters, Raphael soon created his own mature idea of beauty in a stunning series of Madonnas. One of the best is his striking *Madonna of the Chair*, painted in 1516. Raphael's Madonnas are real flesh-and-blood women in the tradition of Fra Filippo Lippi, some of whom were modeled for by his beloved mistress, Margherita. Raphael's fleshy baby Jesus was also a figure drawn from life. The artist has skillfully captured the special bond be-

tween mother and child as the infant John the Baptist looks on.

Raphael's fame as a painter attracted the attention of Pope Julius II, who invited him to Rome in 1508 at the same time Michelangelo was at work on the Sistine Chapel ceiling. He remained there until his early death at age thirty-seven. One of his most stunning accomplishments during this period in Rome was *The School of Athens*. In this fresco, Raphael paid a glorious humanist tribute to many of the legendary sages of antiquity, including Plato and Aristotle, who are featured in the painting's center. The old man sprawled on the steps is Diogenes, the Greek philosopher who searched for an honest man. Below him, isolated in the foreground, is a mysterious figure whose features are doubtlessly Michelangelo's, one of Raphael's heroes from whom he had learned so much.

In contrast to the moody and often tortured Michelangelo, the handsome Raphael seemed to float serenely through life. He

Raphael, *Madonna della Seggiola* (Madonna of the Chair). Galleria Palatina, Palazzo Pitti, Florence, Italy. Alinari/Art Resource.

Raphael, *The School of Athens*. Stanza della Segnatura, Vatican Palace, Vatican State. Alinari/Art Resource.

was able to create almost effortlessly and his congenial disposition and gentle manners won him a host of friends. Deeply loved and admired by his contemporaries, Raphael's early death from fever in 1520 set off waves of grief in Rome. He was buried in the Pantheon, that marvelous temple to all the gods redesigned by the Stoic Roman emperor Hadrian in 120.

THE BELLINI FAMILY

The fine arts flourished throughout Italy during the Renaissance. Venice in particular rivalled Florence in producing visually exciting masterpieces. The city's rich merchants and religious communities provided abundant patronage. Venetian artists such as Giorgione (c. 1478–1511), Veronese (1528–1588), Tintoretto (1524–1594), and the Bellini family helped develop a rich artistic tradition. Of special interest is the Bellini family. Giovanni Bellini (c. 1430–1516) was arguably the most influential Venetian artist of the fifteenth century. His father, Jacopo (c. 1400–1464), and older brother, Gentile (c. 1426–1507), were exceptional artists who taught him a great deal. The superb Paduan artist Andrea Mantegna (c. 1431–1506) was his brother-in-law and also helped shape his early development, as did Antonello da Messina (c. 1430–1479), whose oil paintings Giovanni greatly admired.

Giovanni Bellini had one of the longest careers of any Renaissance painter. From the time he was old enough to hold a paintbrush, he was active in his father's shop. Giovanni is recorded as a painter before 1460, and he was painting up until the time of his death. Of the great figures of Renaissance art, only Michelangelo and Titian surpassed the length of his pictorial career. Highly innovative, Bellini used color in a more deliberate and effective manner than earlier Venetian masters. Throughout his career, Bellini's dramatic style was constantly evolving. His use of nature was quite imaginative. For example, he was one of the first to show movement by painting water flowing under a bridge. Bellini had a profound impact upon his two most famous students: Giorgione and Titian.

THE PROLIFIC TITIAN (c. 1488–1576)

Of the many fine artists working in Venice, Titian was clearly one of the greatest painters of the Venetian School during the Renaissance. He was born in the town of Cadore, high in the Dolomite mountains. Little is known of his youth until 1508 when he assisted the talented Venetian artist Giorgione in painting exterior frescoes on the German commercial headquarters in Venice. He also learned from the great Giovanni Bellini. Titian became the first known painter to use the brush as a way of converting the direct perception of light through color into an unimpeded expression of feeling. He also used many layers of glazes to tone down the brilliant colors that were part of his unique style.

His artistic talent, abundant energy, and shrewd investments made him rich and famous. After the death of Raphael, Titian became the most widely sought out portraitist in Europe. Prominent individuals wanted to have themselves immortalized in painting and sculpture by renowned artists, something few of the rich had dared to even think of in the Middle Ages, which stressed humility and self-effacement. To commission a portrait of oneself was considered a sign of immodesty, pride, and vanity. This changed with the Renaissance, a time when many prominent people even paid artists to place them in group paintings of biblical scenes or with the saints.

Titian, *Portrait of Emperor Charles V.* Alte Pinakothek, Munich, Germany. Foto Marburg/Art Resource.

As one of the greatest portraitists of the age, by 1531 Titian had secured so many commissions from the affluent that he was able to buy a mansion in Venice with a fine view. Later he was made a count by Holy Roman Emperor Charles V, for whom he served several times as a court painter. Titian's superb portrait of the mature, seated emperor captured much of his dignity, earnestness, and somber piety. This was a prince who, because of his strong sense of duty and his enormous responsibility as Holy Roman emperor and king of Spain and its colonial empire, had the weight of the world on his shoulders. Charles was a devout Catholic who had to endure what for him was the embarrassment of the first phases of the Lutheran Reformation. Titian's portrait seems to reveal all this and more.

In addition to painting insightful portraits, Titian was attracted to religious scenes and themes from classical Greek and Roman mythology such as his marvelous rendering of the *Venus of Urbino*. In this painting, finished in 1538 for the duke of Camerino, Titian's sensual goddess of love has just been awakened and looks at us with a calculating stare. She lies upon her couch with her little dog asleep at her feet. With one hand she holds a nosegay while her rich and silky golden-brown hair floods over one of her delicate shoulders. In the background a servant looks for something in a clothes chest while another splendidly dressed woman looks on. Little wonder that Titian's work dazzled many of his contemporaries, despite Michelangelo's snide comment that while "he liked his coloring and style, it was a pity that good design was not taught at Venice from the first." Titian's long and successful career spanned the High Renaissance through the religious tensions of Mannerism and into the period known as the Baroque.

SOFONISBA ANGUISSOLA (c. 1532–1625)

As Titian's career illustrates the rise in status and wealth of some widely recognized artists, the career of Sofonisba Anguissola reveals a greater public recognition of

Titian, *Venus of Urbino*. Uffizi, Florence, Italy. Giraudon/Art Resource.

women artists at the end of the Renaissance. Rich and powerful women such as Isabella d'Este played a great role as patrons during the Renaissance even if their contributions to art were seldom acknowledged. The situation was worse for those females who actually produced art. Daughters and wives of male painters labored in the workshops of Renaissance Italy, but they were not formally apprenticed or allowed to become members of art guilds. No woman artist was profiled by Giorgio Vasari. Their contributions therefore remain anonymous. All this changed with the career of Sofonisba Anguissola, followed by that of Artemisia Gentileschi.

The eldest of six daughters, Sofonisba was born into an aristocratic family in the northern Italian town of Cremona. Following the kind of advice found in Castiglione's *The Courtier,* her parents made sure she and her two elder sisters became accomplished in painting and music. Because she and her sister Elena showed signs of major talent as painters, they were able to study formally with an important local painter, Bernardino Campi. Elena eventually gave up her painting to become a nun, but Sofonisba continued to develop her talent as an artist and was encouraged to do so by her father, Amilcare. In 1557 he asked Michelangelo in Rome to send his daughter several of his drawings to be copied in oil paint and returned for his criticism. Michelangelo was so impressed that he allowed Sofonisba to study with him informally for two years in Rome.

During this period she painted such a splendid portrait of the duke of Alba that he recommended her to his liege lord, King Philip II. For nearly twenty years, Anguissola worked as court painter and friend of the royal family in Spain. In 1569 she married the Sicilian nobleman Fabrizio de Moncada with a dowry which the late Queen Isabella had provided. King Philip gave her in marriage and presented her with numerous, costly gifts. When her husband died, she returned to Genoa by ship, where she had a whirlwind romance with a merchant who became her second husband. In that prosperous maritime city, Sofonisba continued her prolific career as a painter, painting portraits of the nobility as well as religious subjects to great acclaim.

Over fifty of her works have survived, including the *Portrait of a Couple* shown below. In this portrait, Anguissola revealed her distinctive style with the husband and wife gazing mysteriously at the viewer. He holds her with a combination of tenderness and control, which suggests all sorts of possibilities in their relationship. The brilliant Flemish painter Anthony van Dyck (1599–1641) made a pilgrimage to visit her as one of the last remaining giants of the Renaissance. Sofonisba Anguissola's life and

Sofonisba Anguissola, *Portrait of a Couple.* Galleria Doria Pamphilj, Rome, Italy. Alinari/Art Resource.

work inspired a host of other artists, including Lavinia Fontana (1552–1614) and Artemisia Gentileschi.

ARTEMISIA GENTILESCHI (1593–c. 1632)

Born in Rome, Artemisia was the eldest child and sole daughter of the painter Orazio Gentileschi and his wife, Prudentia Malone, who died when Artemisia was twelve. None of her three brothers showed any aptitude as artists, so her father trained Artemisia as a painter. Orazio may have also used her as the model for his striking *Portrait of a Young Woman as a Sibyl*, which shows a strong sense of color and reveals the emotional complexity of its subject. If Artemisia was indeed the model, the sometimes strained relationship between artist father and daughter is strongly suggested in the mysterious look and expression of the sibyl.

Artemisia Gentileschi received additional instruction in the painter's art from the renowned master Caravaggio (1569–1610), a friend of her father. Orazio recognized that his own talents were limited and that the great Caravaggio had even more to teach his talented daughter. Caravaggio's powerful biblical scenes, such as his *David with the Head of Goliath*, had a profound impact on her developing style and choice of subject matter. She also seems to have been influenced by his dramatic use of light and shade to heighten emotions and his strong sense of composition.

In the year of Caravaggio's death, when Artemisia was only seventeen, she completed her first known painting, *Susanna and the Elders*. Based on the biblical

Orazio Gentileschi, *Portrait of a Young Woman as a Sibyl*. Samuel H. Kress Collection. Photo courtesy of The Museum of Fine Arts, Houston, Texas.

Caravaggio, *David with the Head of Goliath*. Galleria Borghese, Rome, Italy. Alinari/Art Resource.

story of a vulnerable young woman in a dangerous world of men, *Susanna* would prove tragically prophetic. In May of 1611, Agostino Tassi, a painter friend of her father's and one of her teachers, raped Artemisia. Her father sued him eight months later. During the ordeal of a seven-month trial, Artemisia, despite being tortured with thumbscrews, testified that Agostino had been trying to seduce her and became infuriated when she preferred her painting to his advances. She actively resisted him and at one point wounded him with a knife. After raping her, Tassi promised to marry her. Finding that he had other prospects, she consented to sexual relations with him in the hope that he would marry her. "What I was doing with him, I did only so

that as he had dishonored me, he would marry me."[5]

Tassi, a veteran seducer, denied having assaulted Artemisia. He had been previously charged with having murdered his wife and had already been imprisoned for incest with his sister-in-law, by whom he had three children. Following the usual custom of the day, Tassi assumed the court would find him more believable than a teenage girl and brought in phony witnesses to attempt to disparage Gentileschi's character. One of them, Pietro Stiattesi, later broke ranks and supported Artemisia's version of the events in question. The court finally concluded that Artemisia was the one telling the truth. Tassi was found guilty, but released from prison after he had served

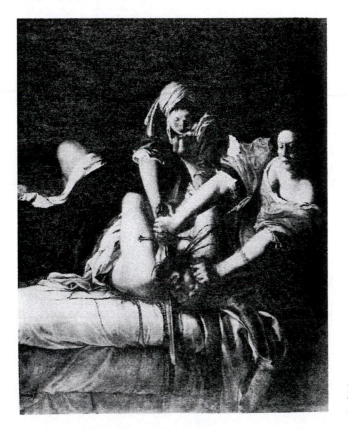

Artemisia Gentileschi, *Judith Slaying Holofernes*. Uffizi, Florence, Italy. Alinari/Art Resource.

only eight months. Since women were not valued fully as humans, the all-male courts of the period did not always consider the rape of a non-noblewoman to be a particularly serious offense.

For Artemisia it was a devastating experience from beginning to end and she could not remain in Rome with its painful memories of her public humiliation. Although relations with her father had become strained, he used his contacts in Florence with the Grand Duchess Christina de' Medici, mother of Duke Cosimo II. Assured of Medici patronage, she moved to Florence with her new husband, the painter Pietro Stiattesi, the former friend of Tassi's who had testified on her behalf at the rape trial. She married him a month after the trial ended "to restore her honor."

They both worked as painters in Florence and had two daughters. Despite the responsibilities of a family, Artemisia's art flourished and in 1616 she became the first woman admitted to the prestigious Florentine Academy of Art. Among her supporters was Duke Cosimo II, the scientist Galileo, and the grandnephew of Michelangelo. It was during her Florentine period that she painted her powerful masterpiece, *Judith Slaying Holofernes*. Gentileschi was fascinated by the biblical heroine Judith and painted at least six different versions of the story. According to the Old Testament, as an act of war Judith had supper with the Assyrian tyrant Holofernes, murdered him, cut off his head, and brought it back to the Hebrews.

Commissioned by the Grand Duke Cosimo II, Gentileschi's rendering of the scene was extremely vivid and dramatic. A fiercely committed Judith, assisted by a maidservant, cuts off the head of the tyrant with grim determination. Blood spurts from the head of Holofernes onto white bedding in a depiction which is much more graphic

than a similar work by Caravaggio, her mentor, in 1598. As a victim of sexual assault, Gentileschi may have felt herself to be avenging in a sense all the wrongs she had suffered. Judith is a strong heroine with whom the artist clearly identified. The painting reveals not only her passion for justice, but also her incredible talent and such technical abilities as the mastery of dramatic composition, *chiaroscuro*, modeling, and bold use of color.

In 1621 Gentileschi separated from her husband, whose career she threatened to eclipse, and left Florence shortly after the death of her patron, the Grand Duke. Reunited with her father, she went on to undertake commissions in Genoa, Venice, Rome, and Naples. Between 1638 and 1641

Artemisia Gentileschi, *Self-Portrait as the Allegory of Painting*. Kensington Palace, London, United Kingdom. Collection of Her Majesty the Queen.

Artemisia painted at the court of King Charles I and Queen Henrietta Maria of England. The ravages of the English Civil War forced her to return to Naples, where she lived her remaining years. Most of her subject matter was biblical, including a tender *Madonna and Child* of 1609, but Artemisia Gentileschi had a special interest in strong women and painted spectacular portraits of Cleopatra, Lucretia, Minerva, and Mary Magdalene.

She was also courageous enough to paint herself as the living embodiment of painting. In *Self-Portrait as the Allegory of Painting* (1630), Gentileschi depicted herself bearing the widely recognized attributes that identify the allegorical figure "Painting." The artist's unkempt, dark hair shows her obsession with painting over appearance. On her gold neck chain is a mask that represents imitation. She holds a paint brush in one hand and a palette in the other, as light floods in on her face from an unknown source. Gentileschi's stunning self-portrait and the career of Sofonisba Anguissola help mark the beginning of a new era for women artists. No longer would all women artists continue to labor in obscurity. Painting had become a woman's art as well as a man's, and all the world should be able to see and know that.

Chronology

c. 1266–1337	Life of Giotto.		c. 1488–1576	Titian.
c. 1400–1455	Fra Angelico.		1495	Leonardo begins *The Last Supper* in Milan.
c. 1400–1464	Jacopo Bellini.			
1401–1428	Masaccio.		1508	Michelangelo begins the Sistine Chapel ceiling.
c. 1406–1469	Fra Filippo Lippi.			
c. 1416–1492	Piero della Francesca.		1511–1574	Life of Giorgio Vasari.
c. 1428–1516	Giovanni Bellini.		c. 1532–1625	Sofonisba Anguissola.
c. 1431–1506	Andrea Mantegna.		1534	Michelangelo begins the *Last Judgment*.
1444–1510	Botticelli.			
1446–1524	Perugino.		1569–1610	Life of Caravaggio.
1452–1519	Leonardo da Vinci.		1593–c. 1632	Artemisia Gentileschi.
1475–1564	Michelangelo.		1616	Artemisia Gentileschi admitted to the Florentine Academy of Art.
c. 1478–1511	Giorgione.			
1482–1520	Raphael.			

Further Reading

GENERAL WORKS

Paul Barolsky, *The Faun in the Garden: Michelangelo and the Poetic Origins of Italian Art* (1994).

Michael Baxandall, *Painting and Experience in Fifteenth-Century Italy* (1972).

Lorne Campbell, *Renaissance Portraits: European Portrait-Painting in the Fourteenth, Fifteenth, and Sixteenth Centuries* (1990).

Kenneth Clark, *The Art of Humanism* (1983).

Bruce Cole, *The Renaissance Artist at Work* (1983).

Samuel Edgerton, *The Heritage of Giotto's Geometry: Art and Science on the Eve of the Scientific Revolution* (1992).

John Hale, *Italian Renaissance Painting from Masaccio to Titian* (1976).

Marcia Hall, *Color and Meaning: Practice and Theory in Renaissance Painting* (1992).

Frederick Hartt and David Wilkins, *History of Italian Renaissance Art,* 4th ed. (1994). The sumptuously illustrated, widely used textbook.

Paul Hills, *The Light of Early Italian Painting* (1987).

George Holmes, *Art and Politics in Renaissance Italy* (1994). A collection of his essays.

———, *The Florentine Enlightenment, 1400–50* (1969).

Peter Humfrey, *Painting in Renaissance Venice* (1995).

Norbert Huse and Wolfgang Walters, *The Art of Renaissance Venice* (1990).

Norman Land, *The Viewer as Poet: The Renaissance Response to Art* (1994).

David Landau and Peter Parshall, *The Renaissance Print 1470–1550* (1994).

E. Ann Matter and John Coakley, eds., *Creative Women in Medieval and Early Modern Italy* (1994).

Linda Murray, *The High Renaissance* (1967).

Patricia Lee Rubin, *Giorgio Vasari: Art and History* (1994).

James Saslow, *Ganymede in the Renaissance: Homosexuality in Art and Society* (1986).

Laurence Schmeckebier, *A New Handbook of Italian Renaissance Painting* (1981).

Alistair Smart, *The Dawn of Italian Painting, 1250–1400* (1978).

Giorgio Vasari, *Lives of the Painters, Sculptors and Architects,* ed. by Edmund Fuller (1968). Written by a Renaissance artist, but must be used with caution because of his fondness for legends. See the discussions in Paul Barolsky and Patricia Rubin.

Martin Wackernagel, *The World of the Florentine Renaissance Artist* (1981).

John White, *Art and Architecture in Italy, 1250–1400,* 3rd ed. (1993).

PATRONAGE

Clifford Brown, *Our Accustomed Discourse on the Antique: Cesare Gonza and Gerolamo Garimberto: Two Renaissance Collectors of Greco-Roman Art* (1994).

D. S. Chambers, ed., *Patrons and Artists in the Italian Renaissance* (1971). A revealing primary source collection.

Rona Goffen, *Piety and Patronage in Renaissance Venice* (1986).

F. W. Kent and P. Simon, eds., *Patronage, Art and Society in Renaissance Italy* (1987).

Guy Lytle and S. Oregl, eds., *Patronage in the Renaissance* (1981). Valuable essays by a variety of scholars.

Clare Robertson, *"Il Gran Cardinale": Alessandro Farnese, Patron of the Arts* (1992).

INDIVIDUAL ARTISTS

Mosche Barash, *Giotto and the Language of Gesture* (1987).

Carlo Bertelli, *Piero della Francesca* (1992).

Bruce Cole, *Masaccio and the Art of Early Renaissance Florence* (1980).

Charles Dempsey, *The Portrayal of Love: Botticelli's Primavera and Humanist Culture at the Time of Lorenzo the Magnificent* (1992).

Gloria Fossi, *Filippo Lippi* (1989).

Luba Freedman, *Titian's Portraits through Aretino's Lens* (1995).

Mary Garrard, *Artemisia Gentileschi* (1989).

Gail Geiger, *Filippino Lippi's Carafa Chapel* (1986).

Creighton Gilbert, *Caravaggio and His Two Cardinals* (1994).

Carlo Ginzburg, *The Enigma of Piero: Piero della Francesca, the Baptism, the Arezzo Cycle, the Flagellation,* tr. by Martin Ryle and Kate Soper (1985).

Rona Goffen, *Giovanni Bellini* (1989).

Howard Hibbard, *Michelangelo* (1986).

William Hood, *Fra Angelico at San Marco* (1993).

Roger Jones and Nicholas Penny, *Raphael* (1983).

Ronald Lightbrown, *Botticelli,* 2 vols. (1978).

Ilya Sandra Perlingiere, *Sofonisba Anguissola* (1993).

John Pope-Hennessy, *Fra Angelico* (1981).

LEONARDO DA VINCI

James Beck, *Leonardo's Rules of Painting* (1979).

Serge Bramly, *Leonardo, The Artist and the Man* (1995).

Kenneth Clark, *Leonardo da Vinci* (1975).

Martin Kemp, *Leonardo da Vinci* (1981).

——, Jane Roberts with Philip Steadman, *Leonardo da Vinci* (1989).

Jane Roberts, *Leonardo da Vinci* (1989).

Notes

1. Giorgio Vasari, *Lives of the Painters, Sculptors, and Architects*, tr. A. B. Hinds, ed. Edmund Fuller (New York: Dell, 1968), p. 182.
2. Cited in Kenneth Clark, *Leonardo da Vinci: An Account of His Development as an Artist* (Baltimore, Md.: Penguin, 1959), p. 147.
3. Vasari, *Lives*, p. 348.
4. Ibid., p. 349.
5. Cited in Mary Garrard, *Artemisia Gentileschi: The Image of the Female Hero in Italian Baroque Art* (Princeton, N.J.: Princeton University Press, 1989), p. 22.

7

RENAISSANCE SCULPTURE, ARCHITECTURE, AND MUSIC

The Fatiguing Art: Sculpture

The achievements of Renaissance painters were complemented by stunning creations by sculptors, architects, and musicians. Many of the great artists of the period excelled in a variety of mediums. Others chose to specialize in a particular art and were not above disparaging the arts of their colleagues. Leonardo da Vinci, jealous of the growing fame of his younger rival Michelangelo, wrote:

> I do not find any difference between painting and sculpture except that the sculptor pursues his work with greater physical fatigue than the painter, and the painter pursues his with greater mental fatigue. This is proved to be true, for the sculptor in producing his work does so by the force of his arm, striking the marble or some other stone to remove the covering beyond the figure enclosed within it. This is a most mechanical exercise accompanied many times with a great deal of sweat, which combines with dust and turns to mud.[1]

Unlike painting, of which few classical examples had survived, Renaissance Italy was filled with surviving models of ancient sculpture. However, Renaissance sculptors did more than just imitate classical models; they also made their own unique contributions to the art of sculpture. The ingenuity of sculptors such as Ghiberti, Donatello, and Michelangelo showed that Leonardo was wrong. Great sculpture required both brains and brawn.

LORENZO GHIBERTI (c. 1381–1455)

Lorenzo Ghiberti of Florence was one of the first to imitate and adapt classical models. He first achieved prominence by winning the famous competition of 1401 and getting the commission to cast a complete set of doors for the baptistery of St. John adjacent to the Florentine Cathedral. The competition was sponsored by the Wool Merchants Guild in thanks to God for saving the commune from the plague of 1400.

Seven important Tuscan sculptors competed for the commission including Ghiberti and the multitalented Filippo Brunelleschi. Each competitor was to sculpt a bronze panel depicting how the faith of the biblical patriarch Abraham was tested when God asked him to sacrifice his only son, Isaac. Although trained as a painter and still not a graduate of any guild, the young Ghiberti's panel was declared the winner. Brunelleschi was so angry at losing to his younger rival that he left Florence to study ancient architecture in Rome. If he could not be Florence's best sculptor, he would become its greatest architect.

Ghiberti's winning panel showed the first truly Renaissance nude figure in direct imitation of ancient Roman models. The nude figure of Isaac is kneeling on the right side of the panel while his father, Abraham, is poised with his knife pointed toward his son. With a single gesture, the angel floating directly above them stops the sacrifice. On the left is a ram resting quietly in a thicket while servants converse below. Ghiberti's panel revealed a clarity of composition, which combined classical and natural elements. His figures were also hollow and less expensive to produce, a fact that was probably not lost on the practical minded among the judges.

Ghiberti spent the next twenty-three years of his life designing, modeling, and sculpting the full bronze doors, whose subject matter was changed to scenes from the New Testament. After their completion

Lorenzo Ghiberti, *Sacrifice of Isaac*. Bargello, Florence, Italy. Alinari / Art Resource.

in 1424, he was awarded a commission for a second set of bronze doors showing episodes from the Old Testament. When completed in 1447, the second set of doors were considered an even greater success than the first. Michelangelo later declared that the second set of baptistery doors were worthy to serve as "the gates of paradise." Ghiberti also sculpted monumental, heroic statues of *St. John* and *St. Matthew* for the banking guild's niches at the Orsanmichele, a public structure in Florence that served as a shrine, wheat exchange, and granary.

DONATELLO (1386–1466)

Although Ghiberti serenely confessed in his autobiography that "few things of importance were made in our country [Florence] that were not designed and planned by me," his student Donatello surpassed him as a sculptor and continued the wonderful tradition of art as part of the civic revival of Florence after the political crisis at the beginning of the century.[2] He was a member of the stone and wood workers guild, but also studied goldsmithing and worked for a long time in Ghiberti's busy studio. He became a close, lifelong friend of Brunelleschi and studied classical monuments and statues in Rome. However, Donatello was not interested in either Brunelleschi's concern for strict proportions nor Ghiberti's interest in graceful line. Instead, he chose to depict the inner life of his subjects in dramatic force and power.

Much of Donatello's early sculpture in Florence was done in relation to architectural settings; however, he is famous for having sculpted the first freestanding nude statue in the round since antiquity. Donatello's revolutionary *David* of 1425 to 1430 was sculpted for the Medici palace gardens, where viewers could see it from all angles. In contrast to other heroic Davids, including

Lorenzo Ghiberti, *Gates of Paradise.* Baptistery, Florence, Italy. Alinari/Art Resource.

one of his own done earlier in his career in marble, this bronze David is a slight boy of twelve or thirteen, clothed only in leather boots and a shepherd's hat. He holds a sword in his right hand, while his left hand relaxes at his hip. His right foot rests upon a wreath, but his left foot toys idly with the severed head of the giant Goliath. David (Florence) has triumphed over Goliath (Milan) with the help of God and is utterly relaxed in victory.

In the early 1440s Donatello departed for Padua and remained there for over a decade. There he sculpted a colossal equestrian statue in bronze of Erasmo da Narni, the Venetian mercenary general known as Gattamelata (the "Honeyed Cat"). The dead general's family paid an enormous sum for this tribute, as stipulated in his will. Donatello's models included the great ancient equestrian statue of the Stoic Roman Emperor Marcus Aurelius, which he had studied in Rome. When finished in 1453, the statue was placed in the square in front of the Basilica of St. Anthony, where it still stands today as a monument to Donatello's genius.

Gattamelata shows the artist's mastery of equine, as well as human, anatomy. The powerful horse with his swelling veins, open jaws, and flaring eyes and nostrils is firmly under the general's command. His

Donatello, *David*. Bargello, Florence, Italy.
Alinari/Art Resource.

Donatello, *Monument to General Gattamelata*.
Piazza del Santo, Padua, Italy. Alinari/Art
Resource.

rider, dressed in fifteenth-century armor
with Roman details, holds a general's baton
and is armed with a huge broadsword. *Gattamelata*'s face, with its firmly set jaw, arched
eyebrows, and widespread eyes, reveals the
force and confident personality of this accomplished general. It is a masterful portrayal of the power of command.

Growing weary of the adulation he received in Padua, the bachelor Donatello returned to the more critical atmosphere of
Florence, where he spent his last years
sculpting and arguing with clients over fees.
The temperamental Donatello is reputed to
have destroyed some of his own compositions when he failed to receive the proper
compensation. Fortunately, enough of his
work survives to assure his reputation as the
greatest sculptor of the Renaissance before
Michelangelo. His dramatic depictions also
had a profound influence on painters such
as Botticelli and many others.

MICHELANGELO AS A SCULPTOR

The young Michelangelo had long been impressed by the sculptural mastery of Ghiberti, Donatello, and other Florentines. He
had also studied available classical models
and made his own intensive studies of human anatomy. Immersed in Neoplatonic
idealism from his time with the Medici and
an associate of Marsilio Ficino and the Platonic Academy, he was interested in the life

of the human soul as expressed in the structure and movement of the human body. For Michelangelo, the body was the "mortal veil" of divine intention. Only by creating bodies could he dare do something analogous to God's creation of body and soul.

In June 1496 Michelangelo left Florence for Rome. An art agent had paid him thirty ducats for a sleeping cupid done in Roman style. The agent then buried it in the earth to give it the appearance of age and sold it for 200 ducats to a Roman cardinal as an antique. When Michelangelo learned of the fraud, he quickly dashed off to Rome to correct the problem. He stayed for five years and received a number of excellent commissions, including one from a French cardinal for the *Pietà*.

Images of the dead Christ on his mother's lap were common in France and the Holy Roman Empire but were virtually unknown in Italy. Michelangelo made his first trip to Carrara to find marble of the highest quality for this statue. In the Vatican *Pietà*, the twenty-five-year-old artist showed his deep religiosity and a technical virtuosity that surpassed even the mature Donatello. Never had anyone sculpted with the refinement and delicacy of touch as shown in the torso and limbs of the dead Christ and the complex arrangement of the drapery. Michelangelo's tender Mary seems years younger than her son, whose wounds have virtually disappeared. Their purity of soul has removed all traces of injury and age. Typical of Renaissance self-promotion, the artist sculpted his name across the chest of Mary.

In 1501 the government of Florence commissioned the now famous sculptor to create a David out of a block of Carrara marble that other sculptors had rejected as cut too narrowly for a fully rounded, free standing statue. Michelangelo went into seclusion with the marble for two years and

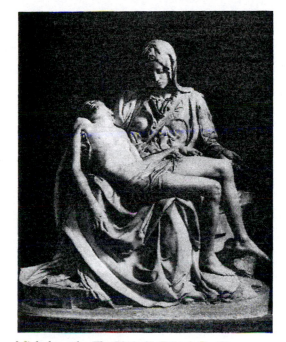

Michelangelo, *The Pietà*. St. Peter's Basilica, Vatican State. Alinari/Art Resource.

emerged with a giant *David* that defiantly glorified the naked human body. David is shown before his battle with Goliath, his sling over his shoulder and a stone resting in his right hand. His muscles are taut, but his face is confident and defiant. Gone is the young Hebrew boy in desperate need of God's help; instead, Michelangelo has sculpted a god-like classical hero. The sculptor has pushed beyond the limits of classical realism to create a colossal superhuman, who belongs to the world of the mannerists. The Florentine government placed Michelangelo's *David* in front of the town hall as a valued symbol of the city, but they also prudishly insisted on placing a brass girdle with twenty-eight copper leaves around the defiant hero's waist!

In 1506 Michelangelo returned to Rome, where he spent the three most productive decades of his life in the service of

Michelangelo, *David*. Accademia, Florence, Italy. Alinari/Art Resource.

four Renaissance popes, beginning with the crusty warrior-pope Julius II (Papa Terrible). Julius commissioned Michelangelo to create a gigantic tomb for him to stand three stories high and to be filled with dozens of statues of saints, apostles, cherubs, and sybils. "Let it cost any amount and you shall have it," bragged Papa Terrible. The reality was that Michelangelo frequently had a difficult time collecting his money, despite assurances from church officials that he was "our most dear friend."[3]

The pope also interrupted Michelangelo's work on the tomb to force him to paint the ceiling of the Sistine Chapel, as discussed in the previous chapter. Even this work was interrupted by the restless pope, whose inner demons almost matched Michelangelo's and who inspired so much dread among his enemies. For years Julius had been attempting to expand the papal state in central Italy. When he had finally cleared the Romagna of foes and entered Bologna in triumph, he ordered Michelangelo to sculpt a huge bronze, seated figure of the pope with the keys of the kingdom in one hand and a gesture of benediction in the other. The Bolognese hated it as a symbol of their humiliation and later melted it down to make cannon balls during an attempt to throw off papal rule.

Despite these interruptions Michelangelo worked with great speed to advance the tomb, although only three of the statues were ever brought even close to completion. One of the finished works was a heroic and heavily muscled *Moses*. In this work Michelangelo depicts Moses as the man who saw and talked to God on Mount Sinai. There the biblical hero received the Tablets of the Law, which he holds under his right arm. He is shown with "horns," as was traditional, based on a deliberate mistranslation of the Hebrew word for "rays" by St. Jerome. When Moses came down from Mount Sinai for the second time, rays of light shone from his face. St. Jerome, the translator of the Vulgate Bible, refused to attribute light to anyone who preceded Christ.

Michelangelo's rendering of Moses was not traditional in most of its details, including the unusually spectacular beard that tumbles down his chest. Meant to be viewed from below because it was intended for the second level of Pope Julius's tomb, Michelangelo's *Moses* reveals the artist's fascination with the male human body and his ability to create superhuman figures. In an effort to illustrate how Neoplatonic notions permeated his art, he once claimed that he could envision the completed figure inside the marble slab and what he had to do was to chip away the exterior. Few others have ever been able to release such incredible sculpted figures upon the world.

Michelangelo received patronage from

Michelangelo, *Moses*. S. Pietro in Vincoli, Rome, Italy. Alinari/Art Resource.

Julius's successors, but later returned to Florence to work on the facade for San Lorenzo. When that project was cancelled, he began work on the Medici Chapel. For the chapel he sculpted not only giant portrait sculptures of dukes Lorenzo (d. 1519) and Giuliano de' Medici (d. 1516) and their more famous predecessors of the same names, but he also added the mysterious, allegorical figures of *Day*, *Night*, *Dawn*, and *Twilight*. The full, gigantic project was never completed because he was called to Rome by the reformer Pope Paul III (r. 1534–1549) for the painting of the *Last Judgment* on the altar wall of the Sistine Chapel. Michelangelo spent the last thirty years of his life in Rome, turning down invitations from all over Europe and even one from the ruler of the Ottoman Empire, Süleyman the Magnificent, who had received some training

as a goldsmith and valued great art and architecture.

Since sculpture was too physically demanding for a man in his sixties who had suffered so much from years of inner turmoil and bad eating habits, Michelangelo turned most of his attention to the less exhausting work of drawing architectural plans and composing lyrical and metaphysical love poems. He fell deeply in love with a handsome young Roman aristocrat, Tommaso dei Cavalieri, for whom he wrote passionate sonnets. Michelangelo also had a close, platonic friendship with the religious poet Vittorina Colonna. He died in his ninetieth year still working on a dome of St. Peter's Basilica, one of his greatest architectural efforts.

BENVENUTO CELLINI (1500–1571)

According to Benvenuto Cellini, Michelangelo saluted him as "the greatest goldsmith we know of; and now I recognize you to be a sculptor of like talent."[4] A supreme egoist, Cellini did not dispute this judgment by the artist he most admired besides himself. Cellini was a native of Florence, where he had been born the son of a musician and instrument maker. Apprenticed to a goldsmith, Benvenuto showed a great talent for the craft, as well as a violent temper that resulted in numerous scrapes with the law throughout his life. In 1519 he journeyed to Rome, where he eventually found work as an artist for Popes Clement VII (r. 1523–1534) and Paul III (r. 1534–1549). He claimed in his *Autobiography* to have played a heroic role in the defense of the papal castle during the sack of 1527 by imperial troops.

Accused of stealing jewels from the papal tiara, he was imprisoned, escaped, recaptured, tortured, and threatened with hanging. King François I of France requested that Pope Paul III release him to his care in 1540. After five years of service to the French king, Cellini returned to his native Florence where he continued to have trouble with the law while continuing his successful career as an artist. In 1558 he began composing his famous *Autobiography*. There he details his adventures, crimes, religious conversion, and artistic triumphs. Although the artist did support his widowed sister and her six children, he fathered seven illegitimate children and coolly abandoned at least one young woman when leaving France for Italy.

In addition to his unfinished and widely circulated *Autobiography*, Cellini also wrote an important technical treatise on the art of goldsmithing. While many of his masterpieces have disappeared, likely because thieves coveted the precious metals and jewels he used, enough remains to confirm Michelangelo's assessment of him. His *Perseus and Medusa*, commissioned by Duke Cosimo I de' Medici in 1557, stands in the sculpture loggia adjacent to the City Hall of Florence and Michelangelo's *David*. It is a dramatic rendering of Perseus, a son of Zeus, displaying the severed head of the gorgon Medusa. Cellini is also well known for a gold and enamel saltcellar he created for his French royal patron. According to Cellini, when he had shown the king a wax model of the saltcellar, François exclaimed, "This is a hundred times more divine a thing than I had ever dreamed of."[5] Because of his extraordinary talent, Benvenuto Cellini was forgiven for a great deal and was honored with a magnificent funeral in Florence.

Architecture

In addition to the glories of Italian painting and sculpture, the Renaissance was also an incredible time for architecture. The highly influential architect, artist, musician, and theorist Leon Battista Alberti (c. 1402–1472) had called for the building of beautiful cities worthy of humanistically inclined men and women of virtue. In his seminal book, *On Building* (c. 1452), Alberti praised architecture as a social art, concerned with the health and welfare of people. No structure should be designed as an isolated unit; each building should be planned in relation to its social functions and setting. According to Alberti, a disciple of the first century A.D. Roman architect Vitruvius, creative design should utilize classical forms because their principles had been proven to work over time.

FILIPPO BRUNELLESCHI (1377–1446)

Alberti applied these ideas in his own designs, as did his supremely gifted contemporary Filippo Brunelleschi. The son of a notary, Brunelleschi had served an apprenticeship as a goldsmith, but departed from Florence upon losing the baptistery sculpture competition to Lorenzo Ghiberti in 1401. In Rome in the company of Donatello, he studied the great designs and monuments of classical architecture. With his mind filled with ideas, Brunelleschi returned to Florence in 1407 at the very time the city government had decided to complete the construction of the dome of the cathedral of Santa Maria del Fiore (St. Mary of the Flowers). The Florentines were still in the throes of their struggles with Milan and wanted to use public art to express their thanks to God for delivering them from the Milanese and to express their confidence in the future.

After lengthy wrangling, Brunelleschi's design for the dome was accepted and construction was finally begun in 1420 and was completed in 1436. His dome was the largest ever built since the time of the Roman Pantheon, towering nearly 180 feet. Brunelleschi was able to displace some of the ceiling weight of the dome by making it

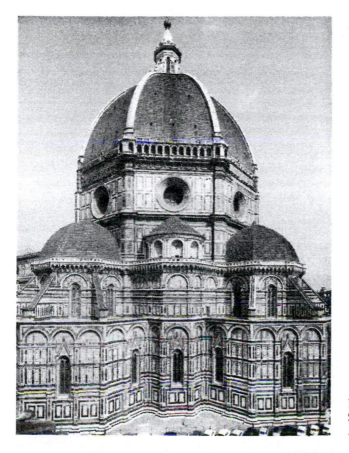

Brunelleschi, Dome of the Cathedral of
Santa Maria del Fiore. Florence, Italy.
Alinari/Art Resource.

Brunelleschi, Interior
view down the nave
toward apse, San
Lorenzo, Florence, Italy.
Alinari/Art Resource.

higher than a fully rounded dome. He also used such innovative features as an inner and outer shell, ribbed vaulting, smaller support domes, and a thick drum at the roof base. Brunelleschi's dome for the cathedral was so successful that he soon became the most celebrated architect in Florence.

Brunelleschi's architectural legacy included the graceful Pazzi Chapel, a strikingly original Hospital of the Innocents, and several revolutionary churches, including the Medici's San Lorenzo. In contrast to Gothic architecture with its emphasis on verticality, Brunelleschi's design with its flat ceilings and horizontal lines emphasized the control of space. He was intrigued with the simple three-aisle system of early Christian basilicas that he had observed so carefully in Rome. In addition to his work as an architect, Brunelleschi made invaluable contributions to painting with his explanations of the working of linear perspective. He also came up with several clever mechanical devices and advised his fellow inventors not "to share your inventions with many, share them only with a few who understand and love the sciences."[6]

MICHELOZZO MICHELOZZI (1396–1472)

Brunelleschi submitted plans for a sumptuous new Medici palace to Cosimo de' Medici, who rejected them as too grand. Instead, the commission went to Michelozzo Michelozzi, who also supervised the completion of San Lorenzo. Michelozzi, the son of a tailor, began his artistic career as a sculptor, working in bronze, silver, and marble with Donatello and Ghiberti. His skill, moderation, and good taste won the admiration of Cosimo de' Medici, who commissioned him to design his family palace. Michelozzi's modest and graceful design is much less grandiose than Brunelleschi's larger Pitti Palace, which was built partly with

Michelozzi, Palazzo Medici-Riccardi. Florence, Italy. Alinari/Art Resource.

slave labor, and more in keeping with Cosimo's determination not to flaunt his wealth beyond the bounds of good taste and civic virtue. The rough cut stones of the ground floor suggest an urban fortress. The Medici coat-of-arms is prominently displayed on the building's corner. The finished building was so successful that it became a model of Renaissance domestic architecture. Michelozzi went on to become one of Italy's most important architects.

BRAMANTE (1444–1514)

Donato d'Agnolo Bramante was the leading architect of the second half of the fifteenth century. A native of Urbino, he was trained as a painter in Mantua and Milan. Bramante made his first appearance as an architect in 1485 when he undertook the rebuilding of the church of Santa Maria Presso San Satiro in Milan. His design was so well received that he soon became the leading church architect of the Sforzas. With Ludovico il Moro's fall in 1499, Bramante left for Rome hoping for better luck and new patrons in the papal city. One of his greatest masterpieces is the circular Tempietto (little temple) commissioned by Ferdinand and Isabella of Spain in 1502. Bramante based his design on ancient round temples he had observed in Rome and Tivoli. His Tempietto has no single elevation; it exists in space like a work of sculpture and has come to be regarded as a paragon of Renaissance architecture.

The success of the Tempietto helped bring Bramante to the attention of the papal court. He soon became the leading papal architect and reached the climax of his architectural career with his designs for the new St. Peter's basilica and a grand renovation of the Vatican Palace. When completed later in the century using mostly the plans of others, St. Peter's became one of the greatest monuments to the genius of a host of Renaissance architects, artists, and patrons. As the largest and most expensive house of worship in western Europe, the cost of its construction helped to spark the Protestant Reformation.

Bramante and others, Exterior of St. Peter's. Vatican State. Alinari/Art Resource.

WOMEN IN SCULPTURE
AND ARCHITECTURE

What contributions women made to Renaissance sculpture and architecture are not as yet fully known. Even the exact role of noblewomen in architectural patronage is unclear. Architecture and sculpture were considered male monopolies and because those arts were even more public than painting, it was impossible for females to gain commissions to sculpt or design buildings. Most Renaissance men assumed that women were not to be trusted with the expenditure of large sums of money and the supervision of male construction workers. Not until the nineteenth century do we hear of female architects.

Potential women sculptors were barred from the field by the fifteenth-century requirement that all sculptors be familiar with human anatomy, especially the nude male. Sweaty sculptors' workshops were considered even less suitable for females than workshops that focused on other arts such as glassmaking or painting. Young women in the Renaissance found it impossible to receive training as sculptors even from the most supportive of males. Therefore, Michelangelo could offer Sofonisba Anguissola training in drawing and painting, but not in architecture and sculpture.

The Sounds of the Universe:
Music

Renaissance humanists also had a passion for music. Had not the revered Greek philosopher Pythagoras (sixth century B.C.) shown that harmony was the essential component of the universe? Music was a critical ingredient of medieval worship from the Gregorian chants onward. The Renaissance Neoplatonist Marsilio Ficino had argued that music was a way to approach God and heal disease. Renaissance courts relied heavily on musicians for entertainment and enrichment. Progressive humanist schools such as that of Vittorino da Feltre included music as part of the experience. Musical instruments such as the lute, viol, flute, and harp were used primarily as accompaniment for songs or dances. Eventually, instrumental music also became popular, especially at civic festivals and public events, where trumpets, trombones, and oboes were used with great effect.

Francesco Landino (1325–97), the blind organist of the church of San Lorenzo in Florence, was one of the greatest musicians of the early Renaissance. He was a skilled performer with the lute, recorder, and organ and also wrote hundreds of madrigals (a complex, unaccompanied vocal piece), ballads, and other mostly secular music. Landino also won fame as a humanist, philosopher, and mathematician. The cadential formula, *Landino sixth*, is named after him.

Building on the growing reputation of Florence as a center for music, Lorenzo de' Medici founded a "School of Harmony," which attracted musicians from all over Italy. Isabella d'Este brought many singers to her court at Mantua. She had learned to sing and play instruments and appreciate music growing up at the court of her father, Duke Ercole, in Ferrara. He was an avid musical enthusiast. Ferrara's reputation as a leading musical center continued into the late sixteenth century when the duke organized a group of "lady singers" in 1580, who proved to be the first professional female court musicians. One of them, the virtuoso singer and instrumentalist Tarquinia Molza (1524–1617), wrote arrangements for voice, lute, viol, and harp. Tragically, her compositions have all been lost, but the fashion for "lady singers" spread to Mantua, Rome, and elsewhere.

GIOVANNI PALESTRINA (c. 1525–1594)

Giovanni Palestrina was, arguably, the most talented composer of the sixteenth century. Influenced by Flemish as well as Italian traditions, he spent most of his life at various churches in Rome, eventually becoming the papal organist and director of the papal choir. There Palestrina composed masses, motets (choral compositions on a sacred text), madrigals, and settings for the biblical Song of Solomon. Not an innovator, he brought to a head the century-and-a-half development of polyphonic (vocal counterpoint) music. Inspired by the Catholic Reformation and the Council of Trent, Palestrina later sought to purge his music of all secular elements. His later compositions are not nearly as sensuous or as complex as his earlier ones, but they are still powerful expressions of the growing power of music.

Papal Rome continued to be a great source of patronage for musicians long after the death of Palestrina in 1594.

CLAUDIO MONTEVERDI (1567–1643)

Claudio Monteverdi was the seminal figure in the dramatic development of opera. Born in Cremona, he was attached to the sophisticated court of the Gonzaga's in Mantua for many years. There Monteverdi came up with the idea of combining singing, acting, dancing, and instrumental music with elaborate stage designs and costumes. His first opera, *Orfeo* (Orpheus), was performed at Mantua in 1607. It created a sensation and was followed by other grandiose open-air productions. In 1613 Monteverdi moved to St. Mark's Cathedral in Venice to serve as its master of music. He remained in Venice for the rest of his life, composing sacred music, operas, madrigals, and motets in his harmonic style. His legacy continues to enrich us today.

Chronology

Further Reading

SCULPTURE

Bonnie Bennett and David Wilkins, *Donatello* (1985).

Bruce Boucher, *The Sculpture of Jacopo Sansovino* (1991).

Charles de Tolnay, *Michelangelo* (1975). By the leading authority.

Michael Hirst and Jill Dunkerton, *The Young Michelangelo: Making and Meaning, The Artist in Rome, 1496–1501* (1994).

Richard Krautheimer, *Lorenzo Ghiberti* (1970).

Anita Moskowitz, *The Sculpture of Andrea and Nono Pisano* (1986).

Roberta Olson, *Italian Renaissance Sculpture* (1992).

John Pope-Hennessy, *The Study and Criticism of Italian Sculpture* (1980).

Charles Seymour, Jr., *Sculpture in Italy, 1400–1500* (1994).

William Wallace, *Michelangelo at San Lorenzo: The Genius as Entrepreneur* (1994).

Sarah Blake Wilk, *Fifteenth-Century Italian Sculpture* (1986).

Diane Zervas, *The Parte Guelfa, Brunelleschi and Donatello* (1988).

ARCHITECTURE

James Ackerman, *The Architecture of Michelangelo* (1986).

Eugenio Battisti, *Filippo Brunelleschi* (1981).

Joan Gadol, *Leon Battista Alberti: Universal Man of the Early Renaissance* (1969).

Richard Goldthwaite, *The Building of Renaissance Florence* (1986).

Deborah Howard, *The Architectural History of Venice* (1980).

Frances Kent, *A Florentine Patrician and His Palace* (1981). A study of the Rucellai Palace in Florence.

Peter Murray, *The Architecture of the Italian Renaissance* (1986).

Howard Saalman, *Filippo Brunelleschi: The Buildings* (1993).

Christine Smith, *Architecture in the Culture of Early Humanism: Ethics, Aesthetics and Eloquence, 1400–1470* (1992).

David Thomson, *Renaissance Architecture: Patrons, Critics, and Luxury* (1993).

MUSIC

Allan Atlas, *Music of the Aragonese Court of Naples* (1985).

Paolo Fabri, *Monteverdi* (1994).

Iain Fenlon, *Music and Patronage in Sixteenth Century Mantua*, 2 vols. (1981).

Frederick Hammond, *Music and Spectacle in Baroque Rome: Barberini Patronage under Urban VIII* (1994).

Barbara Hanning, *Of Poetry and Music's Power: Humanism and the Creation of Opera* (1980).

Lewis Lockwood, *Music in Renaissance Ferrara, 1400–1505* (1985).

Nino Pirrotta, *Music and Culture in Italy from the Middle Ages to the Baroque* (1984).

Richard Strohm, *The Rise of European Music, 1380–1500* (1994).

Gary Tomlinson, *Monteverdi and the End of the Renaissance* (1987).

Notes

1. Cited in G. R. Elton, ed., *Renaissance and Reformation, 1300–1648*, 3rd ed. (New York: Macmillan, 1976), p. 67.
2. Cited in De Lamar Jensen, *Renaissance Europe: Age of Recovery and Reconciliation*, 2nd ed. (Lexington, Mass.: D. C. Heath, 1992), p. 166.
3. Cited in D. S. Chambers, ed., *Patrons and Artists in the Italian Renaissance* (Columbia, S.C.: University of South Carolina Press, 1971), p. 35.
4. Cited in Julia Conaway Bondanella and Mark Musa, eds., *The Italian Renaissance Reader* (New York: Penguin, 1987), p. 355.
5. Cited in Lewis Spitz, *The Renaissance and Reformation Movements* (Chicago: Rand McNally, 1971), p. 224.
6. Cited in Kenneth Bartlett, ed., *The Civilization of the Italian Renaissance: A Sourcebook* (Lexington, Mass.: D. C. Heath, 1992), p. 211.

8

ITALY'S
MACHIAVELLIAN MOMENT

When King Charles VIII (r. 1483–1498) invaded Italy in September 1494 with an army of 30,000 men, he changed forever the nature of Italian politics and the culture of the Renaissance. From the French perspective, 1494 seemed like the perfect time to assert their claims to Naples and use that city as a staging area for a crusade against the menacing Ottomans, who had taken well-fortified and massive Constantinople in 1453 and pressed on into the Balkan underbelly of Europe. The once powerful duchy of Milan was in a state of disorder and was no longer a strong guardian of the passes over the Alps. The rest of Italy was divided into regional factions and jealousies. Some Italian politicians such as Ludovico il Moro of Milan even invited the French to intervene on their behalf. The death of King Ferrante of Naples earlier in 1494 gave the young king of France all the excuse he needed to launch an invasion. It came at the very height of the flowering of Renaissance culture, especially in Florence. Disruptions caused by the coming and going of the French would have profound consequences for Italy and the world.

The Fiery Dominican:
Savonarola (1452–1498)

The coming of the French after forty years of relative peace and the subsequent fall of the

Medici had long been predicted by the charismatic Dominican preacher Girolamo Savonarola. A native of Ferrara and the son of a court physician, Girolamo entered a Dominican friary in Bologna after being rejected by a daughter of the wealthy house of Strozzi. Following stints as a preacher in Bologna and then Ferrara, he was called to San Marco's monastery in Florence in 1482. The young ascetic found Florence incredibly beautiful but sinfully worldly. It was while preaching in nearby San Gimignano that his eloquence first began to attract public notice. Lorenzo de' Medici urged Savonarola to return to San Marco's in Florence.

Beginning in August 1490, Savonarola began preaching dire warnings of coming disasters and urged the Florentines to repent of their sins. Disgusted by the extravagance and womanizing of Lorenzo de' Medici and his dissolute son and political successor, Piero, the Dominican spoke of the fall of tyrants and the need for justice for the poor and the oppressed. He also called for reformation in the church. Savonarola's sermons struck a responsive chord and soon he became the leading preacher in Florence, prior of San Marco's, and a frequent guest preacher in the great cathedral. In his Lenten sermons of 1494 he called for the building of another Noah's ark against the floods to come. Then Savonarola claimed to have had a vision in which he saw a hand bearing a flaming sword inscribed with the words: "The sword of the Lord will be over the earth swiftly and soon."[1]

When news reached Florence in September 1494 that King Charles of France had crossed the Alps and arrived in Italy, the people were terrified, and it seemed to many that Savonarola's dark, apocalyptic prophecies were coming true. Savonarola now proclaimed, "Behold the Sword has descended; the scourge has fallen, the prophecies are being fulfilled. Behold it is the Lord God who is leading these armies. . . . Behold, I shall unloose waters over the earth."[2] The Mantuan ambassador reported to his master that "a Dominican friar has so terrified all the Florentines that they are wholly given up to piety." The philosopher Giovanni Pico della Mirandola testified that Savonarola's sermons sent shivers up and down his spine and made his hair stand on end. As an old man, Michelangelo was still haunted by the powerful voice of the Dominican preacher.

When Charles VIII entered Florence on November 17, 1494, with a part of his large army in sumptuous array, it seemed as if the flood had come. Piero de' Medici had already been exiled from the city for his failure to halt the French advance, so it was the popular preacher Savonarola who twice met with the king and begged him to spare the city on the Arno. The Dominican's intercessions seemed to have some effect, for eleven days later the French left Florence for the road south to Naples without having done extensive damage. Savonarola was hailed as the savior of the commune and was compared to Pope Leo I, who had allegedly convinced Attila the Hun not to sack Rome in 454. Florence was made into a less autocratic republic with greater representation on its Great Council of 3,000 members. Savonarola proclaimed that "Florence will be more glorious, richer, more powerful than she has ever been."[3]

Savonarola wanted to make Florence a republic of virtue "filled with true religion," purging it of its vices and sins and rendering justice unto the downtrodden. Toward that end, in 1496 the Dominican inspired a great "burning of the vanities" in which gambling equipment, jewelry, cosmetics, false hair and pads, musical instruments, and lewd books (including Boccaccio's *Decameron Tales*) were put to the torch. Some of the ancient texts of risqué Roman poets such as Catullus and Ovid were destroyed. Even some of the paintings of Botticelli, a follower of the Dominican, were consigned to the flames.

The friar dreamed not only of reforming Florence, but of cleansing the church as a whole. He was especially critical of the corrupt Pope Alexander VI and urged King Charles VIII to depose him. The Borgia pope retaliated by ordering the "meddlesome friar" to stop preaching. Enraged by the efforts to silence him, Savonarola only intensified his attacks on the papacy. The pope then excommunicated him in 1497 and threatened to place Florence under an interdict if the friar were allowed to preach again. Many of the elite, already jealous of Savonarola's power over the populace and fearing for the loss of so many pleasures, began to worry, especially as the city weathered a severe economic crisis in the winter of 1497–1498. They helped stir up public discontent with the saintly but determined preacher.

In the spring of 1498 rival Franciscans challenged Savonarola to an ordeal by fire. He was going to have to prove his faith in God by agreeing to walk on hot coals. Fearing he was losing his hold over the Florentine populace, the reformer reluctantly accepted the challenge, saying he would walk out of the fires unscathed. whereas the Franciscans would burn. When the day of the spectacle arrived, arguments between the Franciscans and the Dominicans delayed the proceedings in front of the town hall until a rainstorm struck and doused the fires. Egged on by Savonarola's political enemies and disappointed that the promised show had been aborted, an angry crowd turned against their former hero.

Emboldened, Savonarola's opponents in the government now ordered his arrest and condemned him to death by hanging. On May 23, 1498, after days of torture, Savonarola and two young supporters were hanged in the public square, the site of the "burning of the vanities" and the ordeal by fire. Their bodies were then burned and tossed into the Arno River, which flows through the heart of Florence. The historian Francesco Guicciardini wrote of Savonarola:

> Although his detractors searched industriously during the investigation, they could not find even the slightest moral defect in him. The work he did in promoting decent behavior was holy and marvelous; nor had there ever been as much goodness and religion in Florence as there was in his time.[4]

Lions and Foxes: The French Invasion of 1499 and Its Aftermath

Louis XII (r. 1498–1515) ascended the French throne at almost the same moment that Savonarola died in Florence. From the house of Orléans, Louis was usually a kindhearted, plain-speaking if sometimes gullible man. Fond of hunting and the martial arts, he gained popularity in France as a "father of his people" by reducing the tax burdens of his humble subjects and enacting a number of administrative reforms. His understanding of international politics did not match his skills in domestic policy. Never-

theless, Louis XII felt compelled to assert his claim to the duchy of Milan and wanted very badly to flex his political muscles. His grandmother, Valentina Visconti, was the daughter of the last Visconti duke, Giangeleazzo. In his eyes the Sforzas were usurpers with no legitimate claim to the prosperous duchy and Ludovico il Moro needed to be punished for having turned against the French in 1495 after having invited them to invade.

Louis had already been formally invested with the duchy of Milan by Holy Roman Emperor Maximilian I (r. 1493–1519) in 1495, although he saw this as only a temporary concession. Pope Alexander VI hoped to use the French to extend papal control over the Romagna north of Rome and had dispatched his ruthless son, Cesare Borgia, to the French court. Cesare was armed with a papal dispensation that Louis had requested allowing him to cruelly set aside his deformed and crippled wife, Jeanne (a daughter of Louis XI), and marry his predecessor Charles VIII's widow, Anne of Brittany. Such a marriage alliance would further strengthen his claim to his cousin's throne. Even mighty Venice had reluctantly agreed to aid the French invasion and Florence was still in the French camp.

The Milanese collapsed quickly in the fall of 1499 after heavy artillery bombardment and the desertion to the French of two of their best commanders. Ludovico il Moro fled to Austria, but then returned with a contingent of German and Swiss mercenaries. He was defeated at Novara on April 8, 1500. His Swiss mercenaries, disgruntled over their lack of pay, refused to fight at Novara against the Swiss mercenaries in the army of the French. Ludovico was forced to flee again, but was captured by some of his mercenaries, who sold him to the French. The extravagant and foolish duke died eight years later in a French dungeon.

Encouraged by his victories, King Louis XII moved on toward Naples after signing a Treaty of Granada (November 1500) with King Ferdinand of Aragon to partition Naples between them. The wily Ferdinand already controlled Sicily and Sardinia. Emperor Maximilian was embroiled by an imperial reform movement in Germany and could do nothing to check Louis and Ferdinand. Naples fell easily to the French and Spanish, but soon the victors began to quarrel over the spoils. By January 1, 1504, the Spanish had driven the French out of Naples. Disgusted with the duplicitous nature of international politics, Louis XII renounced all further claims to Naples.

The papacy had been the most immediate benefactor of the French invasion of 1499. Using French cavalry and Swiss infantry, Cesare Borgia had managed to conquer the Romagna and began to threaten Florence. At the height of his power, the wheel of fortune, a popular Renaissance conceit, began to turn and in August 1503 his father, Pope Alexander VI, died. Worse yet, Alexander was succeeded by the Borgia's great enemy Giuliano della Rovere, the warrior-pope Julius II. Without papal support, Cesare's empire quickly collapsed and he was imprisoned in 1504. He died three years later in Spain.

With the passing of the Borgias, Pope Julius II became the dominant figure in Italian politics. Although in his early sixties, "Papa Terrible" possessed incredible energy and was determined to secure the loyalty of the lords of the Romagna and Emilia to the north. With the support of the French, the warrior-pope was also able to conquer Bologna, which surrendered to him in November 1506. He then joined the French, Emperor Maximilian, and Ferdinand of Aragon in the League of Cambrai (November 1508) against the haughty Venetian republic. The French feared Venice as the im-

portant rival for power in northern Italy; the emperor resented having lost Trieste and Fiume to the Venetians after his unsuccessful invasion of Italy in 1508. Pope Julius wanted to reduce Venetian influence in the Romagna and the Aragonese were eager to regain the seaports in the kingdom of Naples which the Venetians had occupied.

Venice proved no match for this powerful combination and was decisively defeated in May 1509 at Agnadello. The Venetians were forced to cede all their mainland possessions, but resisted the league's onslaught against the city itself, which had been placed under papal interdict. After having regained all his towns in the Romagna, Pope Julius II then turned on his French allies and attempted to unite the Italians in order to drive out the "barbarians." The barbarians did not, of course, include the Swiss, the "most dexterous rascal" Ferdinand of Aragon, or the English under Henry VIII, who joined the pope's new "Holy League" against their rivals the French. Such allies were necessary to free Italy.

The French, surprised by the pope's double-dealing and the strength of Italian determination to end their dominance, were mauled at Ravenna by Aragonese and papal forces in April 1512. Although they won the bloody battle, it cost them their brilliant commander, Gaston de Foix, and many casualties. In 1513 the Swiss came down the Saint Gotthard Pass and crushed the French at Novara. Ludovico il Moro's son was made a puppet duke of Milan, which the Swiss controlled to secure their economic interests.

Since 1502 the Florentine republic had stumbled along under the leadership of Piero Soderini (1452–1522), who had been named *gonfaloniere* (banner bearer of justice) for life. In August 1512 the Aragonese captured little Prato, not far from Florence, from the retreating French. Florence was defended from the Spanish by a militia force, which had been recruited by Niccolò Machiavelli. In the face of disciplined Spanish infantry, the Florentine militia fled in disarray. Piero Soderini's republic was overthrown and the Spanish restored the Medici to power in the form of Lorenzo the Magnificent's two remaining sons, Cardinal Giovanni and his younger brother Giuliano. When Pope Julius II died in February 1513, Giovanni de' Medici succeeded him as Pope Leo X. With the sudden return of the Medici to power in Florence, Niccolò Machiavelli lost his job in the Florentine government and began his career as a writer whose words, tempered by his experiences during Italy's great time of troubles, would change forever our view of ourselves and politics.

Santi di Tito, *Portrait of Niccolò Machiavelli.* Palazzo Vecchio, Florence, Italy. Alinari / Art Resource.

Niccolò Machiavelli (1469–1527)

Of all the influential thinkers of the Italian Renaissance, few have ever spoken more clearly to our time than Niccolò Machiavelli. He came from a minor Florentine noble family. His father was a lawyer who practiced a little law and mostly lived off his farm and rental properties. As a boy, Niccolò received an excellent humanist grounding in Latin and Italian literature and a smattering of Roman law. He started as a clerk in the Florentine government in the period following the exile of the Medici in 1494 and by 1498 was appointed chancellor of the Second Chancery concerned with foreign affairs and secretary to the Council of Ten, the department of war. During this period, Machiavelli witnessed the rise and fall of Savonarola. He disagreed with the Dominican about blaming Italy's woes on human sin, but credits him with the gift of proph-

ecy: "much was [truly] predicted by friar Girolamo Savonarola before the coming of King Charles VIII to Italy."[5]

In the fine tradition of civic humanists such as Leonardo Bruni and Coluccio Salutati, Machiavelli loved being able to use his classical education in the service of the state. His talents were recognized by Piero Soderini, who made good use of him. Not only was Machiavelli heavily involved in the voluminous official foreign correspondence of Florence, but he also inspected fortifications, helped organize militia units, and went on numerous diplomatic missions. A great deal of the art and institutions of diplomacy, including the use of resident ambassadors, was developed during the Renaissance. As a diplomat, Machiavelli traveled to the courts of King Louis XII of France, Holy Roman Emperor Maximilian I, and many of the Italian states. He met with

Cesare Borgia three times between 1502 and 1503. Borgia's boldness, cunning, ruthlessness, and handsome—if cruelly scarred—features fascinated him. He wrote of Cesare in 1513, "This Lord is very splendid and magnificent, and so spirited at arms that there is no great thing that does not seem small to him. . . . he never rests, nor recognizes fatigue nor danger."[6]

Machiavelli was also intrigued by the warrior-pope Julius II. At first he disparaged Papa Terrible as untrustworthy: "Those who know the Pope say that with him one cannot place a thing overnight and find it there the next day."[7] Yet as he came to understand more of Julius's abilities as he journeyed with him during his 1506 campaign in the Romagna, his admiration for the pope as a political leader grew. Because of his wide range of experiences as a diplomat, Machiavelli had a first-hand knowledge of many of the important players in the turbulent world of Renaissance politics.

With the sudden return of the Medici to power in 1512, caused in part by the machinations of the warrior-pope's anti-French crusade, Machiavelli lost his position in the Florentine government because he was unfairly viewed as an enemy of the recently restored Medici. After a period of torture and imprisonment by those who had forgotten about his devoted service to Florence, he was allowed to retire to a small farm outside of Florence as a gesture of goodwill when Lorenzo de' Medici's son, Giovanni, was elected Pope Leo X in 1513. Although Machiavelli missed political office terribly, he spent the next fifteen years as a successful if embittered man of letters and gentleman farmer. After a day of farm business, tavern games, and gossip, the retired diplomat repaired to his study in the evenings dressed in the "regal and courtly garments" he had once proudly worn as a public official. There he did the writing that was to have such a lasting impact on thought and letters.

MACHIAVELLI'S WRITINGS

As a literary man, Niccolò Machiavelli produced a well-received book of Italian poetry, several satires, a short story, and three plays. His most successful comedy, *The Mandrake Root*, is a lascivious bedroom farce that is traditionally considered the best dramatic work of the Italian Renaissance. The sensual Florentine had a taste for bawdiness and naughty humor which struck a responsive chord. *The Mandrake Root* played to large, enthusiastic audiences in both Florence and rival Venice, which usually disdained all things Florentine. His literary works reveal him to be a deft satirist who always had a political agenda behind the rude jokes.

As gifted as Machiavelli was as an artist, his ultimate reputation was made by his political writings, particularly *The Prince* (1513), written shortly after his release from prison in an effort to curry favor with the Medici. Convinced that Italy needed a strong ruler to protect it from its enemies and instability, Machiavelli instructs a despot in the art of gaining and holding power. He argued that a prince "must imitate the lion and the fox."[8] The prince must have the strength of a lion to frighten enemies and the cunning of a fox to avoid traps. If necessary to maintain power, a prince must be prepared to lie, dissemble, and even murder, while appearing to seem "merciful, faithful, humane, sincere, and religious."[9] Knowing men such as Cesare Borgia, Ferdinand of Aragon, and Pope Julius II, Machiavelli hardly lacked models for his prince even if none of them alone could measure up to his less-than-ideal savior of Italy.

Most medieval political theorists such as Dante had agreed with Aristotle that "politics is a branch of ethics" and that the state exists to promote "the common good of all."[10] In his *On Monarchy* (c. 1313), which attacked the notion of papal supremacy in secular affairs, Dante asserted that Christian princes must be people of peace and justice, who draw their power from God. In startling contrast, Machiavelli argued that because people are basically bad, their rulers may have to behave in ways totally inappropriate for private citizens. In *The Prince*, Machiavelli boldly asserted that the realities of power politics may have to take precedence over normal standards of good and evil.

Much the same assumptions about human nature are reflected in another of his influential writings, *Discourses on the First Ten Books of Livy*. While most of this work is a perceptive commentary on the thought of the prorepublican Roman historian, Machiavelli repeated his assertion that "all men are bad and ever ready to display their vicious nature."[11] Therefore, he argued for a strong type of government which combines the best elements of a "principality, an aristocracy, and a democracy," so that one form keeps watch over the other. Although Machiavelli wrote that "all forms of government are defective," he thought that for Florence a republic was preferable to a monarchy if it maintained law and order and protected the state from its enemies.[12]

Machiavelli's admiration for his native commune was also shown in his last major work, *The History of Florence*, which traced the city's history from its origins until the death of Lorenzo de' Medici in 1492. Commissioned by the university, he dedicated this history to Lorenzo's nephew, the second Medici pope, Clement VII (r. 1523–1534). Influenced by classical Roman historians such as Sallust and Tacitus, the Florentine was concerned with demonstrating the importance of "good laws and institutions," which could be established by strong and enlightened leaders. Machiavelli wanted to dramatize the contrast between an ancient model of civic excellence and the contemporary model of faction-ridden civic corruption, which left Italy open to the "barbarians" and forced it "back into slavery under such peoples."[13] Are these the words of an Italian patriot deeply disturbed by the political crises of his times? His writings permit an intriguing variety of interpretations, which only contributes to a legacy of controversy and notoriety. He died in 1527, the same year in which troops of the Emperor Charles V sacked Rome.

Francesco Guicciardini (1483–1540)

Machiavelli's sometimes pessimistic outlook and admiration for Tacitus was shared by his fellow historian and diplomatic colleague Francesco Guicciardini. From a venerable Florentine family, Guicciardini had been educated in the humanities and civil law at Florence, Ferrara, Padua, and Pisa. For a number of years he served the Medicis in Florence as a diplomat and then entered the service of the Medici popes, Leo X and Clement VII. He was a papal governor of Modena, Reggio, and then in 1521 Parma. Guicciardini knew the retired Florentine diplomat Niccolò Machiavelli well and spent time with him in 1526 before Machiavelli's death in 1527. Made lieutenant general of the papal army, he failed to prevent the disastrous sack of Rome in 1527. Between 1531 and 1534, Guicciardini functioned as governor of Bologna, where he had to suppress a popular insurrection. In 1534 Guicciardini returned to the employment of the Medici before retiring to his villa three years later.

While in retirement Guicciardini wrote a *History of Florence*, which covers the period 1378 to 1509, a celebrated *History of Italy*, which began with the death of Lorenzo de' Medici, and a fascinating collection of *Maxims and Reflections*. In the *Maxims* he argued that historians should "write so that someone born in a far distant age would have all those things as much before his eyes as did those who were present. That is indeed the aim of history."[14] In his own historical writings, Guicciardini produced models of scholarship and analysis of political and diplomatic events and motivations. He was particularly concerned about the moral choices that individuals make, as well as the role of necessity in determining events. "If you consider the matter carefully, you cannot deny that Fortune has great power in human affairs," he wrote.[15]

In commenting on Machiavelli's *Discourses*, Guicciardini came to even more cynical conclusions about the possibility of a successful republican government:

> Better to be the subject of a prince than of a republic. For a republic represses all its subjects and gives only its own citizens a share of power. A prince acts more equably towards all; the one is as much his subject as the other. Thus everyone may hope to receive benefits and employment from him.[16]

His faith in the people had been shattered by his experience of mob revolt and a lifetime in the service of the Medici. He wrote in his *Maxims*, "To speak of the people is in truth to speak of a beast; mad, mistaken, perplexed, without taste, discernment, or stability."[17] Despite his pessimism, in some respects Guicciardini's histories have still not been surpassed and remain some of the finest historical scholarship produced during the Renaissance. Their greatest impact came long after his death. For example, his *History of Italy* was not published until 1561.

Like Guicciardini's histories, his *Maxims* have also given us a great deal to pon-

der, even though we may be uncomfortable about many of his conclusions about human nature and the nature of power politics. As a historian writing during the Renaissance, he is rivalled only by Flavio Biondo (1392–1463). Biondo combined architectural details along with epigraphic, numismatic, and literary materials in a series of histories of Rome. He also wrote the influential *Italy Illustrated*, a topographical survey of the entire Italian peninsula. Biondo identified the fall of Rome as associated with the invasions of barbarians and severe internal divisions. These lessons had a tremendous impact upon the thinking and writing of both Machiavelli and Guicciardini.

Baldassare Castiglione (1478–1529)

In contrast to the often cynical tone adopted by Machiavelli and Guicciardini, the influential prose writings of Baldassare Castiglione, showing us aristocratic and courtly life, seem almost idealistic. Born near Mantua to a noble family, he was well educated in Greek and Latin at Mantua and Milan, where for a while he served Ludovico il Moro. In 1500 Castiglione entered the employ of the illustrious Gonzaga family at Mantua as a soldier-diplomat. From 1504 to 1516 he served the graceful court of Urbino before returning to Mantua. In 1524 Castiglione became a papal representative in Spain and then bishop of Avila. By then he had already written his most famous Neoplatonic work, *The Book of the Courtier* (1516).

In *The Courtier* Castiglione imaginatively reconstructed a series of discussions held at the glittering court of Urbino in 1507 about the characteristics of the perfect court lady and gentleman. Urbino had become one of the great princely centers of Renaissance artistic and intellectual life under a series of cultivated dukes and duchesses, including the remarkably refined Elisabetta Gonzaga (1471–1526). It was Duchess Elisabetta who presided over the circle of luminaries in Castiglione's renowned guide to etiquette.

According to the sensitive and thoughtful Castiglione, male courtiers were to be handsome and graceful, loyal to their princes, skilled in games and swordsmanship, conversant in Latin and Greek, well read in literature, appreciative of music, and able to draw and paint. They should be honest, but tactful, as well as "genial and discreet" with women. Castiglione also expected a great deal of court women, who were to be paragons of virtue much like Duchess Elisabetta. Ladies of the court should be able to show "a certain pleasing affability . . . a quick vivacity of spirit," and be able "to entertain graciously every man with agreeable and comely conversation."[18] Although many of the courtly men and women of the Renaissance fell far short of Castiglione's ideals, it is clear from the influence of his book that the humanists' notion of educating the "whole person" had taken deep roots in Renaissance culture.

The last section of *The Courtier* contains one of the most important discussions of Neoplatonism produced in the Renaissance. It had a lasting impact upon the aesthetic theory of the High Renaissance, most particularly the notions of artistic grace, decorum, and nonchalance extolled by Giorgio Vasari. With the encouragement of his friend Pietro Bembo (1470–1547), a poet and churchman and the featured speaker in the Neoplatonic last portion of the book, Castiglione sent his manuscript to the renowned Aldine Press in Vienna after hearing in Spain of the death of Duchess Elisabetta. It made an immediate and smashing success. An English translation appeared in 1561 and caused a similar sensation in Eliz-

abethan England. If Machiavelli and Guicciardini showed us the way many of the power brokers of the Renaissance actually behaved, Castiglione portrayed the standards which so many of the elite in the Renaissance could at least aspire to.

The Flowering of Italian Literature

The age of Machiavelli also witnessed the flowering of Italian literature. Although fascinated by the surviving ancient Greek and Latin literature, many of the humanists made important contributions to the development of literature in the Italian vernacular. Indeed, early humanists such as Petrarca and Boccaccio joined Dante in shaping Italian as a respected literary vehicle. The tradition of humanists also writing in Italian continued into the fifteenth and sixteenth centuries. For examples, Giovanni Pico della Mirandola made important contributions to the maturing of Italian poetry and Machiavelli contributed to the rise of drama. The Renaissance in Italy also featured many other distinctive voices such as Ludovico Ariosto, Pietro Aretino, Veronica Franco, and Vittoria Colonna.

LUDOVICO ARIOSTO (1474–1533)

Italian poets such as Ludovico Ariosto became well known for their romantic epics, which combined the style of classic epics by Homer and Virgil with many of the traditions of medieval romance. After a career in military and governmental service in the style of Machiavelli and Guicciardini, Ariosto retired to the lively duchy of Ferrara, where he ran the state theater of the ruling Este dynasty. In 1516 Ludovico Ariosto published his important romantic epic, *Orlando Furioso* (Mad Roland), which expounded on the legends of Charlemagne and Roland (Orlando) and their wars with the Muslims. Although intended to glorify his patrons, the Este family, *Orlando* treats many of the conventions of chivalry in a satirical fashion and takes a wry, bemused look at life.

The versatile Ariosto also wrote comedies, odes, Latin poems, satires, and sonnets. Although his theatrical works were well appreciated, his poetry was never popular in his own lifetime. Only later was his genius as a poet fully appreciated. Ariosto's *Orlando Furioso* remains one of the greatest epics produced during the Renaissance, rivalled only by the precocious Torquato Tasso's (1544–1595) *Jerusalem Delivered*. Published in 1575, Tasso's epic treats the capture of Jerusalem during the First Crusade. Writers of romances thus looked back into the medieval past and helped influence the Renaissance present. Many of those who participated in the Renaissance voyages of discovery and conquest were avid readers of popular romances, especially those far below the quality of Ariosto's and Tasso's. Later in the sixteenth century, some of those involved in Europe's struggles with the non-Christian Ottomans thought of themselves as Christian heroes comparable to Roland and Godfrey of Boulogne.

THE POET AS BLACKMAILER:
PIETRO ARETINO (1492–1556)

Pietro Aretino was one of the most colorful and controversial poets who lived during the Late Renaissance. Born to a poor family, Pietro spent much of his hardscrabble youth on the streets of his native Arezzo, where he had little formal education, although he did learn to read and write. Friends of his mother helped him gain employment with a rich Roman banker, Agostino Chigi, and Pope Leo X. However, his penchant for writing pornography and his scandalous lifestyle soon cost him his Roman patronage and led to a life of adventuring throughout Italy and France. He became known as the "The Scourge of Princes" for his merciless satires of the rich and famous. Some people paid him handsomely to write scurrilous attacks on their enemies, while others paid for his silence. Either way, the talented former street urchin prospered. Indeed, he made enough money through blackmail and his writings that he was able to live "with all the pleasure there is in life" in a fine house on the Grand Canal in Venice from 1527 until his death.

Aretino usually wrote in a superb Italian, witty, naughty, sensual, and compelling. For example, here is an excerpt from one of his letters of 1537:

> As far as I am concerned, I would rather see the snow falling from the sky than to be scorched by the so-called balmy breezes. God's truth, indeed, winter seems to me an abbot who floats downstream in comfortable ease, taking just too much pleasure in eating and sleeping and doing that other thing. But summer is a rich and noble harlot, who, drenched in cheap perfume, throws herself down disgusted and does nothing but drink and drink again.[19]

In addition to his famous *Letters* and his notorious collection of *Lewd Sonnets*, Aretino also wrote several successful comedies and one outstanding drama, the *Orazia* (Horatius), based on the ancient Roman historian Livy's story of the struggle between love and honor. They were considered some of the best plays of the sixteenth century written in Italian. Aretino also composed dialogues, satires, and, most surprisingly, some sensitive devotional literature, although he always insisted that "living well comes first." He also claimed in one of his letters that "all that I have written has been in honor of genius, whose glory was usurped and blackened by the avarice of powerful lords . . . true men should always cherish me, because I always fought for genius with my life's blood."[20]

THE HONEST COURTESAN: VERONICA FRANCO (1546–1591)

Pietro Aretino was not the only colorful Renaissance poet to emerge from difficult circumstances. Veronica Franco, who became one of the most successful courtesans in Venice, was the daughter of a prostitute. Because her soul yearned for more than material comforts, she also became a highly talented poet who wrote movingly of her often difficult life. Franco began her life in prostitution on the lower rungs of the profession, listed in a 1565 travelers' guide to Venice as available for the paltry sum of two scudi. As she grew in beauty, literacy, and social skills, Franco advanced rapidly in the sex business. By the time she reached her twenties, Veronica's clients included members of some of Venice's wealthiest families. In July 1574 she was selected by King Henri III of France (r. 1574–1589) for his entertainment while visiting Venice. Since the king was a practicing homosexual, it is most likely he was primarily attracted to Franco's gifts as a conversationalist and musician. Initially proud of her artistry as a courtesan, she wrote, "So sweet and appetizing do I become when I find myself in bed with he who loves me and welcomes me that our pleasure surpasses all delight."[21]

A number of Franco's clients and friends were men of literary ability and they recognized similar talents in her. After all, courtesan-poets were not unknown in pleasure-loving Venetian society. Earlier in the century, Gaspara Stampa (c. 1520–1554) had composed lyric poetry of high quality. In 1575 some of Franco's friends published a collection of her verses which showed what an accomplished writer she had become. Her love poetry added to her growing fame as a leading courtesan. Although she made a great deal of money as a prostitute which enabled her to live a relatively luxurious lifestyle, Franco increasingly became aware of the limitations of the life she was leading. Her growing anguish is reflected in a letter she wrote to a friend who was thinking of training her own daughter as a prostitute as Franco's mother had trained her: "I tell you, you can do nothing worse in this life . . . than to force the body into such servitude . . . to give oneself in prey to so many, to risk being despoiled, robbed or killed."[22] So that other young women in Venice would not have to take so many risks by staying in the occupation, Veronica Franco opened a house of refuge for those leaving prostitution shortly before her own death in 1591.

VITTORIA COLONNA (1490–1547)

Not all of Italy's talented Renaissance poets worked as courtesans or indulged in blackmail. Some like Vittoria Colonna lived exemplary lives of piety. A member of one of Rome's leading families, the bright, devout, and lovely Vittoria was educated in Latin and Italian. At seventeen, she was married to the Spanish marquis of Pescara. The marriage was not a happy one for long as he was frequently gone on military campaigns and often unfaithful. Widowed when she was thirty-five, she glorified him in a series of sonnets. Moving back to Rome, she was much admired in literary and church reform circles. The influential poet-churchman Pietro Bembo was among the many who admired her skill as a poet.

A Neoplatonist in the tradition of Marsilio Ficino and Giovanni Pico della Mirandola, Colonna became a close friend of the artist Michelangelo, with whom she shared a number of intellectual interests. He wrote of her:

> You have no need, my love, of any chain
> To take me vanquished and make me
>   your thrall,
> For I am sure—I very well recall—
> One glance sufficed to make me your
>   slave.[23]

Her life became more complicated by the tensions induced by the Reformation. Her brother Ascanio became involved in a bitter feud with the papacy over their salt monopoly and was exiled to Naples after an unsuccessful raid on Rome. When the Inquisition was established in Rome in 1542, a number of her friends came under suspicion and one of them, the Capuchin reformer Bernardino Ochino (1487–1564), was forced to flee to Protestant Zurich. She found spiritual consolation under the direction of Cardinal Reginald Pole and in her own increasingly religious poetry. Her Christ-centeredness is reflected in the following sonnet, "The Cross":

> When write the Savior's shoulders on the
>   tree
> And droops the holy body from the
>   weight,
> Is there then no key to fit the gate
> That heaven should not open for to see?
> What grievous pangs he bore from sheer
>   pity
> And for our sakes endured so cruel a fate
> Thus by his guiltless blood to recreate
> Our spirits laved of all impurity!
> Our surcease from war, within, wherever,
> Comes from him, the author of our peace
> He is the sun whose brilliance blinds our
>   eyes
> The father's secrets how he will release
> To whom and where and when none can
>   surmise
> Enough for us to know he cannot err.[24]

From the bawdy Aretino to the pious Vittoria Colonna, the Renaissance produced literature to satisfy all tastes.

Chronology

	Florence; Machiavelli turned out of office, imprisoned.	**1527**	Sack of Rome; death of Machiavelli.
		1540	Death of Guicciardini.
1513	Machiavelli in retirement writes *The Prince;* Swiss defeat French at Novara; death of Julius II; Leo X becomes pope.	**1542**	Roman Inquisition established.
		1546–1591	Life of Veronica Franco.
		1547	Death of Vittoria Colonna.

Further Reading

ITALY'S TIME OF TROUBLES

Frederic Baumgartner, *Louis XII* (1994).

Sarah Bradford, *Cesare Borgia, His Life and Times* (1976).

Andre Chastel, *The Fall of Rome, 1527* (1983).

Eric Cochrane, *Florence in the Forgotten Centuries* (1973).

Garrett Mattingly, *Renaissance Diplomacy* (1955).

Vincent Pitts, *The Man Who Sacked Rome: Charles de Bourbon, Constable of France* (1994).

Lorrenzo Polizotto, *The Elect Nation: The Savonarolan Movement in Florence, 1495–1545* (1995).

Robert Ridolfi, *The Life of Girolamo Savonarola,* tr. by Cecil Grayson (1959).

J. N. Stephens, *The Fall of the Florentine Republic, 1512–1530* (1983).

Donald Weinstein, *Savonarola and Florence* (1970).

T. C. Price Zimmerman, *Paolo Giovo: The Historian and the Crisis of Sixteenth-Century Italy* (1995). Important study of a bishop-historian.

MACHIAVELLI

Peter Bonadella, *Machiavelli and the Art of Renaissance History* (1973).

Sebastian de Grazia, *Machiavelli in Hell* (1989). A striking, imaginative biography.

Felix Gilbert, *Machiavelli and Guicciardini* (1965).

Mark Hulliung, *Citizen Machiavelli* (1983).

Victoria Kahn, *Machiavellian Rhetoric: From the Counter Reformation to Milton* (1994).

J. G. A. Pocock, *The Machiavellian Moment: Florentine Political Thought and the Atlantic Republican Tradition* (1975).

Silvia Ruffo-Fiori, *Niccolo Machiavelli* (1982).

ITALIAN RENAISSANCE LITERATURE

David Quint, *Origin and Originality in Renaissance Literature* (1984).

Richard Waswo, *Language and Meaning in the Renaissance* (1987).

Katharina Wilson, ed., *Women Writers of the Renaissance and Reformation* (1987). An important collection of writings by women authors.

INDIVIDUAL AUTHORS

Albert Ascoli, *Ariosto's Bitter Enemy: Crisis and Evasion in the Italian Renaissance* (1987).

Fiora Bassanese, *Gaspara Stampa* (1982).

Maud Jerrold, *Vittoria Colonna,* rpr. (1969).

Mark Phillips, *Francesco Guicciardini: The Historian's Craft* (1977).

Margaret Rosenthal, *The Honest Courtesan, Veronica Franco* (1992).

Notes

1. Cited in Donald Weinstein, *Savonarola and Florence* (Princeton, N.J.: Princeton University Press, 1970), pp. 69–70.
2. Ibid.
3. See Kenneth Bartlett, ed., *The Civilization of the Italian Renaissance: A Sourcebook* (Lexington, Mass.: D. C. Heath, 1992), pp. 331–336.
4. Cited in Benjamin Kohl and Alison Andrews

Smith, eds., *Major Problems in the History of the Italian Renaissance* (Lexington, Mass.: D. C. Heath, 1995), p. 418.

5. Cited in Sebastian da Graza, *Machiavelli in Hell* (Princeton, N.J.: Princeton University Press, 1989), p. 63.
6. Ibid., p. 303.
7. Cited in J. R. Hale, *Machiavelli and Renaissance Italy* (New York: Collier, 1963), p. 90.
8. Machiavelli, *The Prince* (New York: Norton, 1977), tr. and ed. by Robert Adams, p. 50.
9. Ibid.
10. Cited in Nels Bailkey, ed., *Readings in Ancient History: Thought and Experience from Gilgamesh to St. Augustine,* 4th ed. (Lexington, Mass.: D. C. Heath, 1992), p. 259.
11. Peter Bondanella and Mark Musa, eds., *The Portable Machiavelli* (New York: Penguin, 1979), p. 179.
12. Ibid.
13. Ibid., p. 559.
14. Cited in Bartlett, *Italian Renaissance,* p. 392.
15. Ibid., p. 384.
16. Ibid., p. 390.
17. Cited in Lewis Spitz, *The Renaissance and Reformation Movements* (Chicago: Rand McNally, 1971), p. 247.
18. Baldesar Castiglione, *The Book of the Courtier,* tr. by George Bull (Baltimore, Md.: Penguin, 1967), p. 212.
19. Cited in Bartlett, *Italian Renaissance,* p. 348.
20. Ibid., p. 343.
21. Cited in Bonnie Anderson and Judith Zinsser, *A History of Their Own: Women in Europe from Prehistory to the Present,* 2 vols. (New York: Harper and Row, 1988), vol. 2, p. 71.
22. Ibid., p. 77.
23. Cited in Roland Bainton, *Women of the Reformation in Germany and Italy* (Minneapolis: Augsburg Publishing House, 1971), p. 208.
24. Cited in Ibid., p. 208. Reprinted from *Women of the Reformation in Germany and Italy* by Roland Bainton, copyright © 1971 Augsburg Publishing House. Used by permission of Augsburg Fortress.

9

THE NORTHERN MONARCHIES AND THEIR EXPANSION

Although the north of Europe was not as economically advanced or as urbanized as Italy at the beginning of the fourteenth century, it too participated in and made valuable contributions to the Renaissance. Oil painting, for example, was first developed in the Low Countries and spread to Italy in the fifteenth century. Italian humanists and artists came north as diplomatic envoys, secretaries, and university lecturers. Northerners went to Italy as university students and admirers of Italian culture. The Nuremberg artist Albrecht Dürer was typical of many northern artists who found it necessary to travel to Italy to learn from the work of the Italian masters. Business people went in both directions and helped spread Renaissance humanist ideas throughout Europe. As the north of Europe became wealthier and more urban, it too immersed itself in Renaissance culture.

The Economic Background

Northern Europe was a land of small farming villages, hundreds of small towns, a few large cities, and various territorial states. As in Italy, most people still worked the land, but commercial life grew apace during the fifteenth and sixteenth centuries. Northern cities grew in size, primarily along water trade routes in the Low Countries, on the Baltic coast, and along the Rhine and Danube rivers. Great capitalist families such as the Fuggers and Welsers of Augsburg or the Kresses and Tuchers of Nuremberg emulated the methods of their colleagues in Italy and amassed considerable fortunes. South German towns banded together in the Swabian League to protect their trade caravans from robber knights. Elsewhere, individual entrepreneurs like Jacques Coeur (1395–1456) in France made and lost great sums loaning money to the French king and supplying eastern luxury goods to the court. Coeur had also been arrested for coin clipping and later for poisoning a royal mistress and intriguing with the Ottomans.

Trade in the Baltic and North Sea regions was facilitated by a loose federation of about 200 far-flung towns known as the Hanseatic League, whose members included Bremen, Breslau, Bruges, Brunswick, Cologne, Cracow (Krakow), Danzig, Deventer, Dortmund, Hamburg, Königsberg, London, Lüneberg, Magdeburg, Münster, Novgorod, Osnabrück, Reval, Riga, Stockholm, Thorn, and Visby. The German town of Lübeck served as its capital because of its strategic location on the Holstein isthmus that connected the North and Baltic seas. The league concentrated on trade in consumer goods of western and northern Europe for the furs, timbers, ores, and grains of northeastern Europe and Russia.

Like Italy, the north suffered the ravages of the Black Death in the fourteenth century and saw its population gradually increase back to pre-plague levels by the end of the sixteenth century. Europe north of the Alps also endured a long depression throughout much of the fifteenth century. As its population grew and trade increased,

Renaissance Europe.

the north and center of Europe was poised to make its own substantial contributions to the movements known as the Renaissance and the Reformation. However, those movements took place against a background of increasing social and religious tensions, political instability, and ferocious struggles for power between emerging national monarchies.

The Political World

In contrast to the small states of the Italian world, the drama of the Renaissance in the north was acted out against a political background of large monarchies that had emerged from the decentralized, highly feudalized states of the Middle Ages. Northern monarchs were developing greater control over their mighty subjects by relying more on mercenary armies and less on feudal levies. Royal bureaucracies and court systems had also expanded. As national monarchies became stronger, they sought to extend their influence and often their borders as well. This contributed to the fall of the duchy of Burgundy, which could not compete with the rising power of the French monarchy.

THE DISAPPEARANCE OF BURGUNDY

The duchy of Burgundy was made up of the free county of Burgundy (Franche–Comté), Luxembourg, upper Alsace, and much of the Netherlands. Although scattered, Burgundy had rich farm land, prosperous cities such as Bruges, and a strategic location. During the half-century following the Hundred Years' War, the dukes of Burgundy were among the richest and most powerful princes in Europe. Philip the Good (r. 1419–1467) was a leading patron of the arts. Talented artists flocked to his court, including Guillaume

Dufay (1400–1475), the leading composer of the fifteenth-century.

Philip's son, Charles the Bold (r. 1467–1477), sought to realize his father's dream of an independent middle kingdom between France and the Holy Roman Empire. Toward that end, he conquered the duchy of Lorraine in 1475 and secured claims to Guelders and Zutphen in the Netherlands. However, King Louis XI of France soon organized a coalition with Rhineland and Swiss towns against the Burgundians. During the fall of 1476, the Burgundians were defeated in a series of battles against the French and their allies. Finally, in January 1477, at the battle of Nancy, Charles the Bold was killed. Since he had no male heir, his French territories reverted to the French. Only the marriage of his daughter to Maximilian of Habsburg, son of Emperor Frederick III, prevented Franche-Comté and Flanders from also being gobbled up by France. Power politics in the Renaissance could be a very dangerous game.

FRANCE UNDER FRANÇOIS I (r. 1515–1547)

The French kingdom emerged from the Hundred Years' War as one of the strongest monarchies in Europe and twice launched major invasions of Italy in the late fifteenth century. With the absorption of much of Burgundy in 1477, France was well on its way to becoming the largest kingdom in Europe with a population between 12 and 15 million persons. Although an unattractive personality, Louis XI (r. 1461–1483), known as "the spider king," succeeded not only in taking large sections of Burgundy, but he also reduced the power of the French nobility. Ruthless, energetic, and able, he laid many of the foundations for making France a successful Renaissance monarchy. His son, Charles VIII (r. 1483–1498), was only thirteen when Louis XI died. Weak in mind and body, his capable older sister, Anne of Beaujeau, took control of the government for seven years as regent. When barely literate Charles did finally take the reins of power from his sister, his major accomplishment was the ill-fated invasion of Italy in 1494.

With his premature death at age twenty-eight, the French throne passed to his cousin and rival, Louis of Orléans. Despite the failure of his Italian invasion, Louis XII managed to enact a number of reforms inside France. He saw himself as a benevolent "father of his people" and pursued state-building policies which increased the power of the crown at the expense of the nobility. Since Louis died without a son, the throne passed to his son-in-law François, duke of Angoulême, who launched an even more grandiose era of French history in 1515. He was an energetic young prince, who loved sensual pleasures, the hunt, and the joust. Determined to drive the Swiss out of Milan, François I made an alliance with the Venetians and crushed the Swiss at the Battle of Marignano in September of 1515. Milan was returned to French control, although François gave up all claims to Naples to avoid a continuation of the Italian wars and a confrontation with the Holy Roman Emperor Maximilian a year later.

In addition to his aggressive efforts in foreign policy, the king was also an avid builder of well-designed palaces and a great patron of the arts. King François not only served as Leonardo da Vinci's last patron, he also supported French men and women of letters. His sister, Marguerite, queen of Navarre, was the author of the *Heptameron* and an important leader of humanists. Guillaume Budé (1468–1540), a leading French humanist and legal scholar, was made secretary to the king and master of the rapidly growing royal library. Trained as a lawyer, Budé provided useful studies of Roman law and coinage. His most important work, *Commentaries on the Greek Language*, was

published in 1529. He also persuaded the king to establish the College of France.

François I ruled France with a strong hand, even reducing the power of the French church early in his reign. Although sympathetic to some of the religious reformers, he stayed loyal to the Roman Catholic church and strengthened his ties with the papacy. In foreign policy, the king continued his dynasty's rivalry with England and the Habsburgs. A shrewd pragmatist, he was willing to make alliances even with the feared and reviled Ottomans to avoid being boxed in by his rivals in the west. For most Christian rulers of Europe, to ally themselves with an Islamic state even for commercial and political reasons, was equivalent to a pact with the devil. François was quite likely to put practical economic and dynastic considerations ahead of ethnic and religious prejudices.

Jean Clouet, *François I of France*. Louvre, Paris, France. Giraudon/Art Resource.

ENGLAND UNDER THE EARLY TUDORS

Although defeated by France in the Hundred Years' War and then racked by the civil war known as the War of the Roses, England made a considerable comeback during the reign of Henry VII (1485–1509). A determined monarch with a clear focus, Henry Tudor used the Court of Star Chamber to attack the feudal privileges of the nobility. Levying stiff fines and confiscating the property of recalcitrant nobles, the frugal Henry worked to build up the crown revenues. He encouraged foreign commerce and demanded from foreign merchants who enjoyed privileges in England reciprocal privileges for English merchants. Henry also saw to it that a heavy duty was placed on the export of raw wool in order to promote the English manufacture and export of woolen textiles. The Navigation Act of 1485 gave further encouragement to the development of the English merchant fleet. The act stipulated that wines from Bordeaux in France must be carried in English ships with English, Welsh, or Irish crews.

King Henry VII worked well with Parliament, which had gained the right to vote on personal property taxes, customs, and levies for war. Henry also made favorable marriages with the royal house of Spain and Scotland. His oldest son, Arthur, was married to Catherine of Aragon (1485–1536), the daughter of Queen Isabella of Castile and King Ferdinand of Aragon. In 1499, Henry arranged to have his daughter Margaret (1489–1541) marry King James VI (r. 1488–1513) of Scotland. Although this marriage led to only a temporary improvement in Anglo-Scottish relations, it did lay the foundations for the eventual union of the English and Scottish crowns.

Henry VII's son, the talented and aggressive Henry VIII (r. 1509–1547), inherited a relatively stable and prosperous kingdom, whose international status was on the rise. Henry's older brother Arthur had died of consumption in 1502. Henry VII then arranged for his second son, Henry, to marry Arthur's widow. As king, Henry VIII's extravagance and military buildup soon dissipated much of that hard-won wealth. Eager for military glory, young Henry VIII in 1511 joined his father-in-law, Ferdinand of Spain, and Pope Julius II in the Holy League to drive the French out of Italy. In 1512 he allied with Spain and the Holy Roman Emperor Maximilian I against the French. Leading an English army into France, Henry VIII won the Battle of Spurs and seized Tournai. Having been forsaken by his allies, the English king made peace in 1514 with France, who agreed to pay an annual subsidy.

The new French king, François I, renewed French aggression in Italy, taking rich Milan in 1515 as we have seen. England supported Spain in the ensuing struggles between the Habsburgs and the Valois. In 1522, England went to war with France. English campaigns in France in 1522 and 1523 accomplished little but proved exceedingly costly. Worried about the power of Charles V, Henry VIII made peace with François I in 1526. His new pro-French policy proved unpopular, and the king was unable to secure the finances from Parliament necessary to launch an attack on Charles V. By the end of the decade, the king had become enmeshed in domestic affairs, including his struggles to set aside Catherine of Aragon and secure a male heir. That led to the crisis of the English Reformation.

SPAIN UNDER ISABELLA AND FERDINAND

During much of the Middle Ages, the Iberian peninsula had been under Muslim control. As the Christians gradually pushed the Muslims into the single kingdom of Granada in the south, they had forged a number of separate kingdoms. In 1469 the royal houses of two of the largest Spanish kingdoms were brought together by the marriage of Isabella of Castile (1451–1504) with Ferdinand of Aragon (1452–1516). Both were highly intelligent, energetic, and determined to strengthen royal power. They took steps shortly after their accession to curb the powers of the feudal magnates. Instead of appointing nobles to administrative offices, Isabella and Ferdinand began to rely more on clerics and lawyers. The queen had

her husband appointed to head three prominent Castilian military orders. This added to his prestige in Castile and brought in badly needed revenues.

When the Parliament (*Cortes*) of Castile was summoned, the noble members were frequently not invited to attend and that body became increasingly subservient to the royal couple's wishes. The *Cortes* of Aragon, dominated by the nobility, was frequently ignored. Isabella and Ferdinand made greater use of separate administrative coun-

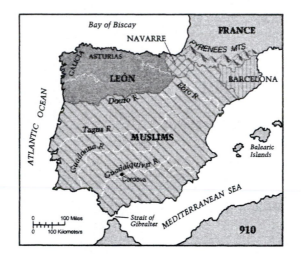

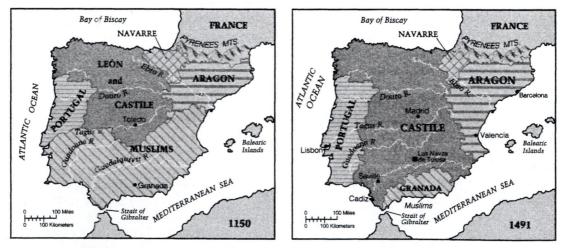

Unification of Spain.

cils for Castile and Aragon, which were controlled by crown appointed officials, most of them jurists.

To further increase the power of the crown and promote religious uniformity, the monarchs petitioned Pope Sixtus IV to establish the Holy Office of the Inquisition in 1478 for Castile. Five years later, it was extended into Aragon. The Inquisition had been used in the Middle Ages as a tribunal to examine the faith and morals of suspected heretics. The Spanish lands had large populations of Muslims and Jews. Isabella was strongly pressured by her advisors to eliminate religious diversity as other European monarchies had tried to do from time to time. Jews were required to wear distinctive insignia and were forbidden to live in certain areas. In March of 1492, a royal edict ordered all Jews to convert to Christianity or leave. Thousands, many of them skilled artisans and professionals, emigrated. The Jews who converted and remained in Spain were supervised closely by the Inquisition.

Even before the expulsion of the Jews, Isabella and Ferdinand had launched a crusade against the last Muslim stronghold, the kingdom of Granada. Isabella herself donned armor and participated in some of the campaigns against the Muslims. By 1490 the Christians had virtually surrounded the city of Granada. In January of 1492, the Muslim king surrendered the keys of the city to Isabella and Ferdinand. The terms of the surrender permitted Granada to maintain its Islamic faith, but soon overzealous church officials instigated a policy of forced conversion. Many Muslims left, but those who converted and remained were often treated with great suspicion and hostility, just as they were in most parts of Europe. Tragically, Spain was not the only European monarchy to expel whole populations. England, France, and parts of the Holy Roman Empire also engaged in expulsions. In those cases, the victims were almost exclusively Jews.

Queen Isabella was so pleased with her victory over the Muslims and her expulsions of religious minorities that she gave the Genoese mariner Christopher Columbus permission to sail and some help toward purchasing three small ships for his voyage of discovery and conquest. Spain's conquests in the Americas brought in enormous wealth. The Machiavellian Ferdinand also extended Spanish influence from Sicily and Naples into other parts of Italy and added the kingdom of Navarre to the Spanish crown.

Isabella sought to make Spain more of a Christian intellectual center. She assembled a large royal library of spiritual and secular books and commissioned the first Castilian grammar. The female scholar Beatriz de Galindo (1473–1535) was brought from Italy to teach the queen Latin. Isabella personally supervised the education of her children, who like the Tudor children in England were well trained in foreign languages.

THE HOLY ROMAN EMPIRE

The Holy Roman Empire was the largest state in Europe, encompassing most of central Europe. Its roughly fifteen million inhabitants spoke a variety of languages and dialects, though various forms of German predominated. In contrast to the hereditary monarchs of England, France, and Spain, the Holy Roman emperors were formally elected by a powerful group of seven electors. The electoral process had become fixed in 1356 when the Emperor Charles IV of Luxembourg-Bohemia (r. 1347–1378) issued a written constitution for the empire known as the Golden Bull. By the terms of the Golden Bull, the archbishops of Mainz, Trier, and Cologne, the king of Bohemia, the duke of Saxony, the margrave of Brandenburg, and the count palatine of the Rhine were to serve as imperial electors and make up the first house of the Imperial Parliament (Diet).

The electoral princes were virtually sovereign in their own lands and could mint their own coins, among other privileges. These privileges were reconfirmed in Frankfurt on the Main River at the election of each new emperor. Because the empire was a complete patriarchy, only males could be elected as emperor or serve as one of the seven electors. The second house of the Imperial Diet was made up of the nonelectoral princes. The third house was made up of representatives from the towns, who in 1489 finally got a vote in imperial affairs. Although Holy Roman emperors had a great deal of prestige as descendants of such legendary monarchs as Charlemagne and Otto I, they were, in fact, dependent on their mighty subjects for special revenues and troops. There was no imperial tax or standing army.

In reality the Holy Roman Empire was a loose confederation of over 300 virtually autonomous principalities and towns. During the Renaissance, the Austrian house of Habsburg succeeded in getting its sons elected as Holy Roman emperors. Since 1273 nearly every emperor was a Habsburg, a dynasty that made their influence felt throughout Europe by their extraordinary success in marrying well. The Habsburgs followed the old motto: "Others may fight and die, thou happy Austria marry!" Among the many able Habsburg dynasts, few were as successful in playing the marriage game as Maximilian I (r. 1493–1519), "an odd little man, whose chin stuck out like a shelf."[1]

In 1491 Emperor Maximilian began negotiating a double marriage treaty with Isabella and Ferdinand of Spain. His daughter, Margaret, married the Spanish heir,

Juan, while his son, Philip, married Juan's unstable sister, Juana. Although Juan died shortly thereafter, Philip and Juana (later called the Mad) produced a son, Charles, who inherited Spain, Austria, and the inside track on his grandfather's imperial title. A second grandson, Ferdinand, was engaged to King Vladislav of Hungary's daughter Anna, thus adding Habsburg claims to both Hungary and Bohemia.

As Holy Roman emperor, Maximilian attempted to strengthen the power of the crown, a move strongly resisted by the German princes. He also opposed French advances in Italy and warded off French attempts to seize the Low Countries. The Swiss Confederation won its independence from imperial control in 1499 and Maximilian also failed to mount a crusade against the Ottoman Turks. He was more successful as a patron of the arts, supporting such well-respected artists as Albrecht Dürer and Hans Burgkmair and such humanists as Johann Cuspinian and Conrad Peutinger. His own writings were mostly autobiographical in nature, such as his *Theuerdank*, which tells of his journey to claim Mary of Burgundy as his first wife. Few of his predecessors had written much more than their names on royal documents, although Frederick II (r. 1211–1250) did write a handbook on falconry. His political achievements would be overshadowed by the reign of his grandson Charles in the empire and Spain.

SCANDINAVIA AND MARGARET OF DENMARK

The Scandinavian countries of Denmark, Norway, and Sweden were not as populous as the monarchies to the south, but they did achieve a degree of political power during the reign of Margaret of Denmark (1353–1412). Margaret was one of the two surviving daughters of Waldemar IV (1340–

1375), the aggressive Danish king. She was betrothed at age seven to King Haakon of Norway as part of an alliance. When Margaret was seventeen, she had a son, Olaf (1370–1387). After her father's death in 1375, the leading nobles chose her as regent for her son because they were impressed with her intelligence, commanding presence, and the need for stability. The choice was also approved by the Hanseatic League, the powerful trading association that linked 200 towns throughout the Baltic and North Sea regions and the north of Germany. League officials figured the unification of the Norwegian and Danish thrones would be good for business and they were right.

Queen Margaret proved an able and assertive ruler; when her husband and then her son died, both the Danish and Norwegian kingdoms named her their sovereign for life. In 1389 she added Sweden to her realm and created the Union of Kalmar, which provided for separate institutions in all three kingdoms but unified them under Margaret's authority. Styled "the lady king" by her subjects, Margaret succeeded in curbing the power of her fractious nobility and ushering in an era of relative peace and prosperity. Although the Union of Kalmar never functioned as well under her successors, it did last until 1523 and gave the rugged Scandinavian lands a degree of stability and prosperity.

EASTERN EUROPE

Eastern Europe was dominated by the threat of the Mongols, followed by that of the Ottomans. In the second half of the fifteenth century, Hungary was ruled by the able Matthias I Corvinus (r. 1458–1490). Matthias broke the power of the feudal magnates, held the Ottomans at bay, and supported humanism and the arts. His capital at Buda became one of the most brilliant courts in Europe outside of Italy. Much of his work was undone by his weak successor, Vladislav II of Bohemia, who resided in Prague.

The Polish monarchy also struggled in the fifteenth century despite the considerable talents of King Casimir IV (r. 1447–1492). Casimir did succeed in gaining a port on the Baltic and reducing some of the power of the feudal barons. Wars with both the Russians and the Ottomans, however, led to a breakdown of royal authority. The noble-dominated national diet became the supreme legislative organ of government and had a hard time coming up with sensible policies. Incessant wrangling among the elite resulted in continued misery for the Polish peasantry, who were bound to the soil by an act of the Polish Diet in 1511. This was at a time when serfdom had almost completely vanished in the West.

RUSSIA

As for Poland's neighbors to the east, the Grand Princes of Moscow had been forced to pay heavy tribute to the descendants of Genghis Khan (1160–1227) until 1480 when Ivan III, the Great (1462–1505), threw off the Mongol yoke and abolished tribute. Ivan then annexed Novgorod in the north and parts of Poland and Lithuania. Preferring diplomacy and intrigue to war, the tall and awe-inspiring Ivan achieved a great deal with a minimum of bloodshed. Not only did he ward off the pretensions of his four brothers, Ivan also married his son to the niece of the last Byzantine emperor. This marriage allowed him to claim the vacant Byzantine throne for his dynasty. Ivan also reduced the powers of his nobility and strengthened the institutions of his government. Despite the improved organization and expansion of the Muscovite state, the Russians were

Mongol and Ottoman Invasions.

still not strong enough to become major players in the ruthless world of European power politics.

The Mongol position as the great eastern threat was replaced by the Ottomans, who had conquered most of the Balkan peninsula late in the fourteenth century. In 1453, Mehmed the Conqueror took Constantinople, the last bastion of the old Roman Empire in the East and one of the largest cities in the world. After that the Islamic Ottomans conquered Greece, then Serbia, Bosnia, Herzegovina, and Albania. Venice fought the Ottomans for control of the Adriatic Sea and its trade empire. Sultan Selim I (r. 1512–1520) overran Syria, Palestine, and Egypt. In full control of the eastern Mediterranean, the powerful Ottomans were ready and able to exert renewed pressure on the quarreling monarchies of western Europe, which had been unable to achieve sufficient cooperation to mount a successful crusade against them.

The Expansion of Europe

The expanding Ottoman Empire also threatened the growth of European commerce. By the end of the fifteenth century, the Ottomans controlled much of the luxury and spice trade from Asia. Added to the duties imposed by the Ottomans upon Arab overland traders was the profit demanded by the Venetians, who in turn sold their cargoes from the eastern Mediterranean to northern merchants in Venice. Price markups of as much as 2,000 percent were not unusual for valued spices such as pepper and nutmeg. Some spices were literally worth more than their weight in silver. All this led to a feverish desire to bypass the Mediterranean and reach the markets of Asia directly by sea.

HENRY THE NAVIGATOR
AND PORTUGUESE EXPLORATION

Although small in size and population, Portugal took the lead in the European race to the orient. After fighting the Moors in North Africa, Prince Henry the Navigator (1394–1460), the third son of the king of Portugal, became obsessed with finding a new route around Africa to Asia. He established a school for mariners at Sagres Castle, near the southwest tip of Portugal. From there Henry sent out annual expeditions southward along the west African coast. His mariners returned with observations about the winds, currents, peoples, geography, and astronomical readings they had made on their voyages. This information was evaluated by Henry's staff and passed on to succeeding generations of cartographers, navigators, and ocean pilots. Those who studied at Henry's school included Vasco da Gama and Ferdinand Magellan. Henry's mariners also benefited from better ships, the invention of the magnetic compass, and the ability to sail against the wind (tacking).

By the time of Prince Henry's death in 1460, his mariners had reached the westernmost bulge of West Africa at Cape Verde. In 1488 Bartholomew Dias rounded the southern tip of Africa, soon to be christened the Cape of Good Hope by the jubilant Portuguese king. Using information from Dias's voyage, thirty-seven-year-old Vasco da Gama succeeded in 1498 in reaching Calcutta, on the west coast of India, with a fleet of four ships. Da Gama's fleet was out of sight of land for almost ninety days, nearly three times as long as Columbus on his first voyage. Although only two ships returned to Lisbon with a handful of very sick mariners, da Gama's return cargo of pepper and gems was sold for nearly sixty times the cost of the expedition.

Six months after da Gama's return to

Lisbon, Pedro Alvarez Cabral set sail for India with a fleet of thirteen heavily armed ships and more than 1,200 soldiers and sailors. Despite being blown by a hurricane so far to the west that they touched the eastern bulge of South America (Brazil), Cabral's fleet made it to India in six months, less than a third of the time it had taken da Gama. However, his encounters with Arab warships and Indian warriors were even bloodier than da Gama's. Cabral's voyage was considered a great success by the Portuguese because he had returned with rich cargoes of spices, drugs, woods, and jewels.

Arab and Muslim merchants were alarmed at the European incursion into their trading empire. In February 1509, a Portuguese fleet of 20 vessels defeated a combined Egyptian-Turkish-Arab fleet of 100 vessels off the island of Diu on the northwest coast of India. The Portuguese had boldly struck into the center of the enemy fleet and nullified the Muslim advantage in numbers. Most of the Muslim fleet was destroyed and the Europeans were never seriously challenged on the sea road to India

again. European ships had become three-masted and larger than ever before (400 to 1000 tons), and were better armed than most of their opponents by the beginning of the sixteenth century. Advances in ship rigging, naval architecture and construction, and bronze cannons would give Europeans a large advantage over the rest of the world for the remainder of the Renaissance.

CHRISTOPHER COLUMBUS (1451–1506)

The initial financial success of the Portuguese in opening trade with India, and by 1513 with a small part of China through the mouth of the Canton River, led other European monarchs to become interested in sponsoring their own voyages of discovery. In 1492 Queen Isabella of Castile helped the mariner Christopher Columbus (Colon) obtain three small ships and ninety men for his own voyage of discovery. The son of a wool worker in the port city of Genoa, Columbus had left weaving to become an itinerant mariner, working on ships that plied the Mediterranean and the coast of West Africa. After he was shipwrecked off the coast of Lagos, Portugal when he was twenty-five, he found his way to Lisbon, where one of his brothers had a map-making business. Columbus then married Dona Filipa de Perestrelo, the daughter of a prominent ship owner. This fortunate marriage helped make his career by providing him with valuable connections and a dowry.

After years of sailing, interviews with veteran navigators, and an intensive study of the existing travel and geographical literature, Columbus became convinced that Asia was far closer than most people believed and that it could be reached by sailing due west. Influenced as well by his immersion in mystical literature, the mariner came to believe that he was a special man of destiny who had been touched by God. Af-

Sixteenth-century sailing ship. Woodcut. Giraudon/Art Resource.

ter failing to interest the Portuguese king in his plans in 1484, Columbus next approached the rulers of Castile and Aragon with his "small world theory." His proposals were studied seriously, but as Isabella and Ferdinand were preoccupied by their war with the Muslims of Granada, they avoided making a financial commitment. The kings of France and England also turned him down. Finally, in the throes of exultation after the fall of Granada, Queen Isabella of Castile agreed to sponsor his voyage, partly as an act of piety. Columbus's religious zeal had made a favorable impression upon the queen.

On August 3, 1492, Columbus's small fleet of three caravels set sail from Palos. Thirty-three days later he made landfall somewhere in the Bahamas. He encountered a gentle people with "handsome bodies and good faces," whom he attempted to convert to Christianity. After exploring some of the coastline of Cuba and Haiti, Columbus established a small settlement with thirty-nine of his crew and sailed back to Spain. There he was given a warm welcome, but the Portuguese asserted that what Columbus had found was theirs because of their earlier efforts at exploration. Queen Isabella appealed to Pope Alexander VI. The worldly Borgia pope issued several papal bulls that confirmed that whatever discoveries Columbus had made belonged to the crown of Castile and drew an imaginary line of demarcation between the competing claims, which became the basis of later negotiations between Spain and Portugal.

The triumphant Columbus returned to the "Indies" with a fleet of seventeen ships and over 1,500 sailors, soldiers, churchmen, and officials. Even some Spanish gentlemen were eager to make their fortunes and serve God in the New World. On November 27, 1493, they reached Haiti only to discover that the European outpost had been de-

Francesco Salviati, *Portrait of Christopher Columbus*. Palazzo Comunale. Alinari / Art Resource.

stroyed by disease and by attacks from some of the native peoples, who had grown hostile in response to the violence of the Spanish and their demands for gold. A second settlement was established while Admiral Columbus went off on a search for the Asian mainland. Although Columbus never did find Asia, he did explore many of the West Indian islands. In 1498 Columbus made his third voyage of discovery to find his colony on Haiti in turmoil. He was arrested by the royal commissioner and returned to Spain in chains with his two brothers. Queen Isabella freed him and allowed him to make a fourth voyage to the New World in 1502. He spent two years along the coast of Central America trying desperately to find a route to the Asian mainland.

Having survived mutinies, wars with the natives, and shipwreck, a disappointed Christopher Columbus returned to Spain, where he died at Valladolid a year and a half later. Among his mixed legacy was the beginnings of the slave trade. Columbus had brought back several Amerindians with him after his first voyage to impress the Spanish court. He later thought to use the native population as slave laborers in the newly discovered territories. His royal patron Queen Isabella disagreed and soon forbade the sale of native inhabitants and declared them to be direct subjects of the crown of Castile. She ordered her colonial governors to protect and Christianize the "Indians." The queen also allowed the Spaniards the right to collect tributes from the indigenous people and use them as laborers. Estate holders, chartered by the crown, were to care for the Amerindians' spiritual and physical needs. However, even this paternalistic policy proved impossible to enforce on settlers over 3,000 miles from Spain, especially after the queen's death in 1504. The actual treatment of the Native Americans by most of the Spanish colonizers was often extremely brutal, even after their replacement as plantation workers by imported slaves from Africa.

Although Columbus was not the first European to come to the Americas, little had come from the early eleventh-century voyages to Greenland and North America by the Norse led by Eric the Red and Leif Ericson. Other Europeans followed in Columbus's wake, bringing widescale plagues and destruction to the Native Americans and forever changing the world. Among the Renaissance European explorers was the Florentine geographer and cartographer Amerigo Vespucci (1451–1512), who sailed to the New World in 1497, 1499, 1501, and 1503 for Spain. Vespucci realized that what Columbus had found was distinct from Asia. The cartographer Martin Waldseemüller used Vespucci's writings in drawing his influential map of 1507, which

named the New World "America" in honor of the Florentine.

OTHER EUROPEAN EXPLORERS

In 1497 and 1498, Giovanni Caboto (John Cabot) of Venice, chartered by King Henry VII of England, explored the coastline of North America from Labrador to Maryland. These voyages became the basis for England's claim to North America, as European monarchies greedily vied with each other to lay claim to the lands long since settled by Native Americans. In 1513 Vasco Nunez de Balboa crossed the Isthmus of Panama and gazed upon the Pacific Ocean. In September 1519 the brave but arrogant Portuguese captain Ferdinand Magellan (c. 1480–1521) headed west with five ships in the service of Spain. Sailing through the straits that now bear his name at the tip of South America, Magellan's surviving ships and crew endured endless hardships in crossing the Pacific Ocean. They reached the island of Guam in March 1521 and later the Philippines. Unwisely intervening militarily in a local civil war, Magellan was killed, but one of his ships managed to circumnavigate the globe and returned to Seville with eighteen surviving crew members.

THE SPANISH CONQUEST OF THE AMERICAS: CORTÉS

In the same year that Magellan's crew began its monumental journey around the world, the Spanish adventurer Hernan Cortés (1485–1547) left Cuba with 530 armed men and one woman, fourteen pieces of artillery, sixteen horses, and eleven ships for the eastern coast of Mexico. Cortés came from modest origins in Medellin, Castile, and had sailed to Santo Domingo in 1504 to seek his fortune after working for a number of years

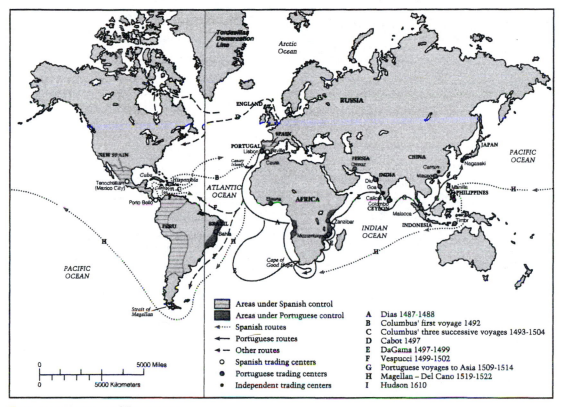

European Voyages of Discovery.

as a notary. He joined Diego Velázquez in the conquest of Cuba and then worked as his secretary when Velázquez was appointed governor. Given land in Cuba, Cortés left the employ of the governor while planning for even better things to come. He was determined to conquer the vast Aztec (Mexica) Empire, which sprawled over 250,000 square miles. After fighting several battles, he established a base in the summer of 1519 at what became the important port of Vera Cruz on the eastern coast. Cortés then journeyed inland toward the heart of the Aztec Empire in central Mexico, fighting several battles along the way and attempting to force Christianity upon the native peoples. Determined "to conquer this land or die," the Castilians were appalled by the ritual human sacrifices commonly practiced in Mexico. They tore down skull racks and toppled statues of gods and replaced them with altars and images of the Virgin Mary.

Cortés was militarily successful against superior numbers of Amerindians because his opponents usually fought to wound not kill. In addition, the artillery, gunpowder and steel weapons, horses, and ruthlessness of the Castilians gave them a great advantage over the tribes of Mexico, who fought largely with obsidian edged weapons and bows and arrows. They had never seen horses, guns, or even beards before and some thought Cortés was a returning god or at the least a great human lord. Cortés's efforts at diplomacy and conversion were greatly aided by a war captive, called Marina, who spoke one of the Aztec dialects. She also became his mistress and was completely loyal to him.

His force of 300 Castilians was joined by over a thousand Tlaxcalans and other former subjects of the Aztecs who had grown tired of paying tribute. Cortés made a peaceful entry into the huge island city of Tenochtitlán, which he described as the most beautiful city on earth. It was also one of the largest, with a population of over 200,000 people. Tenochtitlán was filled with elaborate palace complexes and several massive pyramids. Like the Mayans before them, the Aztecs were also accomplished architects, engineers, mathematicians, and astronomers.

Although he had been welcomed into Tenochtitlán as was the custom of a region that stressed hospitality to all visitors no matter how threatening, Cortés treacherously took Emperor Montezuma II captive. Montezuma was a gifted diplomat, religious leader, and warrior, but he was ill-prepared to deal with such ruthless invaders whose customs differed so greatly from any he had experienced. Highly religious, Montezuma was also done in by his belief that Cortés had come in fulfillment of an ancient prophecy of doom for the Aztecs. While Cortés had to leave Tenochtitlán to intercept a rival Castilian army, his remaining men, fearing an attack, massacred large numbers of Aztecs during a major religious ceremony and inflicted heavy casualties. When Cortés returned, having defeated his rivals, he found himself and his Indian allies under siege. Montezuma was killed trying to restore order and Cortés and his followers were forced to flee the city on July 1, 1520. His local allies stayed loyal and the expedition received reinforcements from Cuba, which allowed them to retake the Aztec capital in the summer of 1521 after ferocious fighting, almost completely destroying the wondrous terraced city in the process. The Aztecs had been severely weakened by an outbreak of smallpox brought by the Spanish.

With the fall of its capital, the rest of the Aztec Empire soon fell to its Spanish and Native American conquerors. Cortés sent out other expeditions to conquer the remains of Mexico as far south as Panama. His lieutenant, Pedro de Alvarado (c. 1485–1541), was especially brutal. A Dominican friar from Seville, Bartolomé de Las Casas (1484–1566), the first priest to be ordained in the New World, reported that Alvarado and his troops "advanced killing, ravaging, burning, robbing, and destroying the country."[2] The sophisticated Mayas and others were thus subdued with great violence and most of their written books destroyed as "seed of the devil." Alvarado, the ruthless conqueror of Ecuador and Guatemala, became the latter's governor from 1530 to 1534.

In direct contrast to Alvarado's systematic cruelty, Las Casas attempted to improve the condition of the Native Americans. He took up their cause in a series of books, pamphlets, and sermons, including his highly influential *History of the Indies*. While some of his statistics and accounts are exaggerated, Las Casas, because of his friendship with Emperor Charles V, had a significant impact on trying to ameliorate some of the features of colonialization. Although he advocated the importation of African slaves to replace the Amerindians as laborers, Las Casas came to repent even that notion. Like almost all of his generation, he assumed that Christianity was "the one, true religion," which all Americans should accept and that Spain had a right to colonize the New World.

As for Hernan Cortés, he was eventually recalled to Spain in 1528 after rounds of incessant quarreling among various Spanish colonial officials. He later died in obscurity in Spain seeking redress of various grievances against the crown officials who had replaced him in Mexico. Cortés would later be eulogized by the Franciscan missionary Girolamo Mendieta as a "Moses" who had led the "Indians" from idolatry to the blessings of Christianity, just as the biblical Moses had led his people out of Egypt to the promised land. For Mendieta, Cortés helped to counterbalance the "evil work" of Martin Luther, who had caused thousands of souls to perish by his splintering of the church. Cortés, as a true Christian soldier, had aided the Franciscans in their mass conversions of Native Americans. According to Mendieta, these gains in the New World would hopefully outweigh the losses to Protestantism in the Old.

FRANCISCO PIZARRO (c. 1475–1541)

The treasure stolen from Mexico was supplemented by that gained by the adventurer Francisco Pizarro's attacks against the Inca Empire of Peru. The illegitimate and illiterate son of an infantry colonel, Pizarro had not been part of Cortés's expedition to Mexico, but had later joined Balboa when he journeyed to the Pacific. In 1525 Francisco Pizarro led an expedition down the west coast of South America, only to be nearly wiped out by native peoples. Two years later, he attempted to conquer the powerful Incas, but failed when a majority of his men deserted him at the island of Gallo near the Equator. He successfully petitioned Emperor Charles V for permission to launch yet another assault on Peru.

In 1533 Pizarro and his small force of 100 infantry and 60 cavalry reached the encampment of the Inca ruler Atahualpa, who was locked in a bitter struggle for the throne with his half brother. Imitating the more sophisticated Cortés, Pizarro kidnapped and ransomed the Inca king and used him to control his people. The Spanish conqueror informed the Inca leader:

> Do not take it as an insult that you have been defeated and taken prisoner. . . . I have conquered greater kingdoms than yours, and have defeated other more powerful lords than you, imposing upon them the dominion of the Emperor, whose vassal I am. . . . We come to conquer this land by his command, that all may come to a knowledge of God and His Holy Catholic Faith . . . in order that you may know him, and come out from the bestial and diabolical life you lead.[3]

Later the Spanish ruthlessly executed Atahualpa.

By November the conquerors were in control of the sophisticated and well-planned Inca capital of Cuzco, a city of 150,000 inhabitants located 12,000 feet high in the Andes mountains. The Incas had been greatly weakened by smallpox. Pizarro sent his lieutenants out exploring, south into Chile, and north to New Granada. Fierce struggles over the spoils eventually broke out and Pizarro and hundreds of his followers died in the fighting. Greed had triumphed over other motivations.

The conquest of Mexico and Peru helped spark a boom in the European economy that lasted throughout the sixteenth century. Commodities such as sugar, dyes, vanilla, cacao, cotton, potatoes, spices, tea, and silver poured into Europe in much greater amounts than ever before. New products from the Americas such as corn, potatoes, chocolate, coffee, tomatoes, pineapple, and tobacco were introduced into Europe for the first time. The Europeans brought sugarcane, chickpeas, wheat, cows, sheep and horses to the Americas, which completely changed the lifestyles of many groups of Native Americans.

Tragically, lethal diseases were also exchanged. Syphilis became widespread in Europe following the return of Columbus and smallpox, measles, and typhus decimated millions of Amerindians. The brutal African slave trade resulted in the deaths of millions more. Even those who survived the dislocations and deaths brought by the wars of conquest, colonization, and the trafficking in human flesh suffered enormously. The world would never be the same or as large again. European arms had triumphed, but at a horrible human cost.

Chronology

1340–1384	Reign of Margaret of Denmark.
1356	Golden Bull of Nuremberg issued by Emperor Charles IV.
1394–1460	Life of Henry the Navigator.
1447–1492	Reign of Casimir IV of Poland.
1451–1506	Life of Christopher Columbus.
1453	Fall of Constantinople to Mehmed the Conqueror.
1458–1490	Reign of Matthias Corvinus in Hungary.
1467–1477	Reign of Duke Charles the Bold of Burgundy.
1469	Marriage of Isabella of Castile to Ferdinand of Aragon.
1485–1509	Reign of Henry VII in England.
1485–1542	Life of Hernan Cortés.
1492	Fall of Granada; Columbus's first voyage to the Americas.
1493–1519	Reign of Emperor Maximilian I.
1499	Da Gama returns from India.
1500	Cabral discovers Brazil.
1504	Death of Isabella of Spain.
1509–1547	Reign of Henry VIII in England.
1515–1547	Reign of François I in France.
1515	Battle of Marignano; François I takes Milan.
1516–1556	Reign of Charles of Habsburg as king of Spain.
1519	Charles of Habsburg becomes Holy Roman emperor; Magellan begins his voyage; Cortés leaves Cuba for Mexico.
1522	Fall of the Aztecs to Cortés.
1533	Fall of the Incas to Pizarro.

Further Reading

THE ECONOMY

Douglas Bisson, *The Merchant Adventurers of England: The Company and the Crown, 1474–1564* (1993).

Philippe Dollinger, *The German Hansa* (1970).

Hermann Kellenbrenz, *The Rise of the European Economy, 1500–1750* (1976).

Peter Kriedte, *Peasants, Landlords, and Merchant Capitalists. Europe and the World Economy, 1500–1800* (1983).

Immanuel Wallerstein, *The Modern World-System, Capitalist Agriculture and the Origins of the European World-Economy in the Sixteenth Century,* 2 vols. (1974).

THE NORTHERN MONARCHIES AND PRINCIPALITIES

BURGUNDY

Walter Prevenier and William Blockmans, *The Burgundian Netherlands* (1986).

Richard Vaughan, *Charles the Bold, the Last Valois Duke of Burgundy* (1973). Vaughan has a series of fine books on the dukes of Burgundy.

FRANCE

Frederic Baumgartner, *Louis XII* (1994).

Richard Jackson, *Vive Le Roi!: A History of the French Coronation Ceremony from Charles V to Charles X* (1984).

Paul Murray Kendall, *Louis XI, the "Universal Spider"* (1971).

R. J. Knecht, *Renaissance Warrior and Patron: The Reign of Francis I*, 2nd ed. (1994).

ENGLAND

S. B. Chrimes, *Henry VII* (1973).

J. R. Lander, *Government and Community, 1450–1509* (1981).

J. J. Scarisbrick, *Henry VIII* (1968).

Neville Williams, *The Life and Times of Henry VII* (1973).

SPAIN

Felipe Fernández-Armesto, *Ferdinand and Isabella* (1975).

J. N. Hilgarth, *The Spanish Kingdoms*, 2 vols. (1978).

Peggy Liss, *Isabel the Queen: Life and Times* (1992).

Derek Lomax, *The Reconquest of Spain* (1978).

Marvin Lunenfeld, *Keepers of the City: The Corregidores of Isabella of Castile (1474–1504)* (1988).

B. Netanyahu, *The Origins of the Inquisition in Fifteenth-century Spain* (1995).

Nancy Rubin, *Isabella of Castile: The First Renaissance Queen* (1991).

Teofilo Ruiz, *Crisis and Continuity: Land and Town in Late Medieval Castile* (1994).

THE HOLY ROMAN EMPIRE

Gerhard Benecke, *Maximilian I (1459–1519), An Analytical Biography* (1982).

F. R. H. Du Boulay, *Germany in the Later Middle Ages* (1983).

Michael Hughes, *Early Modern Germany, 1477–1806* (1992).

Joachim Leuschner, *Germany in the Late Middle Ages* (1980).

Jonathan Zophy, *An Annotated Bibliography of the Holy Roman Empire* (1986).

———, ed., *The Holy Roman Empire: A Dictionary Handbook* (1980).

OTHER STATES

John Fine, Jr., *The Late Medieval Balkans: A Critical Survey from the Late Twelfth Century to the Ottoman Conquest* (1994).

Paul Knoll, *The Rise of the Polish Monarchy* (1972).

Janet Martin, *Medieval Russia, 980–1584* (1995).

Birgit Sawyer and Peter Sawyer, *Medieval Scandinavia: From Conversion to Reformation, circa 800–1500* (1993).

Nancy Shields, *The Making of the Muscovite Political System, 1345–1547* (1987).

Dorothy Vaughan, *Europe and the Turk: A Pattern of Alliances, 1350–1700*, 2nd ed. (1970).

EXPLORATION, CONQUEST, AND COLONIALIZATION

Jerry Bentley, *Old World Encounters, Cross Cultural Contacts and Exchanges in Premodern Times* (1993).

Charles Boxer, *The Dutch Seabourne Empire, 1600–1800* (1965).

———, *The Portuguese Seabourne Empire, 1415–1825*, rpr. (1977).

Peter Hulme, *Colonial Encounters: Europe and the Native Caribbean, 1492–1797* (1986).

Bernard Lewis, *Cultures in Conflict: Christians, Muslims, and Jews in the Age of Discovery* (1994).

James Lockhart, *Spanish Peru, 1532–1560* (1964).

William Maltby, *The Black Legend in England* (1971). Fine study of the legends of Spanish cruelty.

Samuel Eliot Morison, *The European Discovery of America*, 2 vols. (1971–1973).

Anthony Pagden, *European Encounters with the New World* (1992).

J. H. Parry, *The Age of Reconnaissance*, 2nd ed. (1981).

Boise Penrose, *Travel and Discovery in the Renaissance* (1962).

G. V. Scammel, *The World Encompassed: The First European Maritime Empires* (1981).

Stuart Schwartz, ed., *Implicit Understandings: Observing, Reporting, and Reflecting on the Encounters Between Europeans and Other Peoples in the Early Modern Era* (1994). Important essays by a number of scholars.

Roger Smith, *Vanguard of Empire: Ships of Exploration in the Age of Columbus* (1993).

David Stannard, *American Holocaust: The Conquest of the New World* (1992). Impressive scholarship on a horrific subject.

Richard Trexler, *Sex and Conquest: Gendered Violence, Political Order, and the European Conquest of the Americas* (1995).

COLUMBUS AND HIS IMPACT

Alfred Crosby, Jr., *The Columbian Exchange: Biological and Cultural Consequences of 1492* (1972).

Zvi Dor-Ner with William Scheller, *Columbus and the Age of Discovery* (1991). Handsomely illustrated coffee table book.

Cecil Jane, ed., *The Four Voyages of Columbus* (1988). A valuable anthology of sources.

Valerie Flint, *The Imaginative Landscape of Christopher Columbus* (1992).

Djelal Kadir, *Columbus and the Ends of the Earth: Europe's Prophetic Rhetoric and Conquering Ideology* (1992).

Marvin Lunenfeld, ed., *1492: Discovery, Invasion, Encounter: Sources and Interpretations* (1991). A first-rate collection of primary and secondary materials.

William Philips, Jr. and Carla Rahn Philips, *The Worlds of Christopher Columbus* (1992).

Irving Rouse, *The Tainos: The Rise and Decline of the People Who Greeted Columbus* (1992).

Kirkpatrick Sale, *The Conquest of Paradise: Christopher Columbus and the Columbian Legacy* (1991). Polemical but interesting.

CORTÉS AND THE CONQUEST OF MEXICO

Charles Gibson, *The Aztecs under Spanish Rule* (1964).

Serge Gruzinski, *The Conquest of Mexico: The Incorporation of Indian Societies into the Western World in the 16th-18th Centuries* (1994).

Richard Marks, *Cortés: The Great Adventurer and the Fate of the Aztec Mexico* (1993).

Hugh Thomas, *Montezuma. Cortes, and the Fall of Mexico* (1994).

Notes

1. Cited in Jonathan W. Zophy, *Patriarchal Politics and Christoph Kress (1484–1535) of Nuremberg* (Lewiston, N.Y.: Edwin Mellen Press, 1992), p. 28.
2. Cited in Marvin Lunenfeld, ed., *1492: Discovery, Invasion, Encounter: Sources and Interpretations* (Lexington, Mass.: D. C. Heath. 1991), p. 209.
3. Cited in G. R. Elton, ed., *Renaissance and Reformation 1300–1648*, 3rd ed. (New York: Macmillan, 1976), p. 306.

10

THE RENAISSANCE
IN THE NORTH

The Literary Culture of the North

Although the European conquest of much of
the Americas changed the material and political life of Europe enormously, a more
gradual change was occurring in the artistic
and intellectual world of Europe north of
the Alps. Courts, churches, and wealthy
individuals expanded their patronage of
artists and musicians. The Renaissance in
the North witnessed not only the revival
of Greek, Latin, and Hebrew studies by
the humanists, it also saw the development
of vernacular languages such as English,
French, Spanish, and German as literary ve-
hicles. Even though it took the Renaissance
longer to blossom north of the Alps, the
achievements of the northerners were quite
substantial.

CHRISTINE DE PIZAN (1365–c. 1429)

Many writers contributed to the rise of
French as a literary language, but few have
had such a significant impact on the modern
world as Christine de Pizan. Pizan was the
first woman to write professionally and the
first published feminist. Born in Venice, she
moved with her family to France when she
was still a child. Her father, Thomas, who
had achieved fame in Bologna and Venice
as a physician and astrologer, had been

hired to serve King Charles V of France
(r. 1364–1380). Thomas de Pizan soon became a court favorite with the king, who
made him one of his trusted advisors and
court physician.

Despite the objections of her mother,
who feared that too much education would
dampen her matrimonial prospects, Christine was unusually well schooled by her remarkably progressive father. She learned to
read French, Italian, and some Latin before
her marriage at age fifteen to Etienne de
Castel, a young nobleman and courtier from
Picardy. Castel became the king's secretary
and notary and proved to be a good husband for Christine. Her family flourished
until the king's sudden death in September
of 1380. As Christine wrote later, "now the
door to our misfortunes was open."[1]

Her father fell out of favor with the
new king, who withdrew his pension and
cut his salary. His health suffered and he
died sometime between 1385 and 1390. Her
husband, Etienne, became ill while traveling with King Charles VI to Beauvais and
died in the autumn of 1390. At age twenty-
five, Christine de Pizan found herself with a
mother, three children, and a niece to support. She also had to ward off four lawsuits
over debts incurred by her husband.

What was she to do? Few choices were
available to fourteenth century women.

Most remarkably, Christine de Pizan took the unprecedented step for a woman of deciding to pursue a literary career. Petrarca and Boccaccio were among the few men able to sustain themselves in part through their writings, but Pizan was determined to succeed. She began intensive studies of history, poetry, and science to prepare herself intellectually for the task ahead. Armed with this added learning, Pizan began to write poetry which fortunately met with some success beginning around 1393. She also supported her family by copying and producing books, doing illustrations, and possibly by working as a notary.

In addition to verse, Pizan wrote a history of King Charles V of France, written at the request of his brother, Duke Philip the Bold of Burgundy. She composed other biographical pieces upon commission, which were generally well received. Familiar with the world of court politics, her book of advice for princes, *The Body of Policy*, was remarkably respected, given the prejudices against women. *The Book of Feats of Arms and Chivalry* was considered so useful that King Henry VII of England later had it translated into English. Pizan's *Book of Peace* of 1413 stressed the importance of education. An early admirer of Joan of Arc, she wrote the only contemporary tribute to her in *Hymn to Joan of Arc*. Pizan saw Joan as a heroic

Early fifteenth-century manuscript miniature depicting Christine de Pizan presenting her manuscript to Isabella of Bavaria. British Museum, London, Great Britain. Snark/Art Resource.

woman and an example of the triumph of good over evil in politics.

Christine de Pizan also earned a major reputation as a defender of women by critiquing Jean de Meun's conclusion to the *Romance of the Rose,* a popular thirteenth-century allegory in the courtly love tradition. In her treatise of 1399, *The Letter to the God of Love,* she took Meun to task for his mockery of women and his blatant misogyny. This led to a heated literary exchange between Meun's admirers and those who agreed with Pizan, of whom there were many. These arguments set off a debate known as the *Querelle de femmes* (quarrel over the nature of women), which lasted throughout the Renaissance.

Undaunted by the attacks on her reputation and ideas, Pizan continued her defense of women in her most important work, *The Book of the City of Ladies* (1405). In that revolutionary work, she imagined a world in which women could do all the jobs necessary to the running of a city. Pizan took on all the traditional arguments including those from the Bible that had been used to justify women's inferior status. She pointed out that woman "was created in the image of God. How can any mouth dare to slander the vessel which bears such a noble imprint? . . . God created the soul and placed wholly similar souls, equally good and noble, in the feminine and masculine bodies."[2] As for the alleged physical weaknesses of women's bodies, they were more than compensated for by determination and moral strength. Pizan urged women to rely on their own experience and not to be deterred by the "ignorant scribbles of men about what they can achieve."[3]

In 1405 she wrote *The Treasure of the City of Ladies or the Book of the Three Virtues,* a sequel to the *City of Ladies.* This work was a practical guide to etiquette and survival for women ranging from queens to servants and prostitutes. Pizan urged women to follow the three cardinal virtues of "Reason, Rectitude, and Justice," regardless of their social status. Pizan showed surprising insight into the real lives of women from rich to poor and her advice was consistently sensible. She urged women to always stick together, for their lives were never secure.

As her fame as a writer spread, Pizan began to receive offers of patronage from crowned heads all over Europe. Duke Giangaleazzo Visconti of Milan invited her to decorate his court but she refused, as she did a similar invitation from King Henry IV of England. She did allow her son, Jean, to accept an invitation from the earl of Salisbury to become a page at the English court and later to accept a place at the court of Burgundy. King Charles VI and his colorful queen, Isabella of Bavaria, became loyal patrons and presented her with generous gifts, as did other French nobles. Yet as the political scene in Paris deteriorated, Pizan left for life in a convent, perhaps the one at Poissy where her daughter was a nun. She died there leaving a remarkable legacy of accomplishment and her subsequent influence upon the raising of feminist consciousness has been enormous. As Martin le Franc expressed it in 1422: "Though death may draw the curtain around her body, her name shall still endure."[4]

Later French Writers

While the lives and the ideas of few other writers have ever exerted as much influence as have Christine de Pizan's, French literature continued to flourish throughout the Renaissance. Its clearest voices include the convicted thief François Villon, the ropemaker's wife Louise Labé, the graceful Clémont Marot, and the stately Queen Marguerite of Navarre.

FRANÇOIS VILLON (1431–c. 1464)

The greatest French lyric poet of the fifteenth century was the vagabond François
Villon (1431–c. 1464). Raised in the slums of
Paris among beggars and thieves, Villon
eventually became a student at the University of Paris. In 1455 he fatally stabbed a
priest in a drunken quarrel, but was par-
doned for having acted in self-defense. The
following year Villon and four others stole a
substantial amount of money from the College of Navarre. He was later arrested and
spent the summer of 1461 in the prison of
the bishop of Orléans. In 1462 Villon was arrested for theft and brawling and was banished from Paris for ten years. Before his
early death, Villon managed to write several
long poems, and some 40 *ballades* and *ron-
deaux* that revealed his innermost thoughts,
yearnings, and fears more honestly than any
previous poet had done.

Who else but François Villon could
write:

> Have pity, have pity on me
> You at least my friends
> I lie in a dungeon not under holly or
>   hawthorn
> In this exile where I was driven
> By fortune and God's leave
> Girls, lovers, young and fresh folk
> Dancers, tumblers dancing the calfstep
> Quick as arrows, sharp as spurs
> Throats tinkling clear as bells
> Will you leave him here, the poor Villon?[5]

Villon's influence was profound and not until the time of Clémont Marot did French poetry reconcile the traditions of Villon's street
language with French courtly conventions
and classical Latin.

LOUISE LABÉ (c. 1520–1566)

Louise Labé was another unconventional
French literary figure. The daughter of a
ropemaker from Lyon, she received a much
better education than was typical of her
class. Trained in music, letters, languages,
art, needlework, weaponry, and ropemak-
ing, the beautiful Labé urged other women
to "raise their minds somewhat above their
distaffs and spindles" and find pleasure in
study. To experience life more fully, Labé
may have fought in a battle disguised as a
man and worked as a courtesan before marrying a wealthy rope manufacturer. Neither
story can be verified, although the reformer
John Calvin (1509–1564) accused her of
gaining popularity by selling her favors to
local notables. Such tactics were often used
in attempts to silence eloquent women.

We do know that she established a literary circle in Lyon, a major commercial
center with strong ties to Italy. Labé composed several fine sonnets and elegies, as
well as a prose dialogue, *The Debate Between
Madness and Love* (1555). Despite her rather
unusual life, Labé could be quite traditional
in her treatment of subjects such as romantic love. In her "Poor Loving Soul," she extolled the delights of the "illusion of love":

> Him then I think fondly to kiss, to hold
>   him
> Frankly then to my bosom; I that all day
> Have looked for him suffering, repining,
>   yea many long days.[6]

Louise Labé remains one of the most intriguing literary personalities of the French
Renaissance.

MARGUERITE OF NAVARRE (1492–1549)

The most renowned female literary figure of
the period was Marguerite of Navarre, sister
of King François I. Her talented mother,
Queen Louise of Savoy (1476–1531), taught
her French, Spanish, and enough Italian to
read Dante and Petrarca's sonnets. She also
learned Latin and some Greek. Known for

her humanist learning and her physical beauty, Marguerite sometimes served as regent for her brother. After the death of her first husband, the duke of Alençon, she married Henri d'Albret, king of Navarre, and presided over a circle of artists, poets, humanists, and religious reformers. Her circle included the brilliant poet Clémont Marot (1496–1544), who helped bring together courtly French, the language of the streets, and classical Latin. Others in her sphere became leaders of the Reformation in France and elsewhere.

Marguerite's own literary output was remarkable given her many political responsibilities. She wrote intensely mystical poetry of great emotional power, including the well-known *The Mirror of a Sinful Soul*. At the time of her death, the queen was composing her most famous prose work, the *Heptameron*. Influenced by Boccaccio, her seventy-two short stories are risqué and witty reflections of elite French society. The tales range from the bawdy to the spiritual. Resolute in her defense of women, Marguerite of Navarre also demonstrated her interest in reform by describing the abuses of the church and monasteries. She also used her influence to protect a reform-minded group of clerics and scholars at Meaux. Many of them shared her concern about friars, who "can talk like angels, and are for the most part importunate as devils."[7]

FRANÇOIS RABELAIS (c. 1494–1553)

Marguerite of Navarre's description of friars who "can talk like angels" but have a lot of the devil in them might well fit François Rabelais. An extraordinary bundle of contradictions, he was at times a licentious monk, a medical student, a classicist who preferred to write in the vernacular, and a mocker of religious beliefs who was at the same time a true believer. His father, a prosperous lawyer and landowner in central France, provided his son with a good basic education at a nearby Benedictine abbey. Later Rabelais joined the Franciscans at an early age. He found monastic life to be stifling as his studies of Greek were treated with suspicion. Rabelais then worked for a time as a secretary to a Benedictine abbot and bishop, to whose order he transferred. Taking up the life of a student, Rabelais earned his B.A. in 1530 at Montpellier. He studied the humanities as well as medicine, science, and mathematics.

By 1532 Rabelais was practicing medicine in Lyon, corresponding with humanists such as Erasmus, and publishing translations of medical treatises. At that time, he also wrote his first great satirical tale, *Gargantua*, and dedicated it to "most noble boozers and you, my very esteemed and poxy friends."[8] In 1534 *Pantagruel*, its sequel, appeared. These ribald satires were filled with tremendous displays of classical learning as well as an abundant scatological humor. Both were exceptionally popular and quickly condemned by the University of Paris as obscene. Fortunately for Rabelais, he had found a powerful protector in the person of Jean du Bellay, bishop of Paris, who took him to Rome on two occasions as his doctor.

Rabelais later returned to Montpellier, where he earned his doctorate in medicine in 1537. After brief stints at the court of King François I and in Turin, he went to Metz as city secretary. Finding his salary insufficient, Rabelais found additional patronage from du Bellay, now a cardinal, and continued to revise and enlarge his famous tales until his death in Paris. Controversy continues to swirl about Rabelais. He is viewed by many as the greatest comic and satirist of the Renaissance. For example, his Gargantua is a giant, who as a young man founds the Abbey of Thélème, the ideal monastic community for it welcomes members of both sexes and adopts the motto "Do what you wish." Rabelais' targets also included members of the church hierarchy, theologians, lawyers, and philosophers. French humanism had found its comic genius in Rabelais, a man who loved to play with words and ideas no matter how outrageous.

The Emergence of the Vernacular in England

Middle English flowered in the days of Geoffrey Chaucer (c. 1340–1400), whose superb *Canterbury Tales* has long been considered one of the greatest literary achievements of the late Middle Ages. Yet at a time when Italian and French had become relatively stable in the fifteenth century, English continued to change and develop. Not until the second half of the sixteenth century did

Engraved portrait of William Shakespeare. SEF/Art Resource.

English emerge as the primary literary language of England, despite the fine poetry of Sir Thomas Wyatt and others. Even such an important work as Thomas More's *Utopia* (1516) was not translated from Latin to English until 1541. All of this changed, however, during the life of William Shakespeare (1564–1616).

WILLIAM SHAKESPEARE:
THE BARD OF AVON

Shakespeare was born in the town of Stratford-upon-Avon to a prosperous glovemaker and trader who later became a civic official. His mother came from a substantial landowning family. In 1582 William married Anne Hathaway and they had several children. Ten years later he was established as an actor and playwright in London. In 1594 Shakespeare became a charter member of a theatrical company, the King's Men, with which he remained affiliated until his retirement to Stratford in 1611. The earl of Southhampton became one of his most important patrons. Thirty-seven plays and a number of nondramatic poems are attributed to him. Few others have ever managed to produce masterpieces in both tragedy (*Hamlet, King Lear,* and *Macbeth*) and comedy (*A Midsummer Night's Dream, Much Ado About Nothing*). A number of Shakespeare's plays are set in Renaissance Italy (*Othello, Romeo and Juliet, The Merchant of Venice,* and *Two Gentlemen of Verona*). They show to what an extent the Italian world had captured the imagination of northerners.

Shakespeare was also keenly interested in history and showed an excellent grounding in the works of Plutarch as well as historians closer to his own time such as Raphael Holinshed (c. 1525–c. 1580) and Thomas More. His historical plays range from dramas set in ancient Rome, such as *Julius Caesar* and *Antony and Cleopatra,* to some which are closer to his own era, such as *Richard III* and *Henry VIII*. In all his plays, the bard of Avon exhibited an unusually sophisticated understanding of the minds and speech of both men and women of a variety of social classes. He was as familiar with the world of Cheapside taverns as he was with the inner workings of power politics. William Shakespeare is usually considered to be the greatest English writer to date, and his work was of fundamental importance in establishing English as a literary vehicle.

OTHER WRITERS
OF THE ELIZABETHAN RENAISSANCE

The England of Queen Elizabeth I (r. 1558–1603) also featured such remarkable literary talents as the bold dramatist Christopher Marlowe (1564–1593), the poet Edmund Spenser (c. 1552–1599), the poets Sir Philip Sidney (1554–1586) and his sister Mary, countess of Pembroke, among many others. The son of a shoemaker who became a parish clerk in Canterbury, Marlowe earned a B.A. and an M.A. as a scholarship student at Cambridge University. After a brief stint as a diplomat, he pursued a literary career translating the Roman poet Ovid and writing seven plays plus a considerable body of poetry. His most notable included *Edward II, Doctor Faustus, The Jew of Malta,* and *Tamburlaine.* In a great era of playwrights, Marlowe ranked second only to Shakespeare among Elizabethan dramatists. His career was cut tragically short when he was stabbed to death in a tavern brawl. London's theater district on the south bank of the Thames was a rough area filled with brothels and bear-baiting pits.

Sir Philip Sidney was the eldest son of Sir Henry Sidney (later lord deputy of Ireland) and Lady Mary Sidney (sister of the earls of Leicester and Warwick). Educated first at Shrewsbury School, he left Oxford in 1571 without taking a degree. For the next several years he travelled widely throughout Europe, sometimes assisting on diplomatic missions. After losing favor with the queen, he retired to his sister Mary's home and composed his long prose romance, the *Arcadia.* In 1581 Sidney became a member of Parliament and three years later was named governor of Flushing. He died from a wound suffered at the Battle of Zutphen in 1586 against the Spanish. He left a considerable legacy of poetry and an important *Defense of Poetry.*

Mary Sidney (1561–1621) wrote religious poetry, translations of Petrarca, elegies, pastoral dialogues, and a metrical version of the Psalms. She joined the court when she was only fourteen and married the count of Pembroke two years later. Mary impressed the queen with her fluency in languages and her skills in music and embroidery. Like the queen, Mary Sidney dispensed patronage to other poets, including several women. Her courtier-brother's friend Edmund Spenser, considered the greatest English poet since Chaucer, used his major work, the *Faerie Queene,* to pay fulsome tribute to Elizabeth as "Gloriana." Although Spenser spent a number of years in Ireland away from the court, he shared much of the awe of his contemporaries for their brilliant queen. Her reign was, indeed, a glorious time for English letters even though the queen was hardly a champion of free speech. She especially feared dramas that spoke too frankly about the deposition of sovereigns, such as Shakespeare's *Richard II.*

The Golden Age of Spanish Literature

Spanish also emerged as a major literary language during the Renaissance. Miguel de Cervantes (1547–1616) has long been considered the greatest Spanish author of all time. Born at Alcalá de Henares, he was the son of an unsuccessful apothecary-surgeon who became something of a wanderer. Miguel went to school in Madrid and made his debut as a poet. After having fought in a duel, he was forced to flee Spain for Rome, where he entered the service of a cardinal. In 1570 Cervantes joined the Spanish army and fought bravely in the Battle of Lepanto against the Ottomans in October of 1571. He later fought in the campaign for Tunis in North Africa. Sailing back to Spain in September of 1575, his ship was captured by Moorish pirates, who sold him into slavery. Cervantes was finally ransomed in 1580 and returned to tell of his adventures in his *Pictures of Algiers*.

In December 1584 Cervantes married Catalina de Palacios Salazar y Vozmediano, daughter of a prosperous peasant of Esquivias. Her dowry was modest and Miguel was forced to eke out a meager living in Seville by a variety of poorly paid jobs. Although they had no children, their household included two sisters, his illegitimate daughter Isabel, a niece, and a maidservant. Hoping for relief from the pecuniary liabilities under which he struggled, in 1588 Cervantes took a job as one of the many government procurement officers in charge of gathering supplies for the great armada (fleet) sent against Protestant England in that same year. Having seized supplies belonging to the dean of the cathedral chapter at Seville, he was temporarily excommunicated. When discrepancies were discovered in his financial records, he was jailed and then dismissed from royal service. Cervantes spent the rest of his life in poverty but managed to write the masterpiece *Don Quixote de la Mancha,* which did not make him rich but did make him famous.

By 1610 many in Spain were laughing mightily at the mockingly heroic tales. Although intellectuals such as the playwright Lope de Vega dismissed *Quixote* as not worthy of literary praise, it found a vast audience in numerous editions. Cervantes did not benefit greatly financially from its success and a few years before his death he joined the Tertiary Order of St. Francis. After a life filled with difficulties, he died in Madrid on April 23, 1616, the same day on which Shakespeare died in England. His purpose in *Don Quixote* was to ridicule chivalric romances; however, his story created an incredible panorama of Spanish society and showed genuine affection for the knightly ideals of its hero, the knight Don Quixote, the man of La Mancha. Quixote is joined in his adventures by his earthy squire, the practical Sancho Panza. They have become two of the best-known figures in all literature. Cervantes used many of his life experiences in crafting his wondrous tale, including his familiarity with Spanish jails and the rich life found on the Andalusian plains.

Spanish drama also thrived during the Renaissance with significant contributions from Lope de Vega (1562–1635), Tirso de Mólina (1571–1658), and Juan Ruiz de Alarcon (c. 1581–1639). Lope de Vega was a particularly prolific talent, who wrote over 500 comedies and other plays. While he failed to recognize the genius of Cervantes, his own work was enormously influential. Many of his plays are still being performed today. Molina established the character of the insatiable lover Don Juan, loosely based on the half brother of the king of Spain. Although Spanish like English theater was dominated by males (men played all the parts), the Renaissance was one of its greatest periods.

German Renaissance Literature

German literature was slower in maturing during the Renaissance than French or Spanish largely because the Germans resisted the influence of Italian models. German remained a hybrid vernacular in the process of development. Not until the third decade of the sixteenth century did German emerge as an effective literary vehicle under the impact of widespread printing of the writings of the reformer Martin Luther (1483–1546). Luther wrote in a form of German that helped set a literary standard for the language.

Although German poets and dramatists lagged behind their counterparts in most other parts of Europe, several German poets emerged who showed a talent for satire, something in which some of the ancient Romans had also excelled in. Here again the influence of Renaissance humanism is apparent in rediscovering the classic works of Roman satirists such as Juvenal and Martial. Among those authors writing in German who manifested some of the potential literary power of satire were Sebastian Brant (c. 1457–1521) and Hans Sachs (1494–1576).

Brant, a versatile poet and lawyer, was the son of an innkeeper in Strasbourg. After private tutoring, he entered the University of Basel, where he earned a doctorate in canon and civil law in 1489. Until 1500 he stayed in Basel as a professor of law as well as an editor for a local publisher. Brant then returned to Strasbourg and worked for the town government. By then he had become famous for his 1494 poetic satire, *The Ship of Fools.* No segment of society is spared Brant's scorn and derision. Like many of the period's intellectuals he attacked women with great abandon as the following illustrates:

> But wanton wives are far from rare,
> For they dwelleth everywhere . . .
> A leaky roof ere winter's through
> I like a woman who's a shrew.

His targets also included less vulnerable groups such as the clergy, both regular and secular. He wrote of the priesthood:

> No need for scholarship I see
> So long as benefices be,

> Priesthood to them is something slight,
> As through it were a trifling mite;
> Ofttimes young priests are now so crude
> They seem just like a monkey's brood.

Not even the regular clergy escaped his ridicule, as the following excerpt from *The Ship of Fools* reveals:

> Most enter monasteries blind,
> Not old enough to know their mind,
> They enter not by heaven's will
> And only hope to eat their fill.[9]

Although sensitive to the abuses in the church, Brant remained loyal to the church as an institution and was not really a hater of the clergy. It was abuses of power and ignorance that he wanted to eliminate, recognizing that unless humans improve their behaviors we all remain passengers on a ship of fools on our way to destruction.

Hans Sachs (1494–1576) was another great satirical voice of the German Renaissance. The son of a tailor and a native of Nuremberg, he attended Latin school and then began an apprenticeship as a shoemaker in 1508. After a period of wandering and study, both of shoemaking and song, Sachs returned to Nuremberg and remained there as a master cobbler and an incredibly prolific author. He composed more than 4,000 *Meisterleider* ("master songs"), 1,700 tales and fables in verse, and 200 dramas. His writings are distinguished by their colorful use of language, charm, and wit. An ardent supporter of the Reformation, he hailed Luther as "The Wittenberg Nightingale" and ridiculed the clergy for their "fasts by day and feasts by night."[10]

The Fine Arts in the North

The Northern Renaissance also witnessed impressive displays of creativity in architecture, the fine arts, and music. Statebuilding princes such as François I of France proved great builders of palaces. Renaissance courts also attracted a galaxy of talented musicians. In painting, the Flemish master Jan van Eyck (c. 1390–1441) was one of the most important contributors to Renaissance art. We know that Eyck worked in Holland from 1422 to 1424, in Lille from 1425 to 1429, and after that in Bruges, where he died. From time to time Duke Philip the Good of Burgundy employed him as a diplomat as well as a court painter. Some of his famous works were possibly done in collaboration with his older brother, Hubert.

JAN VAN EYCK

Jan van Eyck is most famous for using a form of oil painting. He built pictures up by applying layers of translucent oil over an opaque ground of tempera. This gave his work an unprecedented atmospheric depth and luminosity. The use of oil painting also allowed Eyck to rival manuscript illuminators in the minute detail he could put into his paintings, some of which were done on canvass. Jan van Eyck was able to paint traditional subject matter such as the madonna and baby Jesus with an unprecedented degree of realism. In fact, Mary was one of his favorite subjects as her cult blossomed all over Europe. Many found the mature Jesus a figure to be frightened of, but Mary was always much more approachable and a good intercessor with her sometimes angry son. Her frequent depiction in annunciation scenes with a book in hand was an implied recognition of growing female literacy.

Eyck was also able to flatter contemporaries by placing them in scenes with biblical figures. Imagine how exciting it must have been for a contemporary figure like Chancellor Rolin to be portrayed so realistically in the same space with the mother of God and the baby Jesus. Usually, Jan van

Jan van Eyck, *Virgin Mary and Child*. Galleria Doria Pamphilj, Rome, Italy. Alinari/Art Resource.

Eyck's portraits feature motionless figures set against architectural and scenic backgrounds. His vivid use of color and high level of minute detail had an enormous impact on painting throughout the Low Countries, Germany, and Italy, where oil painting became all the rage in the fifteenth century.

LATER FLEMISH PAINTING

Flemish art continued to be among the finest in Europe in the generations following the deaths of the van Eycks. The Low Countries were one of the most prosperous parts of Europe and wealthy patrons could be found in many places. By the sixteenth century, Italian influences were also being felt in the Low Countries as evidenced by the brilliant work of artists such as Quentin Massys (c.

Jan van Eyck, *Madonna and Child with Chancellor Rolin.* Louvre, Paris, France. Giraudon/Art Resource.

1464–1530) of Antwerp, who used classical themes and Italian settings in a number of his works. He is also known for his biblical scenes and superb portraits, including a marvelous rendering of the humanist Erasmus, which rivals the Erasmus portrait of Hans Holbein. Both of his sons became painters.

Hieronymus Bosch (c. 1450–1516) and Pieter Brueghel the Elder (c. 1525–1569), two of Massys's fellow artists, represent striking new departures from tradition. Bosch's fantastic pictorial imagery is a precursor of Surrealism, while Brueghel dared to concentrate on sometimes bitter scenes of peasant life and landscapes. Bosch's work had a profound influence on Brueghel. Working class men and women were obviously not going to provide an artist with much in the way of patronage. Fortunately Brueghel made

enough money from his more traditional depictions of biblical scenes for patrons such as Cardinal Grandvelle to indulge in his fondness for bucolic life. A master satirist, Brueghel also affords us a vivid record of some of the merciless activities of the Inquisition in the Low Countries. Yet he moved from Protestant-controlled Antwerp to Catholic Brussels.

Peter Paul Rubens (1577–1640) became the greatest figure of the Flemish school in the age of the Baroque. After spending eight years at the court of Mantua in Italy, he opened an enormous studio in Antwerp. Students flocked from all over Europe to learn from a master who made such a good living. He used his students and his assistants to complete the details of massive canvasses which he designed, such as a series of huge scenes of the life of Queen Marie de'

Pieter Brueghel the Elder, *The Peasant Wedding*. Kunsthistorisches Museum, Vienna, Austria. Foto Marburg/Art Resource.

Medici of France. Rubens became one of the most sought after court painters in Europe and worked in Paris, London, and Madrid. He is remembered for his rich coloring and roseate, sensuous nudes. His subject matter ranged from portraits of royalty such as *King Philip IV* of Spain to biblical scenes such as his famous *Descent from the Cross*.

Renaissance Art in Germany

The German-speaking lands of the Holy Roman Empire also produced an abundance of outstanding artists during the Renaissance. Like the Italians and the Netherlanders, German craftspeople had a tradition of quality work. Renaissance artists built on those traditions of excellence with imagination and splendid technique. Patronage improved in Germany as the wealthy sought ways to express themselves by endowing churches and private homes. Some of these German artists, such as Albrecht Dürer, were influenced by developments both in Italy and the Low Countries. Hans Holbein of Augsburg achieved his greatest fame at the Tudor court in England. Lucas Cranach the Elder, a friend of Martin Luther, captured some of the key personalities of the early Reformation movement in Saxony. Sculpture was well represented by Tilman Riemenschneider.

ALBRECHT DÜRER (1471–1528)

Albrecht Dürer of Nuremberg served as one of the most important links between Italian and northern art. He was also the greatest artist of the Renaissance in Germany, a master of an astonishing variety of techniques and styles. The son of a goldsmith, Dürer was at first apprenticed to his father. Having shown an early talent for drawing, he joined the workshop of Michael Wolgemut (1434–1519), a Nuremberg master painter and woodcut designer in November 1486. He remained with Wolgemut for four years before starting his travels about the Holy Roman Empire. In the spring of 1494 Dürer returned to his home town to marry Agnes Frey, an attractive and modest young woman.

Always eager for new knowledge, Albrecht left for Italy in the fall of 1494, where he made a thorough study of some of the glories of Renaissance art. Back in Nuremberg in the spring of 1495, Dürer opened up his own workshop and began getting important commissions. In 1505 he made his second trip to Italy. The handsome Dürer earned a number of commissions from the Holy Roman Emperor Maximilian I. When Maximilian died in 1519, the Nuremberger journeyed to the Netherlands, hoping to secure a continuation of his imperial pension from the new sovereign, Charles V. Dürer stayed for almost a year, studying intensely the works of the Dutch and Flemish masters. He also contracted malaria while examining a beached whale in the swamps of Zeeland, which undermined his health for the rest of his life.

His last years were spent in Nuremberg, where he was an important member of the city's humanist movement and an early supporter of Martin Luther. Dürer thought that Luther had captured the essence of the New Testament message of God's love and forgiveness. After hearing the false news that Luther had been killed after the 1521 Diet of Worms, the artist exclaimed, "Oh God, if Luther is dead, who will expound the Holy Gospel to us with such clarity!"[11]

Success as an artist earned him a comfortable home near the Imperial Castle in the heart of the town and the admiration of his community. He left behind more than 70 paintings, more than 100 engravings, about 250 woodcuts, about 1,000 drawings, and 3 books on geometry, fortification, and human proportions. His media, style, and subject matter varied widely, ranging from realistic depictions of peasants to allegorical works such as *Knight, Death, and the Devil*. Like Leonardo da Vinci, Albrecht Dürer sought to discover the meaning of nature. He wrote, "For truly art is embedded in nature."[12]

His own nature was exceedingly complicated. Prone to bouts of melancholy, Dürer also dared to portray himself looking remarkably Christ-like but prosperous in a fur-trimmed coat. This self-portrait was one of a series beginning with a self-study he finished while still a teenager. His mature self-confidence was surely merited by his achievements, some of which are illustrated in this book and on its cover. Although Dürer's self-portrait shows him in patrician-like splendor, he never lost his interest in the common people. Indeed, his earthy *Dancing Peasants* may seem a long way from the powerful circles in which the artist came to travel; however, he never forgot his artisan background. His feverishly dancing peas-

Albrecht Dürer, *Self Portrait*. Alte Pinakothek, Munich, Germany. Scala/Art Resource.

ants help give concrete reality to the notion of the Renaissance as a dance over fire and water. If his peasants dance on the soil in reality, they can also be imagined dancing over other basic elements.

LUCAS CRANACH (1472–1553) AND HANS HOLBEIN (1497–1543)

Lucas Cranach the Elder and Hans Holbein the Younger, Dürer's contemporaries, also made great names for themselves even if their subject matter and style did not vary as much as the Nuremberger's. Cranach was a northern Franconian who learned the art of engraving from his father. Active in Vienna from 1500 to 1503, he became court painter to Duke Frederick the Wise of Saxony. There he became a member of the city council and a close friend of the reformers Martin Luther and Philip Melanchthon. His portraits of many of the major figures of the early Saxon Reformation and his striking rendition of many biblical themes helped establish his reputation. Although less refined than Dürer's, his art shows an abundance of psychological power and deeply felt religious sensitivity.

Hans Holbein of Augsburg was the son of a well-known artist who sent him to Italy to further his skills. He spent most of the period from 1515 to 1526 in Basel, Switzerland, where he established excellent connections among leading northern humanists. Holbein did a number of book illustrations for Johann Froben, the publisher of Erasmus. He also received commissions for portraits from a number of wealthy merchants and nobles. His reputation as a brilliant portraitist brought him to England, where he painted a number of luminaries, including Erasmus, Thomas Cromwell, and Thomas More. His painting of Anne of Cleves was used to interest King Henry VIII in marrying the German princess. Holbein's mastery of oil painting and ability to convey shrewd psychological insights assure his enormous modern reputation. He was able to flatter his subjects while at the same time reveal the essences of their character.

THE SCULPTOR TILMAN RIEMENSCHNEIDER (c. 1460–1531)

The Renaissance in the north produced no sculptors of the reputation of Donatello or Michelangelo, but there was some first-rate work done, particularly in wood altar-pieces. Tilman Riemenschneider of Würzburg became famous as one of the greatest altar sculptors of the period. Born in Heiligenstadt in the Eichsfeld, Thuringia, he moved to Würzburg to join the guild of painters, sculptors, and glaziers. He became so successful as a sculptor that he was elected several times to the city council and later held other civic offices. Put on trial and tortured because of his expressed sympathies with rebellious peasants during their revolt of 1524 to 1526, Riemenschneider's last years have been described as "dark and empty." Although the Reformation period created a great deal of uncertainty for sculptors in the north because of the feeling of some Protestants that statues were fearsome idols which should be destroyed, some artists found ways of adapting and surviving. Overall, however, the Reformation did not prove a boon to Renaissance art in the north.

Chronology

c. 1457–1521	Sebastian Brant.	**c. 1525–1569**	Pieter Brueghel the Elder.
c. 1460–1531	Tilman Riemenschneider.	**1547–1616**	Miguel de Cervantes.
1471–1528	Albrecht Dürer.	**c. 1552–1594**	Edmund Spenser.
1472–1553	Lucas Cranach the Elder.	**1554–1586**	Sir Philip Sidney.
1492–1549	Marguerite of Navarre.	**1561–1621**	Mary Sidney.
c. 1494–1533	François Rabelais.	**1562–1621**	Lope de Vega.
1494–1576	Hans Sachs.	**1564–1593**	Christopher Marlowe.
1496–1544	Clémont Marot.	**1564–1616**	William Shakespeare.
1497–1543	Hans Holbein the Younger.	**1577–1640**	Peter Paul Rubens.
1520–1566	Louise Labé.		

Further Reading

RENAISSANCE LITERATURE: GENERAL STUDIES

Ernest Grassi and Maristella Lorch, *Folly and Insanity in Renaissance Literature* (1986).

Thomas Greene, *The Light in Troy: Imitation and Discovery in Renaissance Poetry* (1986).

R. A. Houston, *Literacy in Early Modern Europe: Culture and Education 1500–1800* (1988).

Michael Murrin, *History and Warfare in Renaissance Epic* (1994).

David Quint, *Origin and Originality in Renaissance Literature* (1983).

FRENCH LITERATURE

Mikahil Bakhtin, *Rabelais and His World* (1968).

Lucien Febvre, *The Problem of Unbelief in the Sixteenth Century: The Religion of Rabelais* (1982).

Donald Frame, *François Rabelais: A Study* (1977).

Gertrude Hanish, *Love Elegies of the Renaissance: Marot, Louise Labé and Ronsard* (1979).

Michael Heath, *Rabelais* (1995).

George Joseph, *Clémont Marot* (1985).

Raymond La Charité, ed., *Writing the Renaissance: Essays on Sixteenth-Century French Literature in Honor of Floyd Gray* (1992).

I. D. McFarlane, *A Literary History of France: Renaissance France, 1470–1589* (1974).

Zachary Schiffman, *On the Threshold of Modernity: Relativism in the French Renaissance* (1991).

M. A. Screech, *Rabelais* (1979).

Marcel Tetel, *Marguerite de Navarre's 'Heptameron': Themes, Language and Structure* (1973).

Florence Weinberg, *The Wine and the Will: Rabelais' Bacchic Christianity* (1972).

Charity Cannon Willard, *Christine de Pizan: Her Life and Works* (1984).

ENGLISH LITERATURE

John Bakeless, *The Tragical History of Christopher Marlowe*, 2 vols. (1942).

Elaine Beilin, *Redeeming Eve: Women Writers of the English Renaissance* (1987).

Alan Bray, *Homosexuality in Renaissance England* (1982).

Stephen Greenblatt, *Renaissance Self-Fashioning: From More to Shakespeare* (1980).

Peter Holbrook, *Literature and Degree in Renaissance England: Nashe, Bourgeois Tragedy, and Shakespeare* (1994).

Antea Hume, *Edmund Spenser, Protestant Poet* (1984).

M. M. Resse, *Shakespeare: His World and Work* (1980).

Murray Roston, *Sixteenth-Century English Literature* (1982).

Louise Schleiner, *Tudor and Stuart Women Writers* (1994).

S. Schoenbaum, *William Shakespeare: A Compact Documentary Life* (1977).

Patricia Thompson, *Sir Thomas Wyatt and His Background* (1964).

Retha Warnicke, *Women of the English Renaissance and Reformation* (1983).

SPANISH LITERATURE

William Byron, *Cervantes: A Biography* (1978).

Stephen Gilman, *The Novel According to Cervantes* (1989).

Melveena McKendrick, *Theatre in Spain, 1490–1700* (1984).

Paul Smith, *Writing in the Margin: Spanish Literature in the Golden Age* (1988).

GERMAN LITERATURE

Hans Ellis, *The Early Meisterleider of Hans Sachs* (1974).

James Parente, Jr., *Religious Drama and the Humanists' Tradition* (1987). Treats Christian drama in Germany and the Low Countries between 1500 and 1680.

Roy Pascal, *German Literature in the Sixteenth and Seventeenth Centuries* (1968).

Edwin Zeydel, *Sebastian Brandt* (1976).

RENAISSANCE ART IN THE NORTH: PAINTING

Margaret Aston, *The King's Bedpost: Reformation and Iconography in a Tudor Group Portrait* (1993).

Carl Christensen, *Art and the Reformation in Germany* (1979).

Gregory Clark, ed., *A Tribute to Robert Koch: Studies in the Northern Renaissance* (1995).

Walter Gibson, *Bruegel* (1977).

André Hayum, *The Isenheim Altarpiece: God's Medicine and the Painter's Vision* (1992).

Jane Campbell Hutchinson, *Albrecht Dürer: A Biography* (1990).

Joseph Koerner, *The Moment of Self-Portraiture in German Renaissance Art* (1993).

Carol Purtle, *The Marian Paintings of Jan van Eyck* (1982).

Linda Seidel, *Jan van Eyck's Arnolfini Portrait: Stories of an Icon* (1995).

Larry Silver, *The Paintings of Quinten Massys* (1984).

Margaret Sullivan, *Bruegel's Peasants: Art and Audience in the Northern Renaissance* (1994).

Christopher White, *Peter Paul Rubens, Man and Artist* (1987).

Diane Wolfthal, *The Beginnings of Netherlandish Canvass Painting 1400–1530* (1989).

NORTHERN SCULPTURE

Michael Baxandall, *The Limewood Sculptures of Renaissance Germany* (1982).

Jeffrey Chipps Smith, *German Sculpture of the Later Renaissance* (1994).

MUSIC

Howard Brown, *Music in the Renaissance* (1975).

John Metz, ed., *Music in the German Renaissance: Sources, Styles, and Contexts* (1995).

Roy Strong, *Art and Power: Renaissance Festivals 1450–1650* (1984).

Robert Wangermee, *Flemish Music of the Fifteenth and Sixteenth Centuries* (1975).

David Wulstan, *Tudor Music* (1986).

Notes

1. Cited in Christine de Pisan, *The Treasure of the City of Ladies*, tr. and ed. by Sarah Lawson (New York: Penguin, 1985), p. 17.
2. Cited in Gerda Lerner, *The Creation of Feminist Consciousness: From the Middle Ages to Eighteen-seventy* (New York: Oxford University Press, 1993), pp. 144–145.
3. Cited in Julia O'Faolain and Lauro Martines, eds., *Not in God's Image: Women in History from the Greeks to the Victorians* (New York: Harper and Row, 1973), p. 185.
4. Cited in Charity Cannon Willard, *Christine de Pizan: Her Life and Works* (New York: Persea Books, 1984), p. 223.
5. François Villon, *The Poems of François Villon*, tr. by Galway Kinnell (Boston: Houghton Mifflin, 1969),

p. 191. Copyright © 1965. Reprinted by permission of Houghton Mifflin Co. All rights reserved by Galway Kinnel.

6. Cited in James Bruce Ross and Mary Martin McLaughlin, eds., *The Portable Renaissance Reader* (New York: Viking Press, 1970), p. 449.

7. Marguerite de Navarre, *The Heptameron,* tr. by P. A. Chillon (New York: Penguin, 1984), pp. 100–101.

8. François Rabelais, *The Histories of Gargantua and Pantagruel,* tr. by J. M. Cohen (New York: Penguin, 1972), p. 37.

9. Sebastian Brant, *The Ship of Fools,* tr. by Edwin Zeydel (New York: Columbia University Press, 1944),

pp. 215, 243, and 245. Copyright © by Columbia University Press. Reprinted by permission of the publisher.

10. Cited in Jonathan W. Zophy, *Patriarchal Politics and Christoph Kress (1484–1535) of Nuremberg* (Lewiston, N.Y.: Edwin Mellen Press, 1992), p. 78.

11. Albrecht Dürer, *The Writings of Albrecht Dürer,* ed. and tr. by William Conway (New York: Philosophical Library, 1958), p. 158.

12. Cited in De Lamar Jensen, *Renaissance Europe: Age of Recovery and Reconciliation,* 2nd ed. (Lexington, Mass.: D. C. Heath, 1992), p. 421.

11

NORTHERN RENAISSANCE HUMANISM

Europe north of the Alps also witnessed its own unique humanist movement. Although sharing many of the concerns of the Italian humanists with the revival of classical learning, northern humanism had its own special character. Northern humanists were able to build on the work of the great Italian scholars, but also to add their own concerns as well. Some of the northerners were interested in promoting a sense of pride in their particular national identities. Religious ideals drove many northern humanists. In the north of Europe, humanism also came to be infused with an educational movement of great importance.

THE BROTHERS AND SISTERS
OF THE COMMON LIFE

The Brothers and Sisters of the Common Life were concerned essentially with deepening inward religious faith and with cultivating practical Christian living. Education was seen as a tool for promoting these spiritual concerns. The Brothers and Sisters of the Common Life were founded by Gerard Groote (1340–1384), a well-educated lawyer who became a Carthusian monk. Not finding sufficient religious satisfaction inside monastic walls, Groote left the monastery in 1369 and spent the rest of his life trying to reform the clergy, encourage new forms of devotion, and teach the young at his school at Deventer in the Low Countries.

Groote's ministry attracted male and female followers, who eventually created a semimonastic order of laymen and women as well as members of the clergy. The Brothers and Sisters took no irrevocable vows but sought to live holy lives following the ethics of Christ's Sermon on the Mount. Perhaps their best known member was Thomas à Kempis (1380–1471), who lived in the convent of St. Agnes in the Low Countries for more than seventy years. There he composed *The Imitation of Christ*, which records a personal search for God and shows others how to achieve a direct, personal relationship with God (mysticism). Enormously popular, it has been published in over six thousand editions, including one translated into English by Margaret Beaufort, mother of King Henry VII.

The Brothers and Sisters established boarding schools, opened hostels for poor university students, and operated newly invented printing presses to make classics of devotional literature more widely available. Since they found the ethical treatises of ancients such as Cicero and Seneca to be of great value in teaching the young, they became instrumental in promoting a revival of classical studies in the north. Brethren houses spread from the Netherlands into

Germany. The humanists Erasmus and Johann Reuchlin as well as the reformer Martin Luther were influenced by them as were thousands of less prominent Christians on the eve of the Reformation.

German Humanism

CONRAD CELTIS (1459–1508)

Every part of Europe produced its own brand of humanism. In the German-speaking lands, humanism became infused with incipient nationalism. Conrad Celtis was one of the most influential of the German humanists as well as a major lyric poet. Celtis began life in a peasant family near Würzburg. After running away from home, he managed to study at a number of schools and universities in Germany. On April 18, 1487, Holy Roman Emperor Frederick III crowned him Germany's first poet laureate. Armed with this recognition, Celtis wandered about the empire and made his way to Italy, where he was disgusted by the pretensions of the Italians to cultural superiority over the "barbarians" to the north. Later he studied mathematics and poetry at the University of Cracow in Poland. Eventually he became a professor of rhetoric at the University of Ingolstadt and later at Vienna at the behest of Emperor Maximilian I, where he wrote, taught, and died of syphilis at age forty-nine.

In his inaugural address at Ingolstadt, Celtis challenged his fellow Germans to a cultural rivalry with Italy. "Take up arms, O Germans. Rekindle that old spirit of yours with which so many times you terrorized the Romans."[1] He introduced the German world of letters to the writings of the Roman historian Tacitus, who had praised the Germans in his *Germania*, which Celtis published. He also launched an extensive search for the writings of the tenth-century nun and author Hrosvit of Gandersheim. Hrosvit wrote verse, history, and the only dramas we know of composed between the fourth and eleventh centuries. His published editions of her work were intended to demonstrate the antiquity and excellence of German culture. Celtis also wrote his own histories, including his *Germany Illustrated*, to demonstrate the greatness of the Germans.

CARITAS AND WILLIBALD PIRCKHEIMER

Like many humanists, Conrad Celtis enjoyed a rich circle of friends and correspondents. Among his more gifted humanist correspondents were Caritas (1466–1532) and Willibald Pirckheimer (1470–1530), brother and sister humanists from Nuremberg. Caritas came from a prominent patrician family which valued humanistic learning for both its sons and daughters. She won special permission to enter a convent of the Poor Clares in Nuremberg when she was only twelve by dazzling a Franciscan vicar general with her fluency in Latin. The Convent of St. Clare in Nuremberg had a substantial library, a community of literate nuns which came to include one of her own sisters, and a steady supply of talented preachers and confessors assigned from a nearby Franciscan friary.

There she blossomed as a religious and as an intellectual. She provided editorial leadership in producing a *Chronicle* in German and Latin versions detailing the history of the Order of St. Clare and her own convent. She also began to correspond with leading humanists including Conrad Celtis, Johann Reuchlin, and through her brother, Willibald, with the great Erasmus of Rotterdam. Observing monastic modesty and characteristic self-effacement, she continued to downplay her intellectual gifts, writing Conrad Celtis in 1515, "You know that I am not learned, but merely a friend of learned men."[2]

Some of her self-disparagement may also have come from the fact that in 1503 when she became abbess of St. Clare's, one of her Franciscan superiors ordered her to stop writing in Latin. Many in the church were uncomfortable with the notion of learned women who shared their passion for humanistic learning with others outside the cloisters. Although Caritas continued to do some writing in Latin, her output had become carefully circumscribed. Her *Memoirs* became an important source for the history of the early Reformation in Nuremberg. In 1525 Pirckheimer led a spirited defense of her convent, which the Nuremberg City Council wanted to close as part of its adoption of Lutheranism. She used all her humanistic and theological skills to argue the case for her convent and succeeded in reaching a compromise with the city authorities which allowed St. Clara's to stay in existence until 1590.

Caritas's younger brother, Willibald, became an even more famous humanist, but as a privileged male he had many more opportunities. He was allowed to travel with his father on diplomatic missions for the bishop of Eichstätt, whom his father served as a legal advisor. Willibald studied law at the universities of Padua and Pavia from 1488 to 1495. Along the way he mastered Greek and became fully immersed in humanistic studies. In 1496 Pirckheimer was elected to the all male Nuremberg City Council, where he remained until 1523. He also served Nuremberg as an occasional diplomat and military commander.

Pirckheimer was more than just a civic humanist; he was also a patron of the arts, especially the work of his close friend Albrecht Dürer. Pirckheimer also produced major translations of various classical Greek and Latin authors, including Aristophanes, Aristotle, Galen, Plutarch, Ptolemy, Thucydides, and Xenophon. Deeply religious, he also translated the works of a number of important Greek theologians, including his favorite, Gregory of Nazianzus. His own writings included a satire in praise of gout, a historical geography of Germany, a brief autobiography, and various treatises on theological and moral issues. His contemporaries placed him in the company of Erasmus, Reuchlin, and Jacob Wimpfeling as a group from whom one might expect a "better and greater future for all Christendom."[3]

JACOB WIMPFELING (1450–1528)

The leader of the Rhenish humanists, pedagogue, historian, and clerical reformer was born to a prosperous rural family. He was educated at the universities of Freiburg, Erfurt, and Heidelberg in the liberal arts, canon law, and theology. A skilled poet, he became a court secretary to Count Frederick I of the Palatinate and began teaching at the University of Heidelberg. In 1481 Wimpfeling was named vice-chancellor of the university. He wrote a number of advice manuals for princes and in 1500 published his most famous work, *Germania*, which contained a proposal for the creation of a humanist school in Strasbourg and the first national history of Germany.

Troubled by bouts of conscience, Wimpfeling in 1501 left his university post for life in a Williamite monastery in Strasbourg and began to lobby the magistrates for his plan to establish a Latin school. He also tutored a number of Strasbourg patrician boys, including Jacob Sturm (1489–1553), who became one of the political leaders of the German Reformation. Although the Strasbourg city fathers rejected his plan for a school, Wimpfeling continued his own scholarly activities, writing a controversial attack on the legal profession and several treatises on educational reform. He emphasized the constructive role of education in conveying genuine piety and strong moral character. Wimpfeling retired to his hometown of Schlettstadt in 1515. Briefly favorable to Martin Luther, he soon broke with the Evangelicals over their rejection of ceremonial and defended the cult of the Virgin Mary. Like his fellow humanist Johann Reuchlin, Jacob Wimpfeling remained loyal to the Roman Catholic church until his death.

JOHANN REUCHLIN (1455–1522)

The most celebrated of the German humanists was Johann Reuchlin. Like his role model Giovanni Pico della Mirandola, Reuchlin was interested in all aspects of knowledge. "Truth I worship as God," he once declared.[4] He was born in Germany at Pforzheim and educated by the Brethren of the Common Life and later at the universities of Basel, Freiburg, Orléans, Paris, and Tübingen, where he also taught Greek and served as a magistrate. He made three study trips to Italy and came to know the philosophers Marsilio Ficino and Giovanni Pico. He was also a great admirer of the German humanist and Neoplatonic philosopher Nicholas of Cues (1401–1464).

A professional lawyer, Reuchlin worked for many years as chancellor to the duke of Württemberg, where he also served as head jurist of the Swabian League between 1502 and 1512. His last years were spent as a professor of Greek and Hebrew at the universities of Ingolstadt and Tübingen. From all his vast knowledge, Reuchlin became convinced that the study of Hebrew more than anything else brought him close to God. He claimed that "no one can understand the Old Testament unless they know the language it was written in." Reuchlin concluded that Moses and the other Old Tes-

tament prophets had transmitted many divine truths orally through seventy wise men in an unbroken tradition until they were embodied by the medieval Jewish mystics in the *Cabala*. Because of the many references in the *Cabala* to the Messiah or chosen one, Reuchlin believed that the great Jewish mystical book supported Christian revelation.

In 1506 after more than a decade of work in Hebrew sources, the mild-mannered humanist published a Christian-Hebrew grammar. *The Rudiments of Hebrew* was the first reliable manual of Hebrew grammar to be written by a Christian scholar. He followed it with *On the Cabalistic Art* of 1517 in which he sought to demonstrate that Greek Pythagorean theories and Talmudic and Cabalistic works harmonize with Christian beliefs. His studies came to the attention of a recent convert from Judaism to Christianity, Johann Pfefferkorn, who was making a name for himself by attacking the new interest of humanists in Hebrew writings. In his book *A Mirror for Jews*, Pfefferkorn argued that all Hebrew books should be confiscated and received support for this notion from some of the Dominicans of Cologne, who feared that humanism was undermining traditional scholastic understandings of Christianity.

In 1519 Emperor Maximilian I ordered that all Hebrew books should be confiscated. In response to an inquiry from the archbishop of Mainz, Reuchlin offered the opinion that Hebrew books should not be taken away, but instead should be studied more intensely by Christians. Pfefferkorn then attacked Reuchlin directly in a pamphlet accusing him of ignorance. Although he dreaded public controversy, Reuchlin felt compelled to defend his reputation and fired back a treatise aimed at his antagonist, as well as a collection of testimonials on his behalf titled the *Letters of Famous Men*. Despite being overshadowed by Martin

Luther's controversy with church authorities over indulgences, the Reuchlin affair dragged on until 1520 when Pope Leo X condemned the humanist to silence. Although brokenhearted, Reuchlin accepted the church's judgment and died two years later still loyal to the Roman Catholic church.

A HUMANIST KNIGHT:
ULRICH VON HUTTEN (1488–1523)

In defense of Reuchlin and humanistic studies, two of his most ardent admirers, Crotus Rubianus and Ulrich von Hutten, published one of the most famous popular satires of the period, *The Letters of Obscure Men*. The letters, ostensibly written in deliberately faulty Latin in support of the Dominican Orwin Grotius of Cologne, ridiculed the ignorance and foolishness of those who followed Pfefferkorn's lead. Yet they also contained anti-Semitic jibes such as the charge that Pfefferkorn "still stank like any other Jew."[6] It was also filled with many nasty jokes about women, as female bashing was still a favorite pastime among many male humanists.

A stern papal bull forbidding reading *The Letters* only brought more attention to the satire and further increased sales. One of the anonymous authors, the humanist-knight Hutten, went on to fire additional salvoes against the Catholic church. He condemned hypocritical monks, superstitious priests, the luxury of the papal court, and challenged the pope to support the reformation of the church. Hutten also published an edition of Lorenzo Valla's exposure of the *False Donation of Constantine* and offered his sword and pen to the service of the dissident friar and university professor Martin Luther.

Hutten had come by his anticlericalism honestly, for when he was only eleven his noble but impoverished family had placed him in a monastic school at Fulda, apparently convinced that he was not physically strong enough to succeed as a knight. Six years later he left the cloister before taking his vows to begin a career as an itinerant scholar, much to the dismay of his family. Between 1505 and 1511, Ulrich studied at the universities of Cologne, Erfurt, Frankfort on the Oder, Griefswald, Wittenberg, and Vienna. Along the way he began writing poetry and making a good friend of Crotus Rubianus.

From Vienna he traveled to Italy, the home of the Renaissance, his poverty forcing him for a while into service as a mercenary. By 1513 he had entered into the employ of Albrecht of Brandenburg, bishop of Magdeburg. Embittered by the murder of his cousin Hans by Duke Ulrich of Württemberg, who coveted the victim's wife, Hutten launched a series of devastating literary attacks, *Exposures of Ulrich*, in May 1515. Finding that the pen could indeed be mightier than the sword at times, he also wrote a well-received dialogue, *Phalarismus*, against tyranny. Now reconciled to his family, who appreciated his spirited defense of his cousin, he returned to Italy, where he studied law and became proficient in Greek.

His growing literary fame won him praise from Erasmus and the designation poet laureate from Holy Roman Emperor Maximilian I in August 1517. In late 1517 he reentered the service of Albrecht of Brandenburg, now also archbishop of Mainz. In March 1519 Hutten gladly exchanged the pen for the sword to join the successful campaign against his old enemy Duke Ulrich of Württemberg. Ulrich was ousted from his duchy to the joy of Hutten. During his preparations for the campaign, Hutten became intrigued with the robber knight Franz von Sickingen (1481–1523), who promised to help his embattled humanist-hero

Johann Reuchlin. Both offered their swords to Martin Luther at the Diet of Worms. Hutten had already joined Luther on a papal bull which threatened them both with excommunication.

Disappointed by Emperor Charles V's condemnation of Luther at the Imperial Diet of Worms in 1521, Hutten made several raids against church property and hoped to join Sickingen in his campaign against the wealthy archbishop of Trier. Attacked by a recurring bout of illness induced by syphilis, which troubled him for much of his adult life, Hutten was unable to join Sickingen's ill-fated attack on Trier. When the archbishop and his allies counterattacked the knights, Hutten was forced to flee to Basel, then to Mühlhausen, and finally to Zurich, then in the process of being reformed by Huldrych Zwingli (1488–1531). There he died at age thirty-three seeking medical assistance from a doctor on Lake Zurich. Little could be done to help patients infected by syphilis given the limited state of medical knowledge in the Renaissance.

French Humanism

Although some German humanists such as Conrad Celtis resisted Italian influences, humanism in France eventually came to warmly embrace Italian models, especially during the reign of King François I (1515–1547). As we saw in Chapter 10, the king's sister, Marguerite of Navarre, was one of the leading patrons of humanists in France and a major author herself. François Rabelais was another important French humanist. It was also François I who hired Guillaume Budé (1467–1540), the leading French classical scholar, as master of the royal library at Fontainbleau. Budé was a wandering scholar, lawyer, a master of Greek and Latin, and a dedicated teacher. He had been trained in the law at Orléans, but chose to devote himself to humanistic studies. Since Greek texts and teachers were rare in the north, Budé was largely self-taught. Author of a number of translations, his reputation as one of Europe's foremost Greek scholars was fully established by his learned *Commentaries on the Greek Language* of 1529. The following year, with the help of the king, he established his own school, the College of France in Paris.

Budé's reputation as a leading French humanist was rivalled by only that of Jacques Lefèvre d'Étaples (1450–1536). Lefèvre took a doctorate at Paris and then made a pilgrimage to Italy in 1492, where he was greatly influenced by the Neoplatonists Marsilio Ficino and Pico della Mirandola. Like Pico, he was open to all sources of knowledge, including Jewish mysticism and medieval scholasticism. He published French editions of the mystical writings by Ficino and the German mystical philosopher Nicholas of Cues. Lefèvre is known as the founder of the Aristotelian Renaissance in France for introducing humanistic methods of the study of his thought. In his lectures on Aristotle in Paris, he urged that his texts be taught in relation to their historical context.

As he grew older, Lefèvre increasingly became preoccupied with Christian mysticism and thought. Between 1505 and 1536, he published numerous volumes of commentaries, expositions, and textual criticism, including a major *Commentary on the Epistle of St. Paul*. Like Paul, Lefèvre stressed that humans are saved only by God's grace and forgiving mercy. He advised others to "Proceed from [Aristotelian writings] to a reverent reading of Scripture, guided by . . . the fathers."[7] He also published his own French translation of the New Testament and the Psalms.

Although he remained loyal to the Roman Catholic church, Lefèvre was friendly with a number of Protestants. Admired by Marguerite of Navarre, he became part of the circle of Guillaume Briçonnet, the reform-minded bishop of Meaux outside Paris. Briçonnet appointed him his vicar-general in charge of clerical discipline. At one point, hostility to his reforms was so great that Briçonnet had to flee to Strasbourg, where he came to know and influence a number of men who became prominent in the Reformation, including Guillaume Farel and John Calvin.

Spanish Humanism

The greatest promoter of humanism in Spain was Cardinal Jiménez de Cisneros (1436–1517). Jiménez, the son of an impoverished member of the minor nobility, studied law and theology at the University of Salamanca before obtaining a post at the papal court in Rome. His papal service was rewarded by a major benefice in Spain despite the opposition of some in Spain. Jiménez eventually sought a quieter life inside a Franciscan friary, but his reputation for intelligence and holiness brought him to attention of the Castilian court. After the fall of Muslim Granada in 1492, Queen Isabella of Castile made him her private confessor. In 1494 he became provincial of the Franciscan order; in 1495 archbishop of Toledo and primate of Spain. On one occasion he served as regent for Isabella and Ferdinand. In 1508, the powerful Jiménez was named grand inquisitor of Spain.

Cardinal Jiménez used his positions and his powerful patrons at court to undertake a thorough reform of the Spanish church. He insisted on the enforcement of strict discipline upon the secular and regular clergy. In order to enhance the intellectual and moral level of the clergy, Jiménez founded the University of Alcalá near Madrid in 1509. He thought that the study of history, languages, and texts helped make better Bible scholars and Christians. Under the cardinal's patronage, Alcalá became a leading center of biblical scholarship and the study of Greek and Hebrew. Scholars at Alcalá published a Polyglot Bible, which featured Hebrew, Greek, and Latin texts in parallel columns. It was based on a Greek manuscript from the Vatican Library.

Elio Antonio de Nebrija (c. 1444–1522) was among the most talented of those called to Alcalá to work on the Polyglot Bible. A graduate of the University of Salamanca, Nebrija had continued his studies at the University of Bologna. He went to Italy "to restore the long-lost authors of Latin, who have now been exiled from Spain for many centuries."[8] Having absorbed many of the ideas of Italian humanism, Nebrija returned to Spain in 1505 as a professor of grammar at the University of Salamanca. His snobbery and his application of his philological skills to the Bible got him in trouble with some clerical authorities, who were suspicious of him as a layman entering their scholarly domain. He found a powerful protector in Cardinal Jiménez, who allowed him to publish his biblical commentaries and then invited him to join the team of scholars working on the great Polyglot Bible.

An able Spanish humanist with a different vision of reform from Jiménez's was Juan Luis Vives (1492–1540). A native of Valencia, Vives was educated there until he was seventeen when he left to complete his formal education at the University of Paris. He then took a teaching position at the University of Louvain in the Low Countries. The fame of some of his early writings, including *The Fable of Man* of 1518, attracted the attention of the English court and King Henry VIII invited Vives to tutor his daughter Princess Mary. He also became a fellow of Corpus Christi College at Oxford. His comfortable life in England ended abruptly when he fell out of favor with the king after opposing Henry's efforts to annul his marriage to Catherine of Aragon. Vives eventually settled at Bruges in the Low Countries.

In fifty-two published volumes, Vives outlined an extensive humanist program for the reform of education, law, and the church. He thought that the primary purpose of education was to promote morality and goodness, which could best be done by the study of Greek and Latin literature and the application of Christian ideals and piety. Following the lead of Erasmus, his intellectual model, Vives urged that women be educated as well as men, although not in the same way. In his *On the Education of a Christian Woman*, written in 1523 for Princess Mary, Vives omitted rhetoric from any program of study for girls:

> As for eloquence, I have no great care, for woman needeth it not, but she needeth goodness and wisdom . . . if she be good, it were better to be at home and unknown to other folks, and in company to hold her tongue demurely, and let few see her, and none at all hear her.[9]

English Humanism

Humanism also found a welcome reception in England. It not only infiltrated the universities, but it also reached into the heart of the Tudor court, where King Henry VIII hired humanist scholars to tutor his children. John Colet (1466–1519), the founder of St. Paul's School in London, was one of the most influential of the English humanists. He studied at the universities of Cambridge and Oxford, where he earned his doctorate in theology. Colet had spent two years in Italy in the 1490s and made the acquaintance of Ficino and other members of the

Platonic Academy in Florence. In his lectures at Oxford and later at St. Paul's, Colet argued that the new learning would help people to better understand the Bible and strengthen their faith. He very much regretted that he had never learned Greek himself, "without which we can get nowhere."[10] Among the many English scholars influenced by Colet, none became more famous than Thomas More.

THE MAN FOR ALL SEASONS: THOMAS MORE (1478–1535)

Although some of the northern humanists evinced a high degree of dissatisfaction with the practices of the Renaissance church, many others stayed loyal to the papacy. Sir Thomas More, England's renowned humanist-lawyer, was one of the best known of those who defended the teachings and practices of the old church. He began life in London as the son of a prosperous lawyer and developed a taste for the classics in a Latin grammar school. Young Thomas then served as a page in the household of Cardinal John Morton, archbishop of Canterbury. After studying at Oxford for two years, More turned to common law, which he read at Lincoln's Inn in London.

When More was about twenty, he experienced an acute spiritual crisis and gave serious thought to renouncing his father's dream of a legal career and becoming a Carthusian monk. More spent some time living in a monastery, wearing a hair shirt, sleeping with a block of wood for a pillow, and beating himself every Friday in remembrance of Christ's suffering at the hands of Roman soldiers. He later resumed his legal career, but from time to time he would retreat to the monastic world for brief stays.

In 1504, still only twenty-six, he was elected to Parliament. The next year More married Jane Colt, a woman from a good family, and he personally supervised the education of their children including a daughter, Margaret, who was known as a brilliant student of the classics. Since September 1510 More served as undersheriff of London, representing the city's interest in court. More also entered the diplomatic service of King Henry VIII and undertook a number of missions to the Continent. In 1518 he became a member of the king's council, was named a treasury official in 1521, and was elected as Speaker of the House of Commons in 1523.

When Cardinal Thomas Wolsey lost favor because of his failure to secure an annulment of the king's marriage to Catherine of Aragon in 1529, the multitalented More was chosen to succeed him as lord chancellor of England. A staunch Roman Catholic, he later resigned when Henry rejected papal supremacy. In 1535 More was executed for having followed his conscience and defied the king. His strength of convictions has become the stuff of legends.

Despite his spectacular public career, More took the time to pursue his intellectual and spiritual interests. He was a very close friend of leading humanists such as John Colet and the witty Dutchman Erasmus. Erasmus in fact wrote his famous satire, *Praise of Folly*, at More's home. *Praise of Folly* (*Encomium Moriae*) can also be rendered as "Praise of More." More's humanist friends encouraged his continuing study of the classics and his writings, including an important *History of Richard III*, which served as one of the sources for Shakespeare's play.

The fantasy *Utopia* (Nowhere) of 1516 was Thomas More's most significant published work. In the first part of *Utopia*, he criticized the political and social abuses of his times, such as the harsh punishments of the criminal code, the sufferings of the rural poor from the enclosing of land, the incessant wars between Christian states, and materialism. More wrote that "as long as there is any property and while money is the standard of all things, I cannot think that a nation can be governed either justly or happily."[11] In the second part, he described the social arrangements of an imaginary island called Utopia set in the then New World.

More revolutionized Plato's *Republic* by describing his perfect republic in exact detail and stressing a greater degree of equality than had the Greek. In More's fantasy world, ordinary people work only a six hour day and live in nice houses with glass windows, fireproof roofs, and gardens. The water supply is unpolluted and even marketplaces and hospitals are clean. Reason and righteousness rule the land. There is no private property and the goods in the shopping centers are free for the taking. Everyone is required to work. Even the lawgivers dress like everyone else except priests. Women are somewhat subordinated to men, but receive military training. Wars of conquest are not allowed, except for the purpose of claiming unused land. Religion is flexible and undogmatic. The contrasts with More's England are obvious and even he failed to live up to the ideals of his Utopia. For example, as lord chancellor, More vigorously persecuted Lutherans. Nevertheless, the *Utopia* remains as a fascinating vision of a humanist patriarch's dreamworld.

Erasmus (c. 1466–1536), The Prince of the Humanists

Desiderius Erasmus was generally acknowledged as the most respected northern humanist of the sixteenth century. Popes, emperors, kings, princes, and rich merchants wished to be among his patrons, universities offered professorships, and scholars sought out his company. His manners and conversation were "polished, affable, and even charming."[12] No one could match his knowledge of the classics or the writings of the church fathers. His own writings were prodigious. All this was quite an accomplishment for a man who started life as the illegitimate son of a priest and a daughter of a physician. His mother placed him and his older brother at a school in Deventer, a major center of the Brothers and Sisters of the Common Life. Later Erasmus studied at a Brethren school at Bois-le-Duc for two years.

Shortly after both of his parents died from the plague, he entered an Augustinian monastery. Six years later Erasmus accepted ordination as a priest as a way out of the cloisters. In 1494 he became secretary to the bishop of Cambrai and later enrolled at the College de Montaigu in Paris. Later he claimed to hate both its "stale eggs and stale [scholastic] theology."[13] The year 1499 found him in England as a tutor, where he heard the brilliant humanist John Colet lecture on Paul. Colet urged Erasmus to study Greek as a preparation to more serious study of theology. Erasmus also began a strong friendship with Thomas More.

Returning to the Continent, Erasmus settled first in Paris and then in Louvain, where he published 800 Latin *Adages* in 1500. This collection of wise sayings culled from the classics was enormously popular because it made some of the wit and wisdom of the classics available to the non-classically trained elite. The *Adages* were followed by his *Handbook of the Christian Soldier* (1503), which stressed the importance of faith; editions of Cicero's and Saint Jerome's letters; and a critical edition of Valla's *Annotations on the New Testament*. In 1505 Erasmus was back in England to begin working on his own translation of the New Testament. From 1506 to 1509 he worked in Italy as a tutor and immersed himself deeply in classical studies while drawing inspiration from the work of Italian humanism.

Back in England in 1509 while resting

Hans Holbein the Younger, *Erasmus Writing.* Louvre, Paris, France. Giraudon/Art Resource.

from his Italian journey, Erasmus penned his most popular writing, *Praise of Folly*. In this work he attempted to criticize abuses in the church and society and to promote purer spirituality in religion. Erasmus lambasted "the cheat of pardons and indulgences" and those who worshiped the Virgin Mary "before the Son." Even the papacy failed to escape his censure. "Now as to the popes of Rome, who pretend themselves Christ's vicar, if they would but imitate his exemplary life," poverty, and contempt of the world.[14] The *Praise of Folly* was tremendously popular despite being placed on the Index of Forbidden Books by the papacy in the 1560s.

For the next three years Erasmus taught theology and Greek at Cambridge University. Then he moved to Basel in Switzerland to be closer to his publisher as his nine-volume edition of the writings of St.

Jerome rolled from the presses of Johann Froben, one of the great names in the history of publishing. Erasmus found the Swiss town to be a congenial environment: "I am extraordinarily happy. Every day I enjoy the company of learned men. . . . Nowhere have I found so delightfully instructive a society."[15] In 1516 his influential Greek New Testament issued from the presses, as did editions of the writings of Cato, Plutarch, and Seneca. Erasmus like other humanists thought the classics of Greece and Rome would prepare the mind for the reception of God. In addition, the classics were worth studying in their own right. Scholastics, who felt compelled to reconcile the classics with Christian understandings, were ridiculed as people "extant in their own lifetimes," who were content with using faulty translations and missed the essence of Christianity's message in their preoccupation with complex reasoning.[16]

Although capable of ridiculing most women, Erasmus was one of the first prominent male humanists to recommend study at least for the daughters of the rich after having been impressed by the erudition of Thomas More's daughter, Margaret Roper (1504–1544). She had translated his treatise on the Lord's Supper. Study "is not only a weapon against idleness but also a means of impressing the best precepts upon a girl's mind and leading her to virtue" he wrote. In his "Dialogue between an Abbot and a Learned Lady," Erasmus has his learned housewife inform an ignorant abbot that "if men can't play their parts, they should get off the stage and let women assume their roles."[17]

Erasmus was also a pacifist who hoped Europe would bloom with flowers rather than continued strife. In his *The Complaint of Peace* of 1517, he rejected even the Augustinian notion of a just war. Erasmus argued that "war incessantly sows war,

vengeance seethingly draws vengeance, kindness generously engenders kindness."[18] He was also appalled by the concept of crusades and holy war and the involvement of the church's leadership in alliances and military actions. Erasmus begged the papacy to follow the example of Christ and reign as princes of peace.

Erasmus is well known for his criticisms of a great deal in contemporary church practice. Yet what he criticized in the church, he criticized out of love and with a hope for peaceful reform. Although initially sympathetic with Martin Luther's concern about abuses in the church, Erasmus increasingly became alarmed at the Wittenberger's dogmatism, the violence of some of his followers, and the movement to separate from the church. The Reformation threatened his own humanist network and cost him dearly. As he lamented in a letter of 1523:

> Before this division reached its present bitterness, I used to enjoy literary friendships with nearly all the scholars in Germany. . . . Several of them have now grown cold. . . . I also enjoyed contacts with many who now take a more savage line against Luther than I would wish.[19]

Accused of being a "heretic Lutheran," Erasmus denied authorship of the 1517 satire *Julius Excluded from Heaven*, in which the swaggering warrior-pope is excluded from paradise (a draft was later found in Erasmus's own handwriting). In 1524 he also published against Luther's conception of predestination, arguing for *The Freedom of the Will*. When the Protestant Reformation came to Basel in 1529, the scholarly Erasmus fled to Freiburg, where he lived for six more years. In August 1535 he returned to Basel to edit the works of the third century church father Origen. Still mourning the martyrdom of his friend Sir Thomas More, he died eleven months later.

Chronology

1340–1384	Life of Gerard Groote.	**c. 1466–1535**	Erasmus.
1380–1471	Thomas à Kempis.	**1466–1532**	Caritas Pirckheimer.
1436–1517	Jiménez de Cisneros.	**1467–1540**	Guillaume Budé.
c. 1444–1522	Elio de Nebrija.	**1470–1530**	Willibald Pirckheimer.
1450–1528	Jacob Wimpfeling.	**1478–1538**	Thomas More.
1450–1536	Jacques Lefèvre d'Etaples.	**1488–1523**	Ulrich von Hutten.
1455–1522	Johann Reuchlin.	**1492–1540**	Juan Luis Vives.
1459–1508	Conrad Celtis.	**1504–1544**	Margaret More Roper.
1466–1519	John Colet.		

Further Reading

NORTHERN HUMANISM

Jerry Bentley, *Humanists and Holy Writ: New Testament Scholarship in the Renaissance* (1983).

E. Harris Harbison, *The Christian Scholar in the Age of the Reformation*, rpr. (1984).

Robert Mandrou, *From Humanism to Science, 1480–1700* (1978).

Charles Nauert, Jr., *Humanism and the Culture of Renaissance Europe* (1995).

Eugene Rice, Jr., *Saint Jerome in the Renaissance* (1988).

Erika Rummel, *The Humanist-Scholastic Debate in the Renaissance and Reformation* (1995).

GERMAN HUMANISM

Eckhart Bernstein, *German Humanism* (1983).

Maria Grossman, *Humanism in Wittenberg 1485–1517* (1975).

Charles Nauert, Jr., *Agrippa and the Crisis of Renaissance Thought* (1965).

James Overfield, *Humanism and Scholasticism in Late Medieval Germany* (1985).

Lewis Spitz, Jr., *The Religious Renaissance of the German Humanists* (1967).

FRENCH HUMANISM

Philip Hughes, *Lefèvre: Pioneer of Ecclesiastical Renewal in France* (1984).

Donald Kelley, *The Foundations of Modern Historical Scholarship* (1970).

David MacNeil, *Guillaume Budé and Humanism in the Reign of Francis I* (1975).

Eugene Rice, *The Prefatory Epistles of Jacques Lefèvre d'Etaples and Related Texts* (1972).

Franco Simone, *The French Renaissance: Medieval Tradition and Italian Influence in Shaping the Renaissance in France* (1970).

SPANISH HUMANISM

J. A. Fernández-Santamaria, *The State, War and Peace: Spanish Political Thought in the Renaissance, 1516–1559* (1977).

Carlos Norena, *Juan Luis Vives* (1970).

ENGLISH HUMANISM

Maria Dowling, *Humanism in the Age of Henry VIII* (1986).

John Gleason, *John Colet* (1989).

Richard Marius, *Thomas More, A Biography* (1984).

Louis Martz, *Thomas More: The Search for the Inner Man* (1990).

ERASMUS

Cornelius Augustijn, *Erasmus: His Life, Works, and Influence* (1991).

Roland Bainton, *Erasmus of Christendom* (1969).

Marjorie O'Rourke Boyle, *Christening Pagan Mysteries: Erasmus in Pursuit of Wisdom* (1977).

Léon-E. Halkin, *Erasmus, A Critical Biography* (1993).

Lisa Jardine, *Erasmus, Man of Letters* (1993).

James McConica, *Erasmus* (1991).

John Payne, *Erasmus: His Theology of the Sacraments* (1970).

Erika Rummel, *Erasmus as a Translator of the Classics* (1985).

Richard Schoeck, *Erasmus of Europe: The Making of a Humanist 1467–1500* (1990).

J. Kelley Sowards, *Desiderius Erasmus* (1975).

James Tracy, *The Politics of Erasmus* (1978).

Notes

1. Cited in Lewis Spitz, Jr., *The Northern Renaissance* (Englewood Cliffs, N.J.: Prentice Hall, 1972), p. 19.
2. Cited in Paula Datsko Barker, "Caritas Pirckheimer: A Female Humanist Confronts the Reformation," *The Sixteenth Century Journal*, vol. 26, no. 2 (Summer, 1995), p. 264.
3. Cited in Jackson Spielvogel, "Willibald Pirckheimer," in Jonathan W. Zophy, ed., *The Holy Roman Empire: A Dictionary Handbook* (Westport, Conn.: Greenwood Press, 1980), p. 380.
4. Cited in Lewis Spitz, Jr., *The Renaissance and Reformation Movements* (Chicago: Rand McNally, 1971), p. 280
5. Cited in Erika Rummel, *The Humanist-Scholastic Debate in the Renaissance and Reformation* (Cambridge, Mass.: Harvard University Press, 1995), p. 112.
6. Ulrich von Hutten and others, *Letters of Obscure Men,* tr. by Francis Griffin Stokes, intro. by Hajo Holborn (Philadelphia: University of Pennsylvania Press, 1964), p. 157.
7. Cited in Erika Rummel, "Voices of Reform from Hus to Erasmus," in Thomas Brady, Jr., Heiko Oberman, and James Tracy, eds., *Handbook of European History 1400–1600: Late Middle Ages, Renaissance and Reformation* (Leiden: E. J. Brill, 1995), p. 69.
8. Ibid., p. 67.

9. Cited in Merry Wiesner, *Women and Gender in Early Modern Europe* (New York: Cambridge University Press, 1993), p. 127.
10. Cited in Rummel, *Handbook,* vol. 2, p. 74.
11. Thomas More, *Utopia,* tr. by Paul Turner (Baltimore, Md.: Penguin, 1965), p. 65.
12. Cited in Spitz, *Renaissance and Reformation,* p. 295.
13. Cited in De Lamar Jensen, *Renaissance Europe: Age of Recovery and Reconciliation,* 2nd ed. (Lexington, Mass.: D. C. Heath, 1992), p. 383.
14. Cited in Lewis Spitz, ed., *The Protestant Reformation* (Englewood Cliffs, N.J.: Prentice Hall, 1966), p. 21.
15. Cited in M. D. Hottinger, *The Stories of Basel, Berne and Zurich* (London: J. M. Dent and Sons, Ltd., 1933), pp. 65–66.
16. Erasmus, *Praise of Folly and Letter to Martin Dorp 1515,* tr. by Betty Radice (New York: Penguin, 1971), pp. 152–156.
17. *The Colloquies of Erasmus,* tr. by Craig Thompson (Chicago: University of Chicago Press, 1965), p. 223.
18. *The Essential Erasmus,* tr. by John Dolan (New York: New American Library, 1964), p. 203.
19. *The Correspondence of Erasmus: Letters 1252 to 1355,* tr. by R. A. B. Mynors (Toronto: University of Toronto Press, 1989), vol. 9, p. 389.

12

SCIENCE AND TECHNOLOGY

Compared to the dazzling achievements of modern scientists in computing, space exploration, or medicine, those of the Renaissance in science and technology may seem crude and minimal. When placed in their historical context, however, the period witnessed some startling advances. At the beginning of the Renaissance, European science and technology lagged behind some other parts of the world such as China. By 1600 the Europeans had made many important technological and scientific advances and laid the foundations for the great breakthroughs of the Western Scientific and Industrial Revolutions of the eighteenth and nineteenth centuries. That European science and technology emerged from an exclusively male intellectual world so firmly attached to ancient beliefs in alchemy, astrology, and magic is all the more amazing. In some ways, Renaissance humanism with its explorations of the thoughts of ancient thinkers and its discovery of lost manuscripts had served to strengthen the attachment of Europeans to the science of Aristotle, Galen, and Ptolemy.

Astrology and Alchemy

People living in the Renaissance had inherited a set of fixed assumptions that seemed to explain clearly how God's creation worked. Nature was thought to be living and could respond to spiritual stimuli, just as humans do. Most Renaissance intellectuals continued to believe, as had most ancient Greek scientific thinkers, that matter was made up of four basic elements: air, earth, fire, and water. Each of these elements in turn possessed characteristics drawn from four basic qualities: heat, cold, dryness, and moistness. These qualities were related to the four basic medical humors that determined health: choleric, melancholic, phlegmatic, and sanguine. Even the planets, as they slid past each other in concentric spheres pulled by angels, partook of these same qualities. Thus Saturn was believed to be cold and dry, whereas Mars was considered hot.

Furthermore, the movement of the planets and stars was believed to have an impact of life on earth. As the planets moved in relationship to each other and the still earth, their movements caused changes in the lives of humans, animals, and crops. By calculating the correct movement of the planets, astrologers could forecast when plagues or famines would occur and determine when was the best time to conceive a child, plant a crop, or go to war. Even such prominent capitalists as the Fuggers relied on their astrologers to help them make business decisions. Astrology was utilized by prominent individuals and governments throughout the Renaissance.

A few bold skeptics such as the humanist Giovanni Pico della Mirandola noticed in the 1480s that the accuracy of astrological weather predictions was low. He once kept a weather diary and found that the astrologers were correct for only seven out of one hundred days. At the end of his life, while retaining his beliefs in ancient mysticism and magic, he dared to write a "Treatise Against Astrology" in which he noted that "Plato and Aristotle, the leaders of the [philosophy] profession, considered astrology unworthy of discussion."[1] He recommended that physicians be trusted more than astrologers on matters of health when they contradicted each other. Yet Pico's reservations about astrology were a minority opinion even among learned humanists who stressed rationality. Astrology seemed to many a useful and time-tested science. Its teachings had been supported by many revered sages and important Christian theologians. It was taught in the universities along with astronomy. Almanacs filled with astrological lore and predictions continued to be in great demand all during the Renaissance and beyond.

Next to astrology and physics, alchemy continued to be a leading "science" of the day. It had long been observed that many substances in nature change over time. For example, flowers bloom and wilt and change colors. Even basic substances can be altered by heating or cooling. Many alchemists became intrigued with the idea of transforming base metals such as lead into gold. If these transmutations seemed more the work of magicians than scientists, it was argued that magic could be both good and bad. In any case, our modern distinctions between magic and science seldom existed in the Renaissance, although some humanists such as Leonardo Bruni and Poggio

Bracciolini attempted to make them. Despite the hopeless muddle, it is interesting to note that in attempting to alter basic substances, alchemists learned a great deal about the properties of those substances and developed much of the equipment used by later chemists.

PARACELSUS (1493–1541)

The difficulty in distinguishing between magic and science is well illustrated by the work of the controversial Swiss-German alchemist and physician known as Paracelsus. Paracelsus was born Theophrastus Bombastus von Hohenheim at Einsiedeln in Switzerland. His physician father introduced him to the practice of medicine at an early age by taking the boy with him on his rounds. When Paracelsus was ten, his family moved to Villach, a mining community in the Tyrol. With his habitual curiosity, he became interested in mining, minerals, and the occupational diseases of miners. Much of his education was informal and practical, although he did study with Johann Trithemius, the learned humanist and abbot of Sponheim, and later at a number of Italian universities. Paracelsus may even have received a doctor of medicine degree from the new university at Ferrara.

For a number of years, he wandered throughout Europe and maybe even to Arabia and Egypt. Paracelsus sharpened his medical skills working as an army surgeon before setting up a medical practice at Salzburg in Austria. There he began a lifetime pattern of public controversy with the authorities followed by a hasty departure. The next year he surfaced at Basel, Switzerland as town doctor and professor at the university, although the latter position was not approved by the faculty, many of whom were hostile to him. Nevertheless, he did manage to achieve a number of practical successes, such as saving the leg of the publisher Johann Froben from amputation. This won him the respect of Erasmus, Froben's most famous author.

Announcing that he alone would restore medicine from its barbarous state, Paracelsus flung copies of the authoritative writings of the Greek Galen (c. A.D. 129–199) and the Muslim Aristotelian Avicenna (d. 1037) into a bonfire in order to symbolize his rejection of traditional medical theory and practice. He boldly asserted, in German lectures rather than the customary Latin, the need for the use of the experimental method in the discovery and treatment of disease. Little had come of the efforts of several fourteenth century Franciscans at Oxford to provide an experimental method for science. Italian universities such as Padua had begun to stress, in theory at least, the virtues of experimentation. Although Paracelsus did make advances in the use of pain-killing drugs and natural healing, he also believed that herbs and chemicals possessed "virtues," or spirits, that could be extracted and used to cure diseases. His system combined alchemy, magic, and mysticism. For him, God was an eternal mind and an eternal center of power, from which all things flow in a kind of life force or universal substance. He referred to himself as a "prince of philosophy and medicine" and claimed to have discovered a "philosopher's tincture" that could transmute metals and prolong human life.[2]

His arrogance in attacking his critics and unconventional treatments resulted in his exile from Basel in 1528. Paracelsus then became an itinerant lay preacher and physician wandering throughout Germany and Switzerland. He continued to publish books that defended his theories, such as his *Great Surgery* of 1536 and his *Seven Defenses* of 1538, plus numerous writings about alchemy. Paracelsus was able to make a fa-

vorable impression on Archduke Ferdinand of Austria, who permitted him to return to Salzburg, where he died. Paracelsus left a mixed legacy, including some useful work on the properties of mercury and the influence of the mind on diseases of the body. Nevertheless, his experimental work contains numerous errors and is such a strange amalgam of science and quackery that others found it difficult to build on much of his murky thinking.

Medicine and Andreas Vesalius (1514–1564)

Some of Paracelsus's anger at the medical practices of his day is most understandable. After all, many still believed that the human body contained four basic fluids: blood, phlegm, red or yellow bile, and black bile. The proper balance of these four humors was believed to be necessary for maintaining proper health as shown in the complexion. Thus bloodletting was commonly used to correct the problems of imbalance among the humors. Anemic people were often bled with disastrous results.

The balance of the humors and life cycles was also thought to be linked to the movement of heavenly bodies. Renaissance doctors, therefore, commonly used astrology to determine the best time for treatment and the nature of that treatment. Further problems arose from the very training most Renaissance physicians received. Medical schools used the writings of the prolific second-century Greek physician Galen as their guide to human anatomy. Galen had made a number of astute judgments about human anatomy, but his work was fundamentally flawed by his belief that human organs were similar to those of animals. Out of deference to the classical and Christian beliefs in the sanctity of the human body, most dissections prior to the fourteenth century had been limited to dogs, pigs, and when available, apes from northern Africa. Only the anatomical treatise of 1316 by the Italian Mondine di Luzzi was based on the dissection of humans.

Given the limitations of the ancient and medieval knowledge of anatomy, it is easy to see why the anatomical studies of Leonardo da Vinci and Andreas Vesalius were so revolutionary. Leonardo, the supremely talented artist-scientist, had to study human anatomy and other natural things in order to portray them accurately. He performed over thirty dissections. As he wrote in his *Treatise on Painting*, "We rightly call painting the grandchild of nature and related to God."[3] For him, painting was a branch of science which sought to communicate with precision the miracles of nature. Renaissance sculptors, as we have seen, also made their own meticulous studies of human anatomy.

The greatest anatomist of the Renaissance was a Flemish born scholar with a passion for science named Andreas Vesalius. A precocious youth, Vesalius studied at universities in Louvain and Paris. Earning his medical degree at Paris, Vesalius worked for a while as a military surgeon. He then made the long journey to Italy to study at the most renowned medical school in Europe, the University of Padua. For the most part, only Italian universities were dissecting human cadavers and conducting autopsies, though on a limited scale. His ability was quickly recognized and he was appointed to teach anatomy at age twenty-three. His method of instruction was revolutionary. Instead of reading Galen's description of the human organs to his students while a barber-surgeon located each one, Vesalius used the scalpel skillfully himself and reverently pointed out errors in his hero Galen. News of his dissections spread,

Titian, *Andreas Vesalius*. Galleria Palatine, Palazzo Pitti, Florence. Nimatallah/Art Resource.

and they became public events of considerable interest.

He had already begun writing his *On the Fabric of the Human Body*, which was published in 1543 when Vesalius was only twenty-eight. It carefully described in words and detailed drawings the parts, organs, and functions of the human body. Regrettably, the Fleming repeated some of Galen's errors, most notably his description of the circulation of the blood. He accepted wholesale Galen's notion of the "septum" as a wall dividing the heart, which he considered porous, and thus facilitating the passage of the blood from the veins to the arteries. The Spanish heretic Michael Servetus (c. 1509–1553) actually had a better understanding of the circulatory system, whose workings were not fully explained until the work of the English physician William Harvey (1578–1657), who also studied in the learned atmosphere of Padua.

Despite its flaws, Vesalius's book has the most accurate anatomical drawings of the time and his understanding of human anatomy represented a considerable advancement. He had managed to correct nearly 200 errors in Galen. His book's marvelously detailed illustrations may have been prepared in the studio of Titian and surpassed even the studies done by Leonardo da Vinci. *On the Fabric* was criticized by some clerics because it showed an equal number of ribs on both sides of the male body; thus he was accused of denying that Eve had been created out of one of Adam's ribs. He was also accused of plagiarism and for going too far in correcting Galen. Despite the mixed reception, his book eventually became an invaluable guide to physicians and surgeons all over Europe.

Shortly after the publication of his masterwork, and deeply hurt by the criticisms it had received, he left Padua to spend the last twenty years of his life as a court

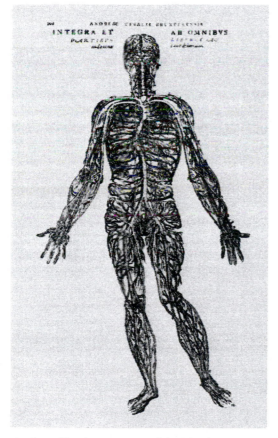

Andreas Vesalius, *Veins and Arteries System.* Collection Fratelli Fabbri, Milan, Italy. Bridgeman/Art Resource.

Andreas Vesalius, *Musculature Structure of a Man.* Collection Fratelli Fabri, Milan, Italy. Bridgeman/Art Resource.

physician to Holy Roman Emperor Charles V and then his son, Philip II, king of Spain. In Spain, Vesalius continued his medical research and made several more valuable contributions to the art of surgery. He also published several new editions of the still-admired work of Galen. He died on a return trip from a pilgrimage to Jerusalem.

The New Astronomy and Nicholas Copernicus (1473–1543)

In 1543, the same year that Andreas Vesalius published his *On the Fabric of the Human Body*, the Pole Nicholas Copernicus published his monumental *On the Revolution of the Celestial Spheres*. Copernicus's work did for astronomy what Vesalius's study had done for anatomy. At the heart of the world-view of the astrologers was an earth-centered understanding of the universe fostered by a host of scholars in the wake of the Hellenistic astronomer Claudius Ptolemy (second century A.D.). Ptolemy's system placed the earth at the center of the universe. This seemed to satisfy the sense, appeal to human egoism, and concur with certain sentences in the Bible. After all, Joshua had ordered the sun, not the earth, to stand still (Joshua 10:12). Before Ptolemy, the revered Aristotle had postulated that the planets move in uniform circular orbits in crystalline spheres.

Copernicus, a Polish mathematician, came to the conclusion that while Aristotle was essentially correct, Ptolemy had erred in placing the earth at the center of the solar system. Copernicus was born the son of a merchant in the busy commercial town of Thorn (Toruń) on the Vistula River in Poland. His uncle, before becoming bishop

of Ermeland in Prussia, had studied at Bologna. He realized the quality of his nephew's mind and sent him to study at the University of Cracow, where he first developed his love for astronomy. In 1496 the young Pole set out for Bologna at his uncle's request to prepare for an ecclesiastical career. A perpetual student, Copernicus studied Greek, mathematics, law, and astronomy at Bologna, canon law at Ferrara (earning his doctorate in 1503), and medicine at Padua. Returning to Ermeland in 1506, he spent the last three decades of his life as a physician to his uncle and a canon of Frauenberg Cathedral.

While using his legal training in the service of his cathedral chapter, Copernicus spent a lot of time in the turret of a nearby castle. Despite rather poor eyesight and poor instruments, he attempted to make observations and mathematical calculations. This led him to his startling conclusion that the venerated Ptolemy was wrong about the location of the earth and its lack of rotation. As he wrote:

> Whatever happens in the course of nature remains in good condition and in its best arrangement. Without cause, therefore, Ptolemy feared that the earth and heavenly things if set in motion would be dissolved by the action of nature, for the functioning of nature is something entirely different from artifice, or that which could be conditioned by the human mind. But why did he not fear the same, and indeed in much higher degree, for the universe, whose motion would have to be as much more rapid as the heavens are larger than the earth?[4]

These conjectures were offered in his breakthrough book, *On the Revolution of the Celestial Spheres*, which was completed in 1530 but circulated in manuscript form only until the year of his death. Copernicus, as a loyal member of the clergy, was concerned that even his mild revision of Ptolemy might not sit well with the church. He humbly dedicated his book to the reform Pope Paul III (r. 1534–1549) with the hope that it would not be considered too upsetting to church dogma. Some Catholics and most Protestants did find his views unsettling. Many found his mathematical proofs insufficient. Nearly a century later, the work of others such as the German astrologer and mathematician Johann Kepler (1571–1630) and the Florentine mathematician and physicist Galileo Galilei (1564–1642) made Copernicus's fundamental discovery more convincing.

Women and Science

The limited progress that science made in the Renaissance was done in a closed world, where women were seldom admitted. Copernicus in his cathedral environment and Vesalius at his university did not have women colleagues with which to consult. There may have been a few women doctors on the medical faculty of the University of Salerno in the High Middle Ages. A legendary twelfth-century woman named Trotula was presumed to have been the wife and daughter of a physician and to have taught and written at Salerno; a widely circulated handbook on gynecology and obstetrics bears her name. In the fourteenth century a number of women in Italy received royal medical licenses, but there is no evidence that they attended formal university courses. Some of them may have been midwives or relatives of male doctors. Costanza Calenda, daughter of the dean of the medical school at Naples, might have attended the University of Florence. In 1422 and 1423, she appeared as a doctor of medicine at her father's university.

North of the Alps, several women learned in medicine wrote useful handbooks. They include Anna of Denmark, wife of the elector of Saxony and daughter of King Christian III of Denmark, and Duchess Eleanor Marie Rosalie of Jaggersdorf and Troppau. Duchess Eleanor's medical treatise was entitled *Six Books of Medicines and Artifices, Chosen for All Human Bodily Weaknesses and Illnesses.* Many less privileged women had long worked as healers and midwives throughout Europe. During the Middle Ages both men and women who practiced medicine were often called "physicians," but by the sixteenth century, only men who had attended medical school could be called "physicians." A similar trend was followed in other professions, even those that did not require university training. For example, women might continue to brew medicines, but only men could use the title "apothecary" and, therefore, charge higher fees for their services. Not until the seventeenth century do we begin to see women scientists in larger numbers and from a greater variety of circumstances.

Renaissance Technology

If science made only halting progress during the Renaissance, technology forged ahead as practical individuals sought to solve everyday problems. As we have seen in Chapter 9, major improvements were made in naval technology during the fifteenth century which permitted Europeans to expand trade opportunities and extend their influence around the world. The European voyages of discovery were made possible in part by new tools of navigation, larger and better rigged ships, and better maps and charts. Similar changes also occurred in military technology. Gunpowder weapons, while often crude and unreliable, fundamentally changed the nature of warfare on land and sea.

AGRICULTURAL TECHNOLOGY

In agriculture, considerable progress was made by the so-called "new husbandry."[5] It was a set of adjustments in agricultural practices that first made their appearances in the Low Countries in the late Middle Ages and slowly spread to other parts of Europe throughout the Renaissance and into the eighteenth century. The basic elements of the new husbandry were all closely related: new crops, staff feeding of cattle, and the elimination of fallowing. The result was that farmers were able to maintain more and better-fed cattle, thereby increasing the supply of animal products. Better-fed animals produced more fertilizer, which helped to increase cereal yields. The new fodder crops, such as alfalfa, clover, and turnips, also turned out to be useful as alternating crops to cereals in better rotations. The European voyages of discovery also brought in new foodstuffs and substantially improved the diets of Europeans.

Improvements also eventually took place in the use of energy. Windmills such as those tilted at by Cervantes's fictional Don Quixote were improved in the course of the sixteenth century. The Dutch took the lead not only in improving the windmill, but in applying wind and water power to fulling and pumping. By applying the windmill to an Archimedean screw (invented by the great ancient Syracusian scientist Archimedes, c. 287–212 B.C.) or a series of buckets, they could not only keep seawater outside their protective dikes but even pump inland lakes. By 1500 the Netherlanders had reclaimed or safeguarded over 285,000 acres of good farmland from the sea. Other parts of Europe followed their lead in draining swamps and marshes.

MINING AND METALLURGY

Mining and metallurgy had been in decline following the Black Death in the middle of the fourteenth century, followed by the long depression which went into the fifteenth century. From about 1450, mining, especially in central Europe. entered an age of advancement unlike anything ever seen before. Expanded demand for metal weapons, clocks, and other devices helped fuel the revival of mining. New techniques for extracting ores and the invention of the blast furnace, which made it possible to manufacture cast iron added to the mining boom. Germans led Europe and the world in mining technology, developing the transmission of waterpower to high-elevation mines, using gunpowder for blasting rocks, using horse-powered treadmills to run windlasses, and developing a variety of pumping devices.

These techniques were spread by the publication from the newly developed printing presses of a large number of how-to-do manuals. The best of these was written by a practicing physician, Georg Agricola (1495–1555). Agricola traveled extensively throughout Bohemia and Saxony and carefully observed the practices and equipment used in mining. Published posthumously in 1556, his wonderfully detailed *On the Principles of Mining* was eventually translated from Latin and widely spread by that most influential of Renaissance inventions, the printing press. Tragically, the rise of mining contributed greatly to the deforestation and pollution of parts of Europe.

THE PRINTING PRESS
AND ITS IMPACT

Few inventions short of the automobile, computer, or television have ever had such an impact on changing cultures as the printing press. Although the Chinese had used a form of printing from hand carved blocks of wood since at least A.D. 800, Europeans had been printing in that fashion only since the twelfth century. Playing cards and coins had long been stamped in Europe. Moveable type, however, did not appear in Europe until the time of Johann Gutenberg (c. 1398–1468) of Mainz. Gutenberg was the son of a goldsmith who worked for the archbishop of Mainz, the leading churchman in the Holy Roman Empire. Little else is known of his early life until 1430 when his name appears in a document which refers to his part in a dispute between patricians and guildsmen. Gutenberg eventually migrated to Strasbourg, where he opened a goldsmith shop.

Experimenting with metals, Gutenberg discovered an alloy of tin, iron, zinc, and lead that could be poured into iron and copper molds to form letters that would not shrink or twist upon cooling. Casting the moveable type was a difficult problem: all letter units had to be of equal length and thickness but of varying width. Gutenberg's inspired solution was to devise molds consisting of two overlapping L-shaped parts. The letter stamps made could then be assembled to form a page of lettering. After printing they could then be broken down and reassembled to form a completely different page. Moveable type could be used to print many copies of the same book or many copies of different books. Even more important, books could be produced for a fraction of the cost of hand-copied manuscripts.

Harassed by legal and financial problems in Strasbourg, Gutenberg returned to Mainz in October 1448. By then he and a partner had already printed a poem on the Last Judgment and an astronomical calendar. By 1454 he began using his moveable type to print a double-columned Bible in Gothic script, with forty-two lines in Latin to

a page. The demand for printed books proved insatiable. Yet what should have been a moment of triumph was marred for the inventor by losing a legal suit for debt repayment. He was forced to hand over his tools and presses. The winners of the lawsuit, including an ex-partner, were the actual publishers of the first printed books. A lifelong bachelor, Johann Gutenberg died a debtor.

Printing presses mushroomed throughout the Holy Roman Empire and then spread to the rest of Europe by the turn of the century. By 1480, there were over 380 working presses in Europe, and in the fifty years following the invention more books were produced than in the preceding thousand years. Printing became a major industry in Europe. By 1500 some nine million copies of 40,000 different titles were in circulation. Over half of the newly printed books were religious—Bibles, commentaries, devotional works, sermons, and the like. Also popular were ancient classics, legal handbooks, philosophical treatises, stories of miracles, astrological predictions, encyclopedias, almanacs, and knightly romances.

Eventually most of the work of the celebrated humanists and literary figures of the Renaissance found its way into print. Marguerite of Navarre's *Heptameron,* for example, was eventually printed in 1554. Erasmus's *Praise of Folly* was published in over 600 editions. The first book printed in Venice, which became the leading printing center in Europe, was an edition of the Roman stoic Cicero's *Letters* in 1469. By 1500 Venice had over 100 printers, more than all other Italian towns combined. The first book printed in English was William Caxton's translation of Raoul le Fevre's *Collection of the Histories of Troy,* printed at Bruges in 1473. The published works of Copernicus and Vesalius eventually reached a wide audience thanks in large measure to the printing press. The media revolution touched off by the invention of moveable type gave written ideas an impact without precedence in history. Without printing, the spread of Renaissance culture and the Reformation of the sixteenth century are inconceivable.

Chronology

c. 1398–1468	Life of Johann Gutenberg.
1422–1423	Costanza Calenda at Salerno.
1445–1450	Invention of moveable type.
1454	Gutenberg Bible printed in Mainz.
1473–1543	Life of Nicholas Copernicus.
1493–1541	Life of Paracelsus.
1495–1555	Georg Agricola.
1514–1564	Andreas Vesalius.
1543	Publication of Copernicus's *On the Revolution of the Heavenly Spheres* and Vesalius's *On the Fabric of the Human Body*.

Further Reading

RENAISSANCE SCIENCE

H. Floris Cohen, *The Scientific Revolution: A Historiographical Inquiry* (1994).

Allen Debus, *Man and Nature in the Renaissance* (1978).

Amos Funkerstein, *Theology and the Scientific Imagination from the Middle Ages to the Seventeenth Century* (1986).

Thomas Goldstein, *Dawn of Modern Science: From the Arabs to Leonardo da Vinci* (1980).

A. Rupert Hall, *The Revolution in Science, 1500–1750* (1983).

David Noble, *A World without Women: The Christian Clerical Culture of Western Science* (1992).

Charles Schmitt, *Studies in Renaissance Philosophy and Science* (1981).

Alan Smith, *Science and Society in the Sixteenth and Seventeenth Centuries* (1972).

MEDICINE

Robert Gottfried, *Doctors and Medicine in Medieval England, 1340–1530* (1986).

Katharine Park, *Doctors and Medicine in Early Renaissance Florence* (1985). Highly readable.

Jonathan Sawday, *The Body Emblazoned: Dissection and the Human Body in Renaissance Culture* (1995).

Nancy Siraisi, *Medieval and Early Renaissance Medicine* (1990).

THE OCCULT "SCIENCES"

Eugenio Garin, *Astrology in the Renaissance: The Zodiac of Life* (1983).

Wayne Shumaker, *The Occult Sciences in the Renaissance: A Study in Intellectual Patterns* (1985).

Lynn Thorndike, Jr., *A History of Magic and Experimental Science: The Sixteenth Century* (1941).

Brian Vickers, *Occult and Scientific Mentalities in the Renaissance* (1986).

INDIVIDUAL SCIENTISTS

Ivor Hart, *Leonardo da Vinci, Supreme Artist and Scientist* (1964).

Thomas Kuhn, *The Copernican Revolution: Planetary Astronomy in the Development of Western Thought* (1971). Intriguing but controversial.

Edward Rosen, *Copernicus and the Scientific Revolution* (1984).

TECHNOLOGY

Carlo Cipolla, *Before the Industrial Revolution*, 2nd ed. (1980).

Ian Friel, *The Good Ship: Ships, Shipbuilding, and Technology in England 1200–1520* (1995).

Otto Mayr, *Authority, Liberty, and Automatic Machinery in Early Modern Europe* (1986).

Joel Mokyr, *The Lever of Riches: Technological Creativity and Economic Progress* (1990). A lively survey.

Lynn White, Jr., *The Expansion of Technology* (1969).

PRINTING

Roger Chartier, *The Order of Books: Readers, Authors, and Libraries in Europe between the 14th and 18th Centuries* (1994).

Miriam Chrisman, *Lay Culture, Learned Culture: Books and Social Change in Strasbourg* (1982).

Mark Edwards, Jr., *Printing, Propaganda and Martin Luther* (1994).

Elizabeth Eisenstein, *The Printing Press as an Agent of Change*, 2 vols. (1979).

Lucien Febvre and Henri-Jean Martin, *The Coming of the Book: The Impact of Printing, 1450–1800* (1976).

Rudolf Hirsch, *Printing, Selling, and Reading 1450–1550* (1967).

Martin Lowry, *Venetian Printing: Nicolas Jenson and the Rise of the Roman Letterform* (1989).

Notes

1. Cited in G. R. Elton, *Renaissance and Reformation 1300–1648*, 3rd ed. (New York: Macmillan, 1976), p. 63.
2. Cited in James Ross and Mary Martin McLaughlin, eds., *The Portable Renaissance Reader* (New York: Viking, 1968), pp. 553–555.
3. Cited in Elton, *Renaissance and Reformation*, p. 67.
4. Cited in Ibid., p. 341.
5. Cited in Joel Mokyr, *The Lever of Riches: Technological Creativity and Economic Progress* (New York: Oxford University Press, 1990), p. 58.

INDEX